We all experience some great times in our lives, we or many of us experience some tough and testing times too.

For those of you that are suffering in silence, please find a friend and speak out about your pain.

Darra & Patrick, this is your monument,

may everyone who reads help build it taller.

Paula
Best wishes in Everything!!

CONTENTS

Introduction

Where does one begin, at the beginning will be the reply from all the smarties in the group, of course the beginning so here we are.

Once upon a time a baby was born and the world did not know what it was in for, but alas it was me. They say a big whopper of a child yet at only 9lbs or somewhere around that mark.

My own very first son, came in at 10lbs 11 or 11lbs 10 always get confused with numbers, yet my self-proclaimed mathematically genius has carried me through many a task of deep numerical quagmire.

Back to serious stuff though, so born yeah! Great out in the world, funny thing as an adult I have the most vivid memories of being a baby, I always ask other adults, new groups of friends do you remember being a baby? Many say NO and I find that strange as I can recall before I ever walked, like it was yesterday I can recall my older brother being told to share his candies with me and I knew he didn't want to and I wanted candy. I will guess my age of that event to be approx. 1 year old.

Now to read and write and put it all on paper finally well aren't we off to a great start, memories from 1 year old, no wonder the book weighs a ton. Let's catch up, this is the internet age so better reference would be "no wonder the download took 7 months" Being witty not the theme here but yes I like to keep things real and call them for the way that I see them, trouble is if you really take a look at the truth or the realness of a situation you are going to find some funny stuff there too and so with life being deep, emotional and miserable it is just as well there is a laugh or two along the way, any who? as they say, back to me. You got the picture born a big lad and it carried me through all my years, not the biggest in the group but a good firm strong built individual to say the least. 6ft and change in the vertically and broad and strong in the wide section, not fat that came with life a little later on.

So why bother reading about me? no reason really you should close the book now and return it for your money back, demand full refund, that is what I say to those of the pessimistic view, why did you pick it up in the first place I mean after all what could be so interesting about me compared to the next Joe schmo? Nothing! That's right nothing.

The reason I am going to share this with you, the reader, is to maybe let one little ounce of this life out to you and maybe just maybe after the record breaking sales of my book one single individual will get it and then it was all worth it.

Rambling again, well you will get used to that and if you like to get lost in a story, then I have tons of them for you, funny thing on that note. A smart well, wise really, guy I came across in my twenties told me, "you know the truth is the hardest thing to believe" I gave it some thought as he persisted, he was a city cop actually and I kept thinking he wanted me to say something I didn't want to say or something. The old Jedi mind trick being used on me, but anyway he insisted, "think about it" if someone tells you a lie you swallow it whole, and cannot wait to run and tell your friends, mates or partners, the story. Now when someone tells you the truth, what is a typical response? "Get out of here" "shut up" "are you for real", "that can't be true" etc. etc. You walk away in no hurry to tell anyone. Funny how it works isn't it. Give it a little thought and you will see, draw on all and or any stories someone ever told you, what was your reaction?

Ok so I have many, many, truths to share with you and some you are going to say are in no way believable and others you will swallow hook line and sinker. Why, it is just the nature of the beast in us. If I could tell you why, I wouldn't be writing it all down to share with you. I would be charging $1000 an hour in a well decorated office in a downtown Manhattan office whilst living care free somewhere around central Park. Just to live the rich lifestyle, of a genius mind reader type guy.

But I do not and so I cannot answer why we tell the truth and nobody wants to believe it. So when reading further keep in mind you might want to set down the auld book as it gets to be too unbelievable which might actually mean you have hit the real truth piece.

I can tell you right now we are gonna become buddies on this one if you stick with it and I will have to call you buddy because I have no way to know your name, are you man or woman, adolescent or elderly or anywhere in between, so take no offense from us getting to know each other through the buddy system. I will call you buddy for want of any better term, none come to mind right now so why not.

Ok the child hood, I was born in the mid-seventies, some of you may identify immediately with the era of growing up, being a fully-fledged kid in the early eighties. I had a great child hood; I mean my innocence was top class. I was so shy you would never believe it, as people used to say I was a fine young handsome man and again being a big strong fit child, all the older folk would pass some comment or other. But my innocence was immense;

I mean I was so, shy and scared as a young boy. I never or rarely would speak in a crowd or answer the teachers question in school, why? I just thought it was better to let someone else answer, someone who would get it wrong and then they could be the embarrassed one, hell no! Not me. I was not going to embarrass myself in a room of 30 other children, that being said because they all viewed me as a genius by about 5years of age they didn't want me to answer anyway because I always had the answer. The other kids got their kicks out of getting their assignments finished before me checking to see if I was finished already, I never cared less, looking back I just did what I needed to do and that was enough.

Chapter 1

I have my father to thank or to blame, who knows which, maybe my older brother too, the same guy who wouldn't share that candy I distinctly remember hearing my mother, say "share with your little brother" but I was standing up in the baby cot waiting for him to come into the room and share but he just didn't. He came in when the candy was gone with a smart Alec type look on his face, so I was destined to be pissed off and disappointed by him from the get go, resentment? Nah, not really, just a vivid baby memory. Why would I thank him, well he is 2 years my elder, so when he had started school at 4 years of age, I was jealous of him doing homework in the evening right around his 4 and half yrs. to 5 mark so me approx. 2 and half heading into three. I wanted home work too. My dad used to sit me up on the opposite end of the table from him and while he was doing the really nasty homework piece I was at the other end learning to write, trying to read and do mathematics. At three years of age, I couldn't wait for my dad to set me up with the home work for the evening, I would try and finish fast because my dad seemed to enjoy it, the harder the math he gave me the quicker I would try and do it. Then it actually became serious, I was rattling of the times tables, long division sums, long multiplication at least that's what it was called back then, to my older brother I was just becoming more and more annoying. But hey I didn't know what annoying was, I was 3 for crying out loud. Looking back my poor dad thought he had an Einstein, thought he produced the next NASA scientist, keep reading you will tie it all together, but to save any suspense, I have never worked for NASA....

So by the time I had started school I was waiting for the others to catch up & within about a month of joining school, the teachers were answering me with things, like yes Aidan I know you know, let's give the others a chance. So there I was off to a flying start in life, bright as a bulb, eager to learn more and loving every minute of it, no idea what arrogant meant or cocky or any of those words, was just me being me.

My class mates struggled through that first year of school learning three time three is nine, three times four is twelve and so on. I was buzzing around a little tyke I can't wait for the 12 times 12 I will smash them on this one, I used to say things like, it's easy just 10 times 10 and add 2 times 2... I really had no idea then obviously I was 4 years of age and I remember turning five, but I had no idea that some people didn't get it, it didn't work for them in their brain. I never thought anyone was less or was stupid, I remember as a child back then I just thought everybody was cool and everybody liked to have fun the way I did, to laugh and make jokes and play sports was all that was important.

And sports it was, I loved every kind of activity they would give us, the list, basketball, Olympic handball, soccer, swimming, Gaelic football, hurling, running around the roads to try and do 5 miles or even ten miles but that was for the bigger kids so I had to wait. But I sure loved sports. I didn't want to wait I wanted to play and I wanted to win. I wanted to play with the bigger, well older children cause I was big for my age and so around 8 and 9 I wanted to be with the 12 and 13 year olds going up against them hard tackles and always thinking, I will out smart you and I am strong enough to win the tackle so no fear there. I liked it I liked to give the full 100%. What did that get me? medals and trophies and achievements like nothing else, I wanted gold I got it, I wanted to win the trophy we got it as a team, they made me captain of the team for no reason other than I was a good thinker and gave it my all and would never shy away from the challenge on the field of play.

When I was not in school or doing homework, although to be honest I rarely did homework as I was going along now at age 8 or 9, because I just needed to read it once and I knew it, maybe the odd poem or two I had to repeat it several times to get it to stick, so what some might or could argue was a little laziness on my part was really just boredom lack of challenge. But in the sports the medals came, on the field of play I was a madman, I was a lunatic, I wanted to win and win always but not to any severe mental case type. I just liked the limelight and got a weird feeling the almost embarrassment feeling or awkward feeling when all the grownups would pat me on the back and say well done.

My dad never pressured me; I would return home and he would say did you win? Yes, I answer & he would say something like "I knew you would" I always believed he really did know that I would win. My dad was never shocked about me winning and I didn't care to try and shock him, so it was easy going as 1,2,3 that's why I said earlier my child hood was great & easy going, things came super easy, no challenge could not be accomplished. My poor mother she came to a soccer match one time, I remember she was there when playing but not really feeling she was there, because hey it was game day. That meant it was time to focus on the task at hand and get the win.

I did my usual routine of keeping the guys motivated, what I didn't know during the match, well forgot about my mam being there, but when we got home and my dad asked my mam at the dinner table Sunday evening, well what did you think, they play well don't they? She said "oh my God, I can't go to another game, that was awful" I was sitting at the dinner table all ready with smiles and thinking my mam was going to be, well speak so highly of how great I was, flattened by her comments, she said that was awful… my dad asked her why, she started off with the "well I never heard such language at a football match not even from adults and these children are playing under 9 age group and my son has to be the one running around the field like a mad man, screaming and cursing f words at every body for the full 90 mins" my dad was laughing which gave me an in to speak and say "Mam you just don't get it. I am the captain I have to keep the lads heads in the game", she said not like that! I said that's soccer, that's the way it is. Her point / argument, it could be done without all the curse words. It didn't bother me, it was funny but it did not even shock me oh yeah my mother was listening to all that... ooooops! We won our league that year, actually now that I think back I do not know did we win the league, the league cup or what we won, I know we got trophies presented to us by the national football team players who were like stars to us and it was a day out to get the presentation, so all good I was a happy little camper at 9 years of age.

I was also taking piano lessons at the same time right around the same age, man did I hate the fricking piano lessons, I mean I could not get it, it didn't make sense to me, ask me the square root of a trillion point 6 and I would love to figure it out, but the piano. This sit up straight business and fingers and timing and just not understanding to read the music and piano was a chore on Saturdays that just held no fun… Saturday mornings used to be get up early and head of to a local swimming pool and swim with the swimming club, about an hour in the morning, of course I won all those races too, but some were not competitive, there was a lot of getting to learn survival and rescue for swimming, it was a lot of fun and kept me super active and I loved the sprints, the races, I would swim my heart out and tip the wall first and look around nobody close and I won again I think I won that like three years in a row. Of course me, I thought nothing of it, I thought it is a race and you are supposed to win, nobody pressured me into that I just understood it to be that way.

By the time I was 11 years of age and all active as a cub scout earning badges for doing tasks and good behaviour, winning swimming medals and soccer medals and taking piano grade exams, where could I go wrong, school getting whatever grade I wanted a's or b's what is the difference I knew that I knew the stuff so no big deal, that is what I thought. So the parish priest came around to our school and comes into our class and says,

"There will be a scholarship up for grabs to go to the Gaeltacht this year sponsored by the parish and from the three schools within the parish all are welcome to try and enter and see who gets it. It will be three weeks speaking Irish, in a rural village in Ireland and you will get to stay with a family and they will feed you for three weeks and you will do classes in a school there, like a summer camp/ summer school".

To explain Gaeltacht, Gael comes from Gaelic which is the Irish language and teach in that language means house, so the scholarship was to be to the "Irish house" for three weeks of the summer.

The catch the parish priest says, the parish will put up 150 pounds, Irish pounds and the winner will have to have their family put up the other 25 as the total costs for the three weeks is 175 Irish pounds. The interviews will be this Saturday in the parish Gaelic football club. From 12 noon to 5 pm.

I went home and that evening after dinner and the home work was done, I said to my mother, I remember being a little nervous to ask for money because we just didn't ask for money in my house, well to be honest looking back we never needed anything so we didn't need money.

I said, "Mam, there is a scholarship up for grabs this Saturday, to the Gaeltacht. I was going to enter for it, basically if I win it you would have to pay 25 and the parish will put up the rest, will you pay 25 pound for me to go the Gaeltacht" she answered me laughing, "25 to get rid of you for three weeks, who do I make the check out to" I said ha-ha ha-ha, I have to win it first but yeah if I do you will pay it. Cool.

Saturday came along pretty quick that week & I had no idea what an interview would be like, but off I went on my bicycle, the day looked like it might rain anytime soon, I needed to cycle about two miles, so I said screw it here I go. Onto the bike and away I went two miles there and two miles back, I showed up for the interview, into a little office type room and then the person inside met me with a greeting in Irish and the whole thing was in Irish, Gaelic language, I remember thinking oh jaysus, I screwed this up for sure. I genuinely forgot or just did not think that the whole interview is going to be in Irish, what a mistake. I was not prepared but looking back it shows me how innocent or stupid I really was, not to look at things in depth or with understanding. Just have at it and try anything, what a great attitude for a child.

I cycled home and my mother & father asked, where did you go you never told anyone? I told them I went for the Irish interview and they wanted to know, well how did you get on with it? I said, hard to know really it was all in Irish. I don't even know what I was saying and so I wrote that off to be a new bad experience and maybe next time I should prepare or something. The following week, the parish priest came around into the class and said there was a winner from one of the three schools, and that person would be going to the Gaeltacht with a scholarship and the winner is, boom, me. Now what do you think of that. I got it; I was going away for the summer by myself to be mixed in with strangers and have a laugh and a good time, oh only stipulation. When you attend the Irish college for the summer school program you are not allowed to speak a word of English, for the full three weeks.

I had been away camping with the cub scouts on numerous occasions for weekends and for a week straight during summers before but this time I was going to be with new people, people I never saw before.

Away I went, for three weeks of speaking Irish and it was an amazing summer fun camp. Irish lessons in the mornings and then home for lunch and then back to the school for sports or activities and then home to the family home for dinner and then back to the school for Irish music and a dance, Irish dance of course, like set dancing I guess, called ceili. Kaylee. This college for the summer was great, beautiful girls, fun times and the only thing different is that we're speaking Irish all the time. I was loving it, every waking minute of each day. In the house I was staying in there were some kids a little older than me two around early teens and three mature students who needed Irish badly for some college course they were failing. On the weekend they had a car so we drove into the local city and got cans of beer, of course I was a big kid, so at that time the age of 11 to 12 I could pass for 15 or 16 so no-one had any hang up about letting me have a couple cans of beer, but boy oh boy did I get nice and drunk off 4 cans of beer and I was already smoking pretty much full time by then anyway. There I was in the west of Ireland in an all Irish school for three weeks, enjoying all the freedom, smoking and drinking like a champion and going to the ceili dancing and trying to kiss the girls, freedom was beginning to feel pretty amazing, what a great place this was. That summer the weather was really nice and so we had nice hot sunny days all through the camp. The bus ride back to Dublin after three weeks was about four hours and my dad picked me up, how was it he asked and I said great, he said that's good can you speak Irish now and so I rattled it off fluent style...

I was home now again and needed to get back to hiding my cigarettes and not smelling of smoke and all because well it wasn't pure freedom anymore, but boy oh boy did I have a hankering for a few beers, so the rest of that summer was about getting a few cans when and where I could .

Chapter 2.

The trouble of being a budding brain box child was it made it easy to always get a few odd jobs or pick potatoes for the farmers, get ahead with a few pound and buy beer. By the end of that summer, I was heading into what they call secondary school which is like high school. Start off around age of 11 or 12, but by the end of those summer holidays I was being a right good drunk, 8 to ten cans of beer on a night, hanging with the older kids, from the local area. Not the immediate area of the village where I grew up and played soccer and where I had gone to school for the past 7 years, a local town a couple of miles away, I knew a few of the people from the cub scouts and some from heavy metal concerts that I went to with my older brother and his friends, yeah I will never forget those, Metallica, anthrax, nuclear assault, a few others, Danzig. Those were fun times.

I had been placed in the brainy box class in the new secondary school based off the entrance exam; they ranked me as clever or something so those were my new classmates, teacher's children and the brain boxes of the future. For me again boring, school just never moved fast enough for me, I have no idea why. It was difficult at times but my interest could not be held. Now I was in the school with the bigger kids, up to 18yrs of age this crowd… and with the girls I had been meeting from the nights drinking during the summer and the metal concerts in the city, these people now really knew I was only a first year…..couldn't fake the age thing anymore, but I still hung out and kicked it with the older crew.

I learned how to dodge school, "mitching" they called it... my mam and dad would drive me to school and head off to work, I would walk to the main entrance door and as soon as I knew their car was gone I would start back tracking thorough the fields towards my house, my parents were gone to work for the day and my other brothers were all at school so the house would be locked, I figured out a way to break in that wouldn't be noticed and would just hang out at home for a while and be sure to get out and pretend I was coming home from school at the right time. I think, thinking back I was enjoying it the idea that they couldn't catch me. My mother used to do fund raising for the cub scouts and so sometimes I would head into where the money was grab a handful of change and off out and buy some cigarettes. On the weekends I would go cut grass for people or wash cars, to get some money and then, 8 cans of beer on a Saturday night, or at that time, there would be the odd occasion I could go to the pubs with the older crew. I would be able to get a few pints of beer, delicious I remember so clear the feeling of being in the pub and the older crew would get me the pints because most of them thought I was about 16 and so no big deal, I was only turning 12 though that's the really messed up piece looking back. Of course with this older teenage hanging out at the weekends, I was not always going home or trying to sneak in without being noticed, and of course with the pub scene and getting drunk on an evening, Saturday night or Friday night hanging out in the cold drinking down 2 litres of cider, came along rolling joints. Smoking hash and getting high. In those times, people who got high were like lepers, kids who got high were either sniffing glue or inhaling gas, smoking hash was this new thing rolling joints drinking beer and having a great time.

I had been missing, dodging quite a bit of school, I had a, I don't give a fuck attitude to everything. One morning, because sometimes I would go to school for the first one or two classes and then just take off and go home. Take a nap or make a big brunch. So this particular morning I remember we had just finished science class and I walked out into the hallway ready to cut out and go home and my math teacher slid up beside me, hey young man, why do you never make it to my class? He asked me would I like it if he scheduled math for the mornings instead and we could shift the whole school itinerary around to accommodate me, I could see his tone was not really about jokes, he was pretty serious with me, he said do me a favour tomorrow Wednesday, we have a double math class in the afternoon, he said, would you please grace us with your presence, do me that favour he asked, I said sure for you and the way you asked nicely, no problem it is a promise, of course he was a little insulted with my attitude, but hey he was cool about it, so why not, that's what I thought. Why not?

Wednesday after noon walk into double math class, sitting waiting, he shows up, "Ok books away, we are going to have a test" "you have 1 hour to complete" I sat there thinking, you sneaky fucking prick, I have not been to this class in about a month.. And now this oh well screw it. I will finish it and walk out.

50 mins later, you were allowed to leave once you had the test completed, I handed my paper in putting it on his desk, he smiled at me all arrogant, like ha! He caught me out; he said thanks for showing up and out I walked, only to get collared by my year head teacher who was like the liaison officer for the class, the one to keep an eye on us.

Because we were being allowed to leave the math class early once the exam was completed the hallways were empty because all regular class time was still going on. So my year head teacher decides I will have to accompany her to her office as she wants to discuss a few things with me. Into her office we go and all I can keep thinking is how this math teacher and his "make me a promise to come to my class" has really gone and thrown a spanner in the works I was floating along just fine until now….of course I didn't miss school when I wasn't there, but I guess school when I wasn't there missed me and so now crunch time with the year head teacher.

The questions started to come, now you have been missing a lot lately, is everything ok at home, it has been rumoured you are drinking alcohol and on and on it went. So all brazen I said yes that's right I like a few pints on the weekend. What's wrong with that? She said, you are 12 years of age that's what's wrong with it. You are missing school, I got argumentative and said if you don't like it, why should I give a fuck, and walked out of her office. Then followed phone calls to my parents, the watchful eye was on me, no more dodging school now they are all watching. I had no choice but to attend. I remember waiting for our history teacher to get to class one day, she was always late, it wasn't break time it was just a break between classes, so I decided I will have a quick smoke while waiting, I light up a cigarette in class, some of the other kids laughed and some were outright disgusted, I got a few puffs into me, about halfway through the smoke, when the teacher showed up, I thought oh fuck she was fast today, why? I had to think on my feet, I remember watching the teacher like a hawk as she settled in with her books and things out of her bag as soon as her nose started to twitch, I put the cigarette in the pocket of a girls coat in front of me and jumped up just before the teacher could ask had someone been smoking, I yell out, Miss this girl is smoking in the class, look come look she just put it in her jacket pocket, you can smell come look. Teacher comes and takes a look there is a lighting cigarette in her jacket, our history teacher sends her to the principal's office and I get off Scott free. Lucky one that one.

I started not going back to school again on different days and then very soon told the head mistress to go fuck herself, who happened to be a nun. I am never coming back, I told my parents I wasn't going back and I was going to get a job, I was touching 12 yrs. of age maybe 12 and half. I started to work in the fields with a local farmer three to four days a week, it got me pocket money and what I didn't know then but was that the school had gotten into an argument with my father that they did not want me back anyway. My father's argument was they should be doing a better job keeping me there every day and less about trying to pry and see are there problems at home, because there were not. The school said they will accept me back based upon a psychological evaluation. Now the shit really started, into the city on the evenings to meet my dad coming from his work. Me, my mam, my older brother and my dad, all sitting in with a shrink having therapy sessions to find out what is wrong with me. Having to get into arguments about why my older brother doesn't want me hanging out with him and his older friends as I am embarrassing to him to have the little brother tagging along. Why won't I go to school, what is wrong with school, why am I drinking alcohol. A big wall to wall mirrored glass wall with a phone mounted on it, where the lady doctor would ask questions and then the phone would ring and she would sit back down with a question "the team would like to know……" so there was a team of doctors sitting behind the mirror analysing me too… like a gold fish. I did not take any of it serious nor did I have anybody to impress I just went along as honest as possible. The police had to come to my house to discuss with me that underage drinking was illegal and if I was caught by them ever I would be in big trouble. I really didn't take that serious either, but I guess it was.

My Dad drove me half way down the country to a private school to take an interview, and I always remember my dad all the way home that evening, "you fucked that interview up on purpose" "slouched down and one word smart answers, to the head master of the school" I answered with all honesty, I didn't screw anything up on purpose, I just answered what they asked.

Chapter 3.

In the local town there is a fleet of fishing boats, one of the older crew I used to go drinking in the bars with was a fisherman, and so I hooked up with him and he called his boss and said I could have a job... Bingo! Now I could have a boat to work on, a boat to eat on and a boat to sleep on all in the one thing, plus they are going to pay me for it... what's not to like about that, so I decided, get some clothes together, say nothing to anyone and just go fishing.

The wages were great, some of the other crews on the other boats were making maybe even double but it was all dependent upon how much you caught, we fished for some fish and prawns, Monday through Friday and then cleaned things up on a Saturday and got paid. I was turning thirteen years of age, getting a pay packet of anywhere from 180 pounds to 350 pounds, at that time some of my old school friends dads, would earn about 70 to 100 pounds a week, just to give an idea of what money was then. At that time, many around the fishing harbour thought I was about 16 or 17 yrs. of age as they had been seeing me around the bars and knew a little about me and nobody said anything to cause me any problems for being young. All the fishing boats had relatively young crew members, guys who had dropped out of school or that was, just their career. With this now came good money cash in the hand on weekends, I didn't have to go home every night and listen to any bullshit or pressure from my parents and so I was free to do whatever I wanted. So what else could follow but more drinking and more getting high on hash and sometimes even acid.

I remember clearly one evening we were going to leave the harbour and go fishing and when I woke up from down below in my bunk bed, the skipper had come down and started the engine and the boats were going out night fishing and needed to get out of the harbour with the flow of the tide as the tide was going out, so I came up to help untie the boat and reel in the ropes. My mother was standing on the harbour trying to see could we have a moment to talk. I remember thinking, what the fuck is she doing here? This is no place for my mother on the harbour with a bunch of smelly fishermen. I said yeah mam but we are going out I will talk to ya at the weekend, and she handed me well almost had to throw it to me, a letter.

I didn't read it right then as I was all embarrassed that my mother was there in the first place. Off we went out on the ocean for the night working away. The next day we came back into the harbour off loaded our catch, and me and my crew mate went to the local bar at the top of the harbour, it was around 11 am and we ordered up a couple of pints of beer, tasty stuff and when you have been working all night, it takes about 2 maybe 3 beers and you feel really drunk. Stroll back down the harbour make a quick sandwich and off down below for some sleep, do it all again the next night. It was the next day I read my mother's letter, a long three pages I remember how it went, why are you doing this to yourself, we love you, come home, you have a family, we love you, you are too smart and too young to throw your life away like this. I thought only one answer for this, a few pints and a few joints and then I will think about it.

So with the timing and my skills for learning I was picking up all there is to know about how these boats work and what needs to be done, and as been the achiever I was enjoying fishing and really wanted to do well in it, but the greedy guy inside wanted more money too. More money means more drink and more drugs and more party.

I had changed boats to an opening on another boat where they earned more money because they caught more but of course meant working longer hours, to explain for example; when you go out fishing for prawns back then in they are known as Dublin bay prawns, it works like this, an hour or more to drive out we call it steaming, but drive to the fishing grounds, in that time you might cook something depending if the waves are big or not, if the waves are big it makes a mess to be spilling tea everywhere and trying to fry some sausages for a sausage sandwich. So when you get to the fishing grounds, you throw the nets into the water and there all steel cables and things to get the nets set right and straight and then you start towing the nets along the bottom. This then kind of gives the boat a bit of extra stability so much easier to grab a cup of tea and cook something to eat, or you go below and grab some sleep. In those times prawns were very plentiful so you would tow the nets along the bottom for about three hours, now the key to getting some sleep in before, whilst towing the net is that once you haul up the net, you empty the prawns onto the deck and put the net back down and tow it again, but this time instead of running below to your bunk for some sleep, you now have to start sorting the catch, so the time spent doing that could take up the full three hours of the tow of the net and so as soon as you finish dealing with the catch you are hauling the net again and then there is more catch to deal with while you tow the net again. So during the finer weather months of the summer from the small fishing town of Skerries, Dublin, the boat might head out on Sunday night and come back on Tuesday evening, head out again Wednesday morning and come back Friday and go again Saturday morning until Monday and then Tuesday morning until Thursday night and then break for the weekend, so every second week would be a weekend off. Each time the boat would come in would be to offload the catch and take new groceries aboard and new ice for keeping the prawns almost frozen so they stay fresh for the two days. Also for most of those days it was the same routine, net to the bottom tow it and haul it, deal with the catch, haul it put it back to tow and deal with the catch, morning noon and night. Rinse repeat, rinse repeat. The job would get very tiring and some of the times in between hauling up the nets would lend some time to grab something to eat or take a quick 30 minute nap maybe. I was loving it, I loved been on the ocean or as they say "out at sea". Every other day when we would come ashore to offload, there would be like 20 boats all with crew of five or six guys, for doing the work, so on those evenings maybe finish up working at 10pm and will be leaving out again at 4am we would congregate on one of the boats, keep the kettle going and brewing tea for everyone and just keep rolling joints and smoking hash like there was no tomorrow. Until your eyes were sinking in your head and then steady step your way back to your boat and collapse into your bunk and wake up at sea the next day starting it all over again.

The new boat I had joined had a crew of guys I didn't really know and of course they were all older than me, and a general rule on the boats used to be that whoever was the last man to join the crew was in charge of keeping the kitchen area clean and the inside of the boat in general to keep it clean at all times as well as doing all the sorting of the fish and prawns on the deck of the boat. Well for this reason the last man to join the crew was always a bit of a, well the "scape goat" or "the skivvy" and this crew really thought it was great fun to take sucker punches at me and use me like a punching bag. For their kicks they would whip me like a slave with a rope that had lead in it so it was pretty hard and caused a lot of bruising for example. I was a big kid and was faced with some situations like I remember thinking, well you wanted to live in a man's world and a man's world is tough so therefore, just take it and don't break down like a child and be crying. They all think you are older so you better act older. I was coming close on 15 years of age, about 14 and half at the time, all the other guys on the crew were 18 to 24 years of age for example but they had been knowing me for a year or more and so they figured that I had to be about 17 now or if not even 18. So the beatings continued for a while. One of my friends from when we were small kids and even when we used to go to the heavy metal concerts, his dad owned one of the fishing boats and he even to this day has kept on his family tradition and owns his own boat now fishing away all the time, but he had heard a rumour I was getting beat up on the boat and so because he used to work with his dad for the summer months, he told his crew mates who were also more older and tougher fishermen.

So on the Friday where we clean down the boat for the weekend off, from 4 of the other boats all their crew came and stood alongside our boat and kept telling the crew they had to come up on the harbour as they were going to beat them up. They had heard I was being used like a punching bag and that these other crews from the other boats were going to punch all kinds of shades of grey out of my crewmen for mistreating me. I remember clearly walking up to the wheelhouse, that's the cockpit of the boat, where the driving is done and looking out the window to see all these guys standing on the harbour. One of the main instigators on my boat was pretending to brush the floor of the wheelhouse but instead he was really hiding so no one on the harbour could see him through the windows. He said to me go and tell them I never hit you, go and tell them or they are gonna beat me up. I felt sorry for him really even though I hated him, when he would be high and whipping me and laughing at me. The boss came and we got our pay and I went up on the harbour and my friend was there and he told me, show these guys the bruises, they are gonna beat up your crewmen, I said nah its ok let's just leave it alone. I didn't want to get beat anymore by the time Monday rolled around.

My friend said absolutely not and he is going to get me a job on his uncles boat and that way we would be on the same schedule and nobody will beat me up there, and that no one will beat me up anymore because now everyone is aware of the situation and that those guys will get a good beating soon for what they had done to me. So I changed to the new boat and nobody even pretended to ever hit me again. I felt such relief, like now I really did fit in and had people who had my back and so I could just do the fishing and get paid and none of the extra beatings. Nobody was treating me like a slave anymore.

But this new life of mine on fishing boats was a tough one and it meant hard drinking and smoking hash and taking acid and now sometimes cocaine or speed, it just depended what was available at the time and where the party was. We used to call them "sessions", where is the session? would be what people would ask, so maybe a stormy day and all the guys that worked on the boats would be here there and everywhere throughout the town, people at their homes or hanging out around the streets or headed into the city to buy drugs, whatever but as soon as we would meet face to face on the street, "hey where you heading?" "I heard there is a session over on xyz boat" because the boats had a galley, which is the kitchen on the boat, usually a kitchen table type setting with room to sit 5 or 6 big guys, and down below in the cabin. The cabin a big open room with bunks set in all around the sides and so what we called lockers wrapped the room which made for bench seating.

Some of the boats at that time could sit 15 or 20 guys in the cabin, maybe we would have stolen a keg of beer from one of the local pubs of the town and then carry it back to the boat. A keg of beer is a heavy barrel of fun, but we managed, as to get high and wasted, one finds the strength to carry such kegs to the harbour, down onto one of the boats and crack it open, everyone gets to drink for free and we get wasted. That was the general gist of things to make a session kick off well.

Chapter 4.

My own confidence was growing by this time and I had one or two fist fights in the streets on weekends. It was nothing abnormal to me, someone started talking crap and then it gets to be a heated argument and then just head butt the guy and catch a nice right hook at the same time almost. Knocking the person out and sometimes as they fell I did indeed kick them in the head on the way down.

How can I explain, this fighting feeling that came over me, I cannot I just found myself in weird situations where it felt to me it is fight or cry and in this hard man world there is no room for crying any more so lash out and fight. This kind of violence looking back of course is unacceptable but at the time I was very immature and around 15 years of age, a tall strong fit young man, no girlfriend, having one definitely might have helped defuse the energy but it was the way it was. I had a weird sense of screwed up loyalty or something, be loyal to my friends and my extended network of friends and only fight those outside of those circles.

I come from a small village and so I felt to always look out for anyone from that village too. If I was in the local town and anyone was getting into any bother from the folks of the local town, I was quick to move in and make a few intimidating gestures to help my village friend out. I have numerous fighting stories but we will get to them, for some reason there I was again just trying to be the best at what I was involved in. I wanted to be the skipper/captain of a boat. I wanted to know everything there was to know about fishing. On the weekends or any stormy days when there was no work I wanted to be the hardest drinker and the guy that could handle the most drugs like nothing could phase me, just be the best at it. The brain works a funny way, when I look back at how the association of who is who and what is what and then how all that can get so distorted when high.

There was a night I was out well that week was a funny week. In and around the Wednesday night the boats were in and I went to a friend's house to have a couple of toasted cheese and ham sandwiches and watch a movie. Oh this was my good friend, he was the best buddy I mean many weekends we would not even be hanging out together and then when I was so wasted and high and screwed up I would head to his house. Their house had a little extension onto the kitchen and I would climb up onto the roof of that extension and start knocking on his window, he would wake up and let me in then I could smoke a joint with him and pass out safe and sound. He felt sorry for me or something, he used to tell me if he was out in the evening with his other friends and we met up, now you have to go home to your mam and dads tonight don't come to my place, I would show up anyway, what was he going to do at 3 am, tell me go away?

He was a fisherman too so we were living the same kind of lifestyle working hard for the cash and drinking hard and smoking hard.

So that Wednesday night we were ashore from sea and up at his house for a snack about 11pm or so a normal week night and we were due to go back out fishing that morning maybe 5 am. Well he had an older sister who had a boyfriend in the army, now the Irish army is not really any great big world military but they, the Irish army in those times were involved with being part of peace keeping troops stationed in Lebanon, something to do with Gadhafi or Sadam or one of them crazy Arabs. Being in the military they used to get military issued treats and one such treats was they used to get movies through the US troops or something, so we had a movie to watch that had not been released yet, because the military got them first. I had heard later in life that some of these movies for example might get made and not go to the cinemas, but could have been released in video to the troops, "the troops overseas" so they would always have new fresh entertainment.

So we were sitting up in his house and the movie was the "silence of the lambs", what a great movie we had our sandwiches and our tea watching the movie, waited for his folks to go to bed and smoked a couple of joints too watching this brand new, not even released yet movie. What a great movie, "Silence of the lambs". If you have never seen it, go and download it now. We finished the movie in an eerie kind of awe and knew it was time to head back down to the harbour and get into the bunk to go asleep and wake up out at sea ready for work the next morning.

We walked out of his house that night and across the street are a couple of flats, smaller housing for the elderly and they had a walkway up to the front door and from our angle of it we could see the pathway with a sheen across it, of flowing substance, after watching the movie and being so high we thought it looked like a river of blood flowing straight out from under the front door and down the pathway of the little flat, we walked across to see, he knew the old lady that lived there Mrs I cannot remember her name to be honest but as we got closer it still looked like what could be a river of blood, the pathway was a typical front pathway to the front door about 4 feet wide with grass on either side, but it was 2 am and dark and the light reflecting in the sheen were those yellow street lamps so exact colour couldn't be determined, when we got there it looked like the water mains had burst and was steadily just forming a little river down the front garden path. We had a good laugh making fun of each other all the way down the street heading over to the harbour. Which one was scared thinking it was blood. From the middle of the town there is a road along the waterfront, businesses and houses on one side and water on the other, the harbour road. Walking along there about 2 am or 2.30 that night a car coming towards us moved to our side of the road and comes to an abrupt halt and the driver jumps out asking us if we know a guy that works on the fishing boats. He wasn't sure of the name but kept saying this guy's name, we said no man you got it wrong, That guy you're asking about works on the ships now and is always away from home, he doesn't work on the harbour or the fishing boats for a few years now at least. Why what's the problem, the guy the driver of the car I am trying to think where do I know him from as I had definitely seen his face before, just as I figured it out, he was the owner of one of the local businesses along the harbour road, the night club owner, he states, I own the night club, and we have an emergency of a guy we needed to get rushed to the hospital as he is nearly dead, he seems to have bashed his skull open on the rocks around the back of the harbour, he jumped into his car and said thanks for the help lads and takes off with a screech. We, me and my buddy continue walking and are wondering to each other what is he talking about someone nearly dead and bashed skull and we are still high and thinking of the movie silence of the lambs and the river of blood on the old lady's pathway and laughing to each other about what an absolutely weird and freaky night.

When we arrive at the boat there is still a few lads up in one of the boats, we could see the light on in the galley so we head over there, seems to be a bit of a smoke session, so in we go and a few of the lads are all stoned and the kettle is on for tea, so we tell them about the movie and the guy supposed to have his head bashed in, a couple more smokes of the good old hash and off to sleep on my boat.

That next couple of days were nothing extraordinary, fishing away sorting the catch, tailing prawns out in the Irish Sea. When we returned to the harbour that Friday evening we were still working away tailing the prawns as this was normal to head into the harbour and get the boat tied up next to the wall and continue sorting the catch right there by the harbour side, some tourists would wander down the harbour to look at the catch and some people would show up with a bag and ask to buy a couple of fresh fish.

This particular Friday we had fished an extra day the Friday as usually when we were going to tie up for the weekend and get time off everything shut down on Thursday but this Friday evening was the quick panic get everything finished up and be done for the weekend, which meant payday also. A local old man who lived in a house up by the night club at the top of the harbour always came down begging for small fish, he always said it was to feed his cats, but many believed he was too embarrassed to admit they were for him and he just didn't want to pay for the fish. He had stepped down the ladder of the harbour onto the deck of our boat and we were tailing prawns right at a work table set up in the middle of the deck, the skipper/captain was helping us to try and get finished quicker by using the shovel and continuing to fill the work table with the catch all the while picking small skinny whiting fish for the old man, the old man says to the skipper, did you know that young man McNally, who lives up by you. The skipper is jovial with him, oh yeah which one of the McNally's. The old guy is making the gossip; young fella lives up by you, used to work here on the boats on the harbour. My boss is smiling and shovelling away and turns to the old man, yeah I know him why... It is a terrible thing, the poor chap a nice young lad I heard, and too bad he died like that… What said the boss man, laughing, he is standing right beside you, the poor old man jumped back with a half a step, what, the whole town is talking about how he died and maybe the night club people had something to do with it. A real good Chinese whisper rumour around the whole town, all the while, while I was out fishing for a day and half from Thursday early in the morning til Friday in the afternoon the rumour was spreading like wild fire. We kept working away and the poor old man was scratching his head and he soon left with his bag of small fish for "the cats". Half an hour or so passed by and while still with about an hour or more working ahead of us sorting the catch and washing things down and weighing in the catch, a couple of the older lads that had been boat captains and fishing for twenty years or more showed up on the harbour looking down on us as we worked.

I looked up my good friend and another good friend standing there saying come up here we want to talk to you. I climbed the ladder of the pier as I was chuffed they had come all the way down to the harbour to talk with me, they were a little drunk the two of them, and they were ready to go and burn the night club to the ground because they also had heard I was dead. They were a little high that night but had a bottle of southern comfort under one arm and a gallon of petrol (gasoline) hidden at the top of the harbour ready to avenge my death. All I could do was laugh. Call it funny call it sad, both of them are dead now, died young. One died, we don't know how, well we know drowning, and his body was found in a harbour. The other, passed away with a heart attack, the heart attack got him and put him in a coma and then there was no option, he lasted a week in a coma. Both of them real true friends of mine and will always be in my prayers. Too young to die only late thirties the drowning and mid-forties a heart attack. There is no rhyme or reason to how it all goes.

So Friday we were paid, finished the work and off home, time to get a quick shower, I should go back and explain about the home life. I had basically walked out of home as I mentioned earlier when I was thinking I knew it all and fishing was the life for me, I had the boats for shelter a place to eat and a means to make money so what did I need a home for. Well as I had explained my mother had come and gave me a letter one evening and other attempts and pressure from many saying just go home and be normal. So through one argument and the next I agreed to go home one evening after finishing up on the boats and had a discussion with my parents where my father had laid out terms, the terms were keep responsible hours, continue with my work, pay my mother weekly for my keep and all amenities would be available to me just like any grown son who would be living in the family home who was working and not attending school. As you can imagine this was not the first argument/discussions with my parents as my attitude, was mostly of the "fuck you" attitude and no one is going to tell me what to do. Looking back seriously on a deep level, what on earth was I born with, what kind of mind had I got that was trying to be all grown up by the age of 11 and 12 years of age. There was no one I would allow to tell me anything. The shrinks I had to go and see for the being allowed back into school, as far as my understanding which was not a high understanding but nonetheless I understood I was given a clean bill of health and that the school were told they could not deny me an education. That was the fight of my father with the school and while he was fighting that fight I was saying fuck you to them all and out on the ocean fishing.

So the basics were I was going home every so often some nights yes some nights no, stay at my friends or be so wasted just wake up on the beach or on the boat in my bunk or even once I remember waking up freezing and stiff from the cold in the doorway of the local church, cold denims from peeing myself and clutching to a litre bottle of gin which was half drank. Those were some-times indeed, to be 14 and just a true martyr for the booze, I loved it.

Anyway back to the house that Friday evening, wages in the pocket in need of a shower, I had just put in a very long week and a half fishing and was thirsty for the party. Record player on Metallica seek and destroy playing and towel wrapped around me walking to my bedroom, I shared a bedroom with my 4 brothers, it was a room with five bunk beds mounted to the walls and going different directions, My dad was an architect who was handy with his hands and he build the beds from scratch and mounted them on the 3 walls of the room, each lower bed had two drawers under it, one bed jutted out so it had four drawers, under the two high bunks were closets and so we all had a drawer and a closet, It was a cool set up really.

So there was a knock on the door, I opened the door and was just coming from the shower, friends of mam and dads, had called up to the house, I said hiya's doing, go on into the kitchen they are just finishing up their evening meal, there is tea on. The couple Noel & Emmer, friends of the folks we had known them years they had a son and a daughter, the son was my age and when we were 7, 8 and nine were made play together while the moms had their coffee mornings or whatever, me and their son took tennis lessons together also so we had a long history of interaction. They didn't reply much and in they came to sit with mam and dad and have evening tea.

I broke out the new denims I had bought a couple of weeks before and was getting fresh ready to hit the pubs. Imagine 15 years of age and getting spruced up on a Friday night I guess the good thing was I didn't even have to shave, face bare as a babies bottom. My mother came down to the room and said I bought you a gift and handed me a denim jacket, Levis oh boy was I loving that, a new denim jacket I was the bee's knees now. She said to me that her friends had a heard a rumour that I was dead and they had called up to sit with my mam and dad to comfort them as they heard me, their son was dead, was the rumour that had been going around the local town for the last couple of days. I laughed what a joke, I said to my mother, "hey mam what would you have done with the denim jacket if I was dead"? "She said a mother knows and I don't listen to rumours, I knew you were not dead, even though you were not here I knew you were out fishing". "Is that why you bought me the jacket"? "No it is because I won five numbers in the lottery this past week and bought something for you and each of your brothers with the winnings"

Jesus what a stroke of luck must have been 1989 or '90 she had won a little over a thousand pounds in the lottery and that was a good chunk of change. Of course if she had the sixth number she would have had a million but that's the way it goes.

45

Chapter 5.

Off I went out on the town, Friday night new clothes all the way and money in my pocket, I really remember that evening walking from my house that it really felt great to be alive, that was on my mind cause of the whole rumour thing. I met up with my buddy BO who we had watched the silence of the lambs earlier in the week and we headed straight to the bar for a few pints. The whole evening people were coming up to me, "oh Jesus, we heard you were dead" "let me pinch you, is it really you", we went to another bar and the same thing, I even met one of my class mates from well where I should have been in school too but they were still there, oh my god they said. Our history teacher had a minutes silence for you and everything during the week and all the teachers even still talk about you. Whenever we hear anything about you, like the rumours you were fighting on the streets over the weekend or you were seen in a bar by the teachers at the weekend and for all of us to keep you in our thoughts, and now this week you are supposed to dead…

Me and my buddy Bo we knew there was a whole mix up as we met the guy the owner of the night club that night Wednesday night early Thursday morning who had said someone had their head bust open. Somehow because we met that guy that night on our walk over the harbour road my name got into the mix and in the whole town was the rumour that I was dead. Bo had said to me on one of our walks between bars on our Friday night pub crawl, "I am getting sick of this fucking everyone saying Oh you are dead etc. etc." I laughed and on we went more drinking to be done.

The walk between the bars was always a good excuse to smoke a joint along the way to get as high as we possibly could, that was just the normal routine. I would guess at that time I was 15 approx. so Bo was about 18 or 19. He was fully legal to be drinking in the bars and I had just been around the older crew from the harbour for so long now that the bar tenders just grouped me in with them and figured I was old enough. By 15 I could walk into the bar and with the nod of my head to the barman a creamy pint of Guinness would be on, there were even times when money was scarce the nod would include a few mumbles to the bar man, give me a pint and the change of twenty, in other words a loan so I could buy cigarettes and have a few cold creamy pints, maybe a quiet week night where we would not be paid until the weekend.

In those days growing up, there were all kinds of different feuds going on between people and different parishes or different towns, the young crowd fighting. I was no exception. I really never started a fight; this was something that always made me confused why I ended up in so many of them. The more I fought the better I got. Somehow someone always started something with someone and because I was in the thick of it in seconds, I would try and do the finishing. The alcohol and the drugs did not help; the short temper of a young strong fit man ready to defend his family or his friends was quick to throw the head and a few fists.

Me and Bo went back to the bar we had started in, to finish up the night and then I remember feeling not so tough and not so ready to fight, when Carson, said to me can I have a word with you outside.

Now they were the words usually used when someone was about to get a beat down, and this fella Carson, well a good bit older than me probably in his twenties, maybe 24 or 25 and rumoured, I didn't really know him as I didn't grow up with him but all the lads from the harbour did and so we had shared a few drinks and been at a few parties together, but the rumour was he was the toughest man for fighting in the town at the time. So when the toughest guy and a head case to boot, says "let me have a word with you outside" It is usually a good idea, say yes I will be right there head for the bathrooms and get out the window or sneak out through the lounge hoping he doesn't walk out from the bar before you. I was well drunk and stoned at

the time that night and Bo looked at me like, "fuck"
I walked behind him out the door and remember
trying to think of all the hard man rules of fighting,
hit first, hit or be hit, catch him by surprise throw
the first punch and make it count. Ah fuck it I
thought I will take my beating for whatever he
thinks I done, my fast brain and tongue are not
going to work here. He opened the door ahead of
me and went through to the street, the pub is located
on a little dead end street so no traffic the lights of
the bar and one street lamp light the street, I stepped
through the door and he was standing there on the
pathway outside and handed me a joint and said
"light that up" I am watching his hands like a hawk
getting ready, thinking he hands me the joint my
hands are occupied, I point my eyes down to light
the joint and boom it will pop off, so I am on an
edge as any young fighting lunatic could be who
has about 8 or 10 pints a few shots of vodka and a
half a dozen joints smoked this evening. I light the
joint and he speaks "you know what" he says, "we
all got a bit of a shock this week when we heard you
were dead" I have to admit and let you know we,
me and my girlfriend were planning a big party for
a wake type of thing in your honour" "That news
was shocking" I said, "oh yeah you heard about that
too". He laughed he has a very distinctive deep
smoky poker player type of laugh... "Heard about it,
the whole town heard about it" I passed the joint

and we laughed together. He said be careful whoever or whatever you get up to and whoever is your enemies, because we all believed someone put a stop to you and I want to say I am so glad to see it is not true and you are alive.

Funny thing about that is I have had several meetings and side by side chats with people along the course of my life and take this guy Carson for example, or the two guys on the harbour, Pulit and Eddy. All older guys who had rumours of being vicious and head cases and tough nuts and violent and all bad things said about them, but the truth being at a very young age I experienced a real true side of these guys a real sense of normal human beings and so the idea of listening to rumours, just like my mother had said to me earlier in the bedroom, "I don't listen to rumours" well from now on neither would I.

We went back into the bar and Bo thought I was going to be all beat up, we called for the few last drinks and the laughs were going great. Friday night everybody drunk "well oiled" and so we headed for the Chinese, a usual favourite after a feed of pints, we were young but we had money, our wages that weekend for example my memory says were 580 Irish pounds that week, now a typical person doing labouring work or a regular job might be earning 100 to 120 a week, so having 580 handed to a young fella, we didn't care about 50 pounds for a night out, to some it was a half a week's wages to us it was nothing.

We made the corner to head for the main street where the Chinese take away was located, still is actually and there were two guys, one of them I recognized. He is from Rush I thought. To explain, I come from a small village called Loughshinny in county Dublin, Fingal area it is known as too. North county Dublin was most famous at that time for the first new potatoes every year to the market competing with the Dutch from Holland for the best and first new potatoes. As far as the people from around the country of Ireland were, most or many would be farming towns, Dublin to the country folk means bright lights big city, to the people of Dublin city, north county Dublin is the countryside, many came in those years to the seaside for family holidays during summer months, as our village Loughshinny has a little harbour of lobster fishing boats, Skerries the local town to the north about two miles from Loughshinny along the coast is where the bigger fishing boats for the prawn fishing, where I worked and to the south about 2 miles again the town of Rush, one or two lobster fishermen there but Rush is mostly a farming community, with a similar feel to any town in Ireland where it is one long main street and all the rest is just fields glasshouses and produce farming.

So I saw this guy from Rush and my head said to me, I remember this past week I heard something about an old classmate of mine from national school had had the windows in their house broken by people throwing rocks, my friend from Loughshinny, well not exactly a friend but when you come from Loughshinny and grew up as close nit as we all did, everyone is your friend or your brother or whatever, so I see this guy standing on the street and I recognize he is from Rush, the guys that broke the windows are supposed to be or alleged to be from Rush....I had no idea why I connected the dots, between this guy, Murphs house and the windows.

Rush, all thoughts racing to connect the dots as quickly as I did but a beat down was the only answer. Now we are in Skerries and I am saying to this guy from Rush, you think you can come to Loughshinny and smash windows and then walk around Skerries like no one will know, fuck you as I throw the punches. His friend tries to get in the middle of it, "mac mac what are you doing"? He is a friend of my older brother and that's what they would have called my older brother. I take a second to focus and see that I know this guy, he is from Loughshinny, I am thinking what the fuck are you doing with this prick from Rush? Nothing is making sense, now my Buddy Bo is roaring at me to stop the fighting and he says he has had enough of me going nuts for no reason and he is taking off.

To explain, the guy from Loughshinny I know and is a friend and class mate of my brothers and he also is best friends with Murph, this makes no sense...needless to say I got it completely wrong, yes the guy is from Rush but he too is best friends with Murph and so all I saw was his face, registered Rush and Murph at the same time and the broken windows popped into my head and that was all I needed but I had it all wrong. Punching this guy around the head, yup BO was right for no reason. Ah to hell with it off I went. Luckily the guy didn't press any charges or do anything about it, a couple of weeks later hanging out at the cross roads in Loughshinny another friend of theirs in common came and threw a few weak punches at me for having that altercation, but it became nothing.

I will openly admit these punch up types of things started to become a little more frequent now and I was a bit of a ticking bomb. The stories are endless and with the continued weekend fighting in the streets comes a bit of a bad name and trouble with the Garda; the Garda are what we call the police in Ireland.

Chapter 6.

By this time I had in my head always and now that
the muscles were starting to develop, that with my
new skills of how to be fast with my hands and
ability to fight I had a few scores to settle. So I
caught up with one of the older guys who used to
beat me up on the boat when I was a youngster, of
course I was still a youngster in the realm of normal
society but by 15 I was a man, I had been "at it" for
a few years now. 15 when I think back or come
across a young man of 15 today these days I do not
put them on the same calibre as me as I just seemed
older in many ways of how I conducted myself. But
I was as dumb as any 15 year old that's for sure,
however for me in a clever way. In around fifteen
years of age in Ireland we have a national exam in
school called the inter cert, they call it junior cert
now. I used to spend days out fishing, at sea where
a day consisted of, you are standing there tailing
prawns well it is just like a factory job really except
the boat keeps going up and down, but may times
would smoke a joint and get into deep thought and I
thought to myself, fuck I have fucked off my brains
and school there is just no going back now and I
should be doing my inter cert this year, staring into
the ocean and thinking dam what have you done. I
thought to myself, to hell with it, the world is made
of two thirds water, I have been learning a skill

becoming a fisherman I can fish all over the world what do I need an education for I am educating myself in what is known as an unskilled labour profession.

Another Saturday evening at the bar at the top of the harbour, the drinks are going down well and what do you know one of the guys who used to always beat me up is at the bar. There were four of us and so we drank a few pints headed outside to share a joint and when he was sitting on the windowsill of the bar rolling another joint I took all my might and bust him straight up under the jaw with an uppercut of great proportion, his head went back the joint went everywhere and I stood there waiting for him to get up and said, "come on get up and beat me now" "get up". He put his head down and his hands up around his head curling up his knee and stayed sitting on the windowsill, "no I am sorry, I am sorry, I don't want to fight you" I could see the blood running from his nose and all I wanted was for him to even lean forward and think as to get up I knew in my head straight through the window is where I will put him. The other two guys, Bo being one of them pushing me back saying come on leave it, he is not worth it, while I kept saying , trust me Fagan, let me think you want to have something with me I will leave you eating through a straw for months, tubes will be feeding you. I walked up the town along the harbour road that evening with a feeling of being unstoppable, this guy used to beat me when I was a new kid on the scene but I wasn't 12 anymore. I was a strong 6ft2 well-built fighter now.

Of course it wasn't all about fighting, I was a fun loving guy I used to tease and make fun of my friends and others and hang out and have the laugh. I loved to be having a good buzz with a few joints and a few beers, what the hell is wrong with that? That is what I always thought. Except now the laughs could turn ugly at any moment because I was ready for the fight regardless. What was life then, chaos would be a good word for it. I would never dare to go near a bar where my dad would go. He had his local and I stayed well clear of that place cause he knew I was drinking, he didn't know much about the drugs side of things, some evenings on a Saturday night he would give me a lift down to the town when he was heading out for a few pints himself and he would lecture me, saying look, I only go out at 9.30 pm because I know I can have 4 pints nice and comfortable in that time frame and go home just a social drink and a bit of craic (crack) it is an Irish word meaning "having a laugh" or "having fun". I would sit sometimes thinking about my dad and his four pints of Guinness and think what the heck; it is 9.30 I better get two into me before ten and then another 4 before 11 and another three or four before closing time.

The drugs were getting to be as a necessity as the booze at this time, I would head off into the city, take a train or the bus into the city, head in around the flats in the middle of the city because that is where you could find someone to buy hash from, now you had to be careful that the inner city street kids wouldn't rob your money first on the way in or on the way out rob your drugs, so yeah the innocence was still there in that sense. In the city people would stab each other rather than fight, if it came to fighting we, well me. I could hold my own but there always was that fear of getting robbed. Me and a crew mate of mine Willie headed into the city one Thursday evening to go and buy some hash for the weekend, we were finished fishing for the week and had our money. We ended up in a guy's flat where he had only a couple of small 10 pound deals of hash we wanted like 100 worth, he hadn't got it. But what he did have was a couple of micro dots, I played along micro dots, yeah sure gives us one each. I had not got a clue what a micro dot was, but we paid for them and off we went. We looked at each other, and said go ahead you take it, alright we take them together then, ok go. I didn't swallow mine, two little things looked like pencil lead he had given us, Willie swallowed his so I said, ok here goes as we walked out the parking area of the flats, the Oliver bond flats in Dublin city. We started to walk along the quays as the Oliver bond flats are along the river Liffey in the centre of Dublin and is near to the Guinness factory, always a great smell of roasting hops from the factory in that part of town. As we started walking down the quays there is a garage there a petrol station and who is filling up their car, a new sports type car well not really sports but a little bullet type car a sporty Volvo or something like that anyway, my uncle yup my dad's brother who lives in the city, he says what are you doing I am waiting for this acid to kick in and trying to make an excuse, ah nothing me and my friend are heading for the train station to head back out home, "come on he says I will give you a lift" we jump in and head down to the train station. Luckily for us the timing is perfect, there is an express train that leaves Dublin going to Belfast and the first stop on the way is Skerries, so we are first stop perfect. My uncle drops us off; we are a little giddy, nothing happening for him yet nothing happening for me, we are a little scared cause we are not sure what is supposed to happen anyway. We jump on the train and away for Skerries, now it is about a fifteen minute ride maybe twenty when on the express the usual commuter train would be about half an hour to forty five minutes. This train goes at I believe 8.10 or 8.15 maybe. We had standing room only, the train is full of suits and business people who commute to the city every day for work, off we get with all the commuters at Skerries and we walk with the crowd under the train tracks there is a little brick tunnel type passageway under the tracks and out the other side to the housing development and we are in Skerries, we are a little giddy still and the crowds are jumping into cars and walking fast and I turn to Willie and say I am tripping dude, he says me too and we laugh our asses off all the way along the pathway down through the neighbourhood, we have no idea what is happening to us most of the commuters are giving us the weird looks, like what is wrong with them, those who recognize us, because Skerries is not really a big place, give us the look of "oh they are from the harbour, the boats, they must be high" it was a stigma attached to the group of us as everyone even the Garda, had said to me one time when they stopped me for a simple routine search procedure, where is the hash we know you all live on the stuff over there on that harbour. Me and Willie were as high as we could ever be. We could not figure out how we were in Oliver bond flats about what felt like five minutes ago, my uncle drove his new care like a race car through the traffic of the city along the quays to the train station and the express had us in Skerries in minutes, we were so high and beginning to freak out that how did we get here and was this even real. Willie came up with the great idea of we need to get indoors so we headed to our local pub where we were regulars.

There was a good crowd in for the night, for a Thursday at least, Willie ordered a beer, Carlsberg more than likely and I had a club orange in a pint glass with ice, club orange is probably one of the sweetest orange drinks you can get but ice cold not much can beat it, I was too afraid to mix the alcohol. We sat at the table, the tables were like big old beer barrels and we sat on the high stools like two perch monkeys freaking each other out about who in the bar knew we were on acid. Who knew the "craic", who knew we were on acid, looking at folks in for their few pints of a Thursday night and smiling and saying hello to people as they went to the bathrooms and passed us by, and then they would return to their company and their drinks, me and Willie are sitting opposite each other trying to convince each other that, they are over there talking about us and they know the "craic", they are cool they won't say anything. So the bar tender that night Willie could not help himself but to tell him that we were so high we didn't know what we were doing and if we did anything strange help us out. Well, the worst thing was telling him, every so often he would come over and empty the ashtray and wipe down the table with a few words muttered out the side of his mouth, things like, "would ya look at two of you, 400 cigarettes smoked in an hour and ashes everywhere, no wonder people are talking about yous" then he would come back again and say "the couple over there want to buy yous a drink but Willie you have one sip out of your beer in the last hour, and your date well look at her on the club orange", that was me. So me and Willie are trying so hard to keep our shit together and people are coming cracking jokes and we are freaked as to think how we are supposed to act and how are we supposed to respond, keep it together is what we keep telling each other. I was sitting there scanning around the whole bar area wondering who really knows that I am higher than I have ever been, and who really cares, when I noticed Willie wasn't even there any more, seemed like an hour I started getting edgy where is he, where did he go, what happened, now I was freaking out. I made a screwed up high decision to go to the restrooms, the toilets, to just get out of the crowded bar, and who do you think is standing in the toilets in front of the mirror like a zombie, good old Willie, he is delighted to see me and I am delighted to see him, what are you doing, I don't know he says, I can't get out of the mirror, I am freaking man you left me behind out there alone, they all know now, the whole place is looking at me weird sitting there on my own. Willie is just staring into the mirror, I said come on man we have to go back out, we both stand there at the door of toilets, inside the toilets, we straighten out or clothes and shirts and take deep breaths are you ready, yeah you, no but let's go, ready on three we open the door and head back out to the bar. This was like we were going on stage for a concert or a play or the theatre or something we had to psych ourselves up to the challenge. The bar tender keeps it going now he is telling us under his breath as he comes to wipe down the table, they know and that couple over there know and so on and so forth. For our first time on acid we were a mess. We headed out to the fish and chip shop and stood there in line and ordered nothing and left, smoked a couple of joints and headed home. I had walked home and it was about 3 am I thought I would never come down, I crept into the house and into my bedroom all my brothers were asleep I woke my older brother, they were all good guys school going children at the time, I woke my older brother anyway and told, hey man I am on acid, you have to try it is amazing, he was all groggy waking up, what? Go to bed and shut up, he said I was pleading with him no seriously you have to try it; eventually I was lying in bed and fell asleep. Acid a weird experience, we got lucky we scored some good acid and had a great trip and all returned to normal the next day, I can tell you it does feel like it might never end. Which does happen, and the reason I can say this for sure is, there were many more trips after that but we found the cheap easy way, where we grew up in the countryside, in Loughshinny there were fields a plenty where magic mushrooms grew. I remember being like 4 or 5 and all the punk rockers used to be in the fields around our house and the story was they were getting mushrooms and getting high, cause the punk thing was big then and so they used to be there with mohawks, pink and green and so you could see them miles away, but we had grown now and it was our turn to be hunting mushrooms. One buddy of mine one day was running through the field eating sheep shit and rubbing it all over himself and trying to get us all to eat with him and laughing, he kept saying "I have a great life", "I have a great life" chasing us around trying to offer us sheep shit to eat. His sister used to hang out with us and we told her take him home, after we were finished tripping for the day we went to his house to check on him he was asleep and his sister, said all the way home he was trying to hitch a ride with every car that passed by waving his dick at the car, and when they finally reached the town he walked into a little shop and the rack that has all the birthday cards he just went behind it and took a piss, Just another fun packed day getting high.

One evening on the mushrooms, we were on one of the boats eating mushrooms as many as we could and getting high high high, and one of the guys started freaking out saying we were all thrash and no good, I was drunk at the time I didn't eat the mushrooms, but we were sitting over there in the harbour on one of the boats, everyone there, ten or twenty of us, rolling joints drinking cans of beer and everybody high and he started freaking out, I went upstairs with him and said hey man what's the problem, if you don't calm down I will beat the shit out of you, he said I don't care every one of you and them down below are all scum. I want nothing to do with you, then someone whispers to me he is out of his head on mushrooms, I am making a pact with him that I will beat the living shit out of him but not today because he is on mushrooms, tomorrow when I see you it is on. He wants me to beat him then and there, as he just keeps talking a whole bunch of tough shit. My friend who I had been drinking with is down below, we had been drinking all day and he comes up and says, nobody wants to come up because I had taken this guy up from the cabin saying no one was to come up from the cabin because things are all aggressive, me and him we are going to settle this in private, we were having a full blown heated argument and I told him tomorrow you are a dead man. Now that guy stayed in his mom's house for about 8 months, his mother didn't know what was wrong with him, he would not even go to the store for a pack of cigarettes. After about five months me and a friend called up to visit him and he was just real blank and watching TV and not talking much, I felt guilty that maybe all my hard talk and threats killed his trip from the mushrooms or whatever, when me and my buddy left from our visit with him, I remember we both said, man those mushrooms are dangerous. Look what they are after doing to him, he still seems high from them, 5 to 6 months later. So yeah the mushrooms and the acid are a dangerous gig. In the town of Skerries we had another known associate for want of a better phrase, one of the guys who would have been eating mushrooms back when I was a kid seeing the punks, well he was permanently high, he would come over the boats some evenings when we would be in from sea and smoking a few joints in the galley and he didn't fish anymore because everyone knew he was just permanently high. He would smoke about 10 cigarettes in ten minutes and tell the wildest stories and every one tolerated him because they knew him from before, but he was out there, he wouldn't smoke any hash with us, because he was into god now, and his teeth were so rotten looking from the smoking, he just chewed cigarettes, he took mushrooms one time and never came down, for years, and years. Joey is his name, the most unfortunate thing and what can bring you up to speed, that night when I was supposed to be the one that was dead, that weekend when everyone thought I was dead, well the guy that bust his head open on the rocks was Joey, he tried to dive head first into the sea or into the rocks who knows, and mashed his whole head up. Maybe he wanted to stop his own madness and finish it or maybe he was just still high and thought he was going swimming, but he didn't die, I had heard updates from time to time about Joey that he was in intensive care and they were going to try and start teaching him to type and write stuff by using a pointer type thing, like a pencil taped to his head where he could punch things out on a keyboard so they could do some therapy and try and teach him to communicate all over again. One of the last times I was home in Skerries, I saw him in a wheelchair being pushed by his sister I believe, for a walk down the harbour and he had a blanket across himself, looking like a vegetable for want of a better expression. So yes indeed the mushrooms were great fun but not everyone can withstand them and the devastation can be catastrophic when someone ends up stuck there on a trip permanently high. My friend Willie, who I or we took our first acid together, is no longer with us, suicide a few years back. Willie another true friend gone. He had a tough run with prison and robberies and beatings and more prison. I will always remember Willie when I was a complete out of control lunatic, standing square in front of me on the boat one evening when I showed up with 6 cans and was all high asking, me what is wrong with you? Do you want to go to prison and fuck up all the rest of your life, what is wrong with you, you need to give it up and stop the madness. Just another great true friend through the entire crazy goings on through our adolescents that, is no longer with us. Always in my mind Willie for the laughs we shared. It didn't stop me of course I couldn't wait to get more drugs and keep it all going.

Chapter 7.

One of the tough times when fishing is the winter, the weather is worse and so less money to be made, so the best way is to save some money and buy some hash in big quantities and sell it locally to keep twenties and fifties flowing when there is less money to be made from the fishing. Me and another buddy Tony, we used to make the trip into the city and spend that little extra and then when someone wanted a twenty we would have the goods and give it to them, everything was ounces and quarters and half ounces and so we would buy maybe like the equivalent of a kilo of hash and dish it out bit by bit, around Christmas time, that way if there was no money from the fishing because the boats were not going out to sea with bad weather if

I wanted to go to the bar, I just needed enough for one pint and then I could sit there sipping and someone would buy something for ten or twenty pounds and I could get a skin full of booze for the night, 15 and enterprising. I happened across a couple of fishing buddies in the city of Dublin one night at a bar who had kilos of speed, methamphetamines I think that is what they call it, powder form, they were so high they gave me about half a kilo and said go on make some money. So that Christmas I had hash and speed for sale and to get high off, of course, but would keep me in money. The hash me and Tony bought is funny in its own story, we had our money saved up and we needed to get into the city and buy 2 kilos of hash. Tony was staying in rented accommodation with a family, a friend of his, their parents were letting him stay there for handing up some cash. One night we decided this other friend, Peter was there and sometimes his mother let him have the car, so we said "hey tell you what drive us into the city to score some hash and we will give you a bit, like a twenty", he said cool I will get my mother's car tomorrow. We headed into the city and he parked on the quays, there is an area of Dublin called sheriff street, there were a block of flats there where we had our dealer who was ready and waiting for us with the kilos, we went to the flat and packed our shorts with the hash leaving the flat and back to the quays to Peter who was waiting. We jumped into the car and like in the movies said go, go, go, he pulled out immediately into traffic.

I was in the passenger seat and I could see my shadow on the sun visor someone behind was flashing lights at us. I could not even sit straight because of all the hash in my shorts and now we are going to get arrested, the cops are behind us. OH fuck, I thought we are screwed beyond belief. I looked at Peter and said do not stop this car until we are back in Skerries for nobody or for nothing. He said hell no this is my mom's car...

We got back to Tony's place and started to take the hash out and roll a couple of joints and smoke them from the cuttings as we were cutting the stuff up into deals of smaller size obviously cause we were getting ready for sales, Peter was higher than he had ever been cause we kept the joints flowing and gave him a nugget of hash, we kept cutting and packaging the deals of hash all the while getting high. Somewhere through the evening Peter broke his high silence, "if I knew there was this much hash I never would have agreed" "man my mother would have killed me" the lucky thing was the flashing lights were someone who was flashing their full beam head lights at us in traffic because when we jumped into the car and said go go go, Peter pulled right out into the lane of traffic and cut off the guy who was flashing out of anger. At that time I really thought jail for sure and cops, but luckily that is all it was, of course we never told Peter, we were going to buy 2 kilos of hash. Needless to say we drank all the profits that Christmas, and had a great time getting high and wasted and we had our own atm machine in the form of little money bags of deals of hash. I remember being at home one night wasted as hell fell asleep in front of the TV and in my denim jacket pocket was an ounce of hash, my mother confiscated it. She had no real clue what it was, turned out it wasn't the first time she confiscated from my pockets, as I learned one day on an intensive search of my mother's old handbags was she had five 20 pound deals too in her bag. I got all the hash back that day, she had been going to work every day in the city for months, carrying a couple of hundred pounds worth of hash, I laughed at her and said, if the Garda had stopped you what were you going to say, they would have you for possession and intent to sell or distribute because of the deals, they would not care about the fact you confiscated it from your son and you didn't really know what it was, you were in possession. Things of a funny nature happen, the day I found that hash on my mother's old handbag I remember lighting a joint filling the bath with hot water and soaking in it. About 11am, nice and high and relaxing, all my brothers at school, my mother and father at work and me no fishing. What better way to spend the mid-morning, when I was dressed and out of the bath, my older brother had come home and he always liked to try and control me, so he came barking at me about the smell of hash, he would have been leaving cert that year so his school schedule was always a little different, barking mad at me anyway about what was I doing smoking hash in the house. I followed him into the sitting room and the door of the sitting room caught the mat just inside the door and came slap right back at me and hit me right in the bone above my eye, sore, I remember, I kicked the door as hard as I could and my shoe went right through it, I turned to walk away and my brother came barking more at me out of the sitting room, a scuffle ensued and I had him pinned in the corner of the hallway by the hall door of the house, with a punch to the head that I gave him his whole shoulder went out through the glass window to the side of the front door. The front door of the house is a big old mahogany door with about 8 feet across between the door and the panes of glass on each side. Of course it was this weird type of frosted glass little bubbles in it, so it was not see through. I thought what the fuck now, I was high but my happy buzz had all but gone and what now I have the sitting room door with a gaping hole in it and a whole pane of glass broke in bits at the front door. This looks bad, I called my dad at the office and explained him the wind had slammed the door and it was my fault and where could I buy the glass so I could replace, of course being the architect, it was not your average glass and he said, leave it alone until I come home, as all the panes would have to either be replaced together as he doesn't think he can find that exact glass anymore…

Another great day when I found the hash and thought I had won the lottery gone to shit, with violence and a mess.

Chapter 8.

I was now turning 16 and this was the time I had been waiting for because there is a fishery school where you can go and get certified to be an able bodied seaman and get some papers to say you are a trained fisherman, but they do not encourage young people to leave school and so you have to be 16 to be allowed to take the course, it means going to Donegal which is the northern tip of Ireland to take classes and live with a family there for three months while you take the course and you get an allowance of pocket money while you are on the course. My dad was in agreement of it and so I couldn't wait, I had the application forms all filled out and was waiting to hear if I was going to be accepted to the course. Of course this meant for my dad I would be off the local streets and all these altercations that kept occurring of people showing up to the house claiming I stole something or I hit someone might stop.

One night of another session and drinking and acting the clown, word comes that there is a girl who is having a 21st birthday party, I managed to find my way to the house uninvited of course but we all knew each other so there I was in the kitchen sneaking out the back for a smoke, I used to have a homemade pipe for putting the hash in and smoking hard and fast then so I was hanging out in the kitchen of this girls party as we would just step out the back door and blast the pipe me and a couple of friends who were at the party, they were invited though, and then back into the kitchen for a beer or two, the house was full of youngsters all her friends and gangs of people at the party. In the kitchen was an island counter top separating the eating area from the cooking area a couple of arm chairs in the living area. The eating area of the kitchen had a fireplace across the back wall of the kitchen. It is a development of houses so they are all pretty much the same a front room and a stairs up to the bedrooms a long hallway from the front door into the kitchen with the front room off to the left. But the house was full of people, the Garda were at the front door because some neighbour had complained about the noise, being that I was pretty tall I could see them at the front door over all the heads in the long hallway and the Garda could see me, they knew me well by now with a bunch of arrests for drunk and disorderly and accusations of assaults, but I had nothing fully charged as all cases were on different kind of appeals. Anytime I would see the Garda I would always think they were looking for me for something, but they left and the party continued. Me and my friend Milli were in and out smoking the pipe and drinking it up when in walks an old friend from the harbour, from the fishing boats, what do you know another good soldier who used to beat and whip me with lead ropes. Turns out he is the boyfriend of the girl turning 21. I just keep swigging my beer in the kitchen by the back door and making fun with Milli and looking straight at this piece of shit guy who is sitting in one of the arm chairs in the living area part of the kitchen, the music is playing everyone is having fun. I am as high as a helicopter, and this guy knows me well and he won't take his eyes off me. One time while out having a smoke I asked Milli why is he here, he explains me he is the boyfriend and I tell Milli I am going to bust him here tonight. Milli pleads with me don't start anything; I said no fucking way I have been waiting years for this fucker. Milli says he does not want any part of it, I said don't worry I can handle myself, I have known Milli since I was about

5 years of age, Milli is older than me but he is a lobster fisherman and I am a prawn fisherman so we don't mix much I work in Skerries he works in Loughshinny. While we are there in the kitchen in the area of the cooker on the island is the cake , happy 21st something or other in colourful icing, I say hey Milli I want a slice of cake, some other girl says oh no we have to wait til later, she will be doing the cake later. I flexed my chest watching her boyfriend over there in the chair his foot his tapping away 90 beats a minute like someone with a twitch or is going to do something about something, I puff the chest up and say I said I want a piece of cake and her birthday doesn't mean shit to me. I went to grab a handful of cake and Milli grabbed my hand to say stop man, leave it alone, come on let's leave and go down town and have a few pints. I picked the cake up and smashed the whole thing in Millis face, with that her boyfriend jumped to his feet, I met him before he was standing straight with a very serious and direct punch to the nose right between the eyes he landed in the fire place ass first, legs hanging out nose bleeding and I stood centre of the kitchen fists clinched saying "get up , get up and fight" girls were screaming and people freaking out, birthday cake was all over the floor and this guy was too chicken to move. I don't know exactly was he knocked out but he wasn't saying anything or moving much. I stood there and spat on him and

said, "Yeah you never thought I would grow up, I am not a kid anymore, anytime, anytime" Milli was pulling on my arm with bits of cake all in his hair, come on lets go they have called the Garda, so we headed out over the back fence and away down the street to the bar down town for a few pints. Just another fun night, with a bit of badness thrown in.

I was bad and getting worse by the day, what was a day or a night out if there was not a nose broken or some blood shed somewhere along the line, funny thing I still maintained except for the pay back the vengeance broken noses, I never started anything, I was out one night myself and a crew member Nicky, we used to run from pub to pub making the sound of motorbikes, as out in the Skerries area they hold two big motorbike racing weekends each year and so motorbikes are a big favourite of many. We used to go from a pub where would play darts for money try and win a few fivers and then head off to the GAA club where they held a poker night. We would go and play in the poker and see could we win, Nicky was good at playing poker, I was just there to keep the vodka and orange flowing and would play the game, and I think I might have made a final table once. Nicky didn't go for the smoking the hash too much cause he liked the beer better and sometimes he would smoke but he would get so high he didn't know his own name. We were both drunk one night and headed back to the fish and chip shop after the pub was finished, I remember barely holding my head up by resting it on the stainless counter as I shuffled along in the line, two other guys came in and were drunk too, and started cracking jokes, these guys knew Nicky a little bit and knew my older brother too or at least knew I was his younger brother, next thing they started making fun of Nicky's shoes. He had on a pair of loafers I guess you could call them, they were popular at the time, they had the little tassel at the front almost like a pair of golf shoes but without the spikes, look at them golf shoes or are they for ballet is the fun remarks they were poking. I was head downwards anyway with an awful drunk on me but I could see the tassels on the shoes of Nicky. When we got to pay for our food Nicky said come on lets go and then he turned around to the guy giggling and making fun of his shoes and real serious and stern like, said, "you wanna watch your big mouth" Nicky wasn't into fighting much but he had a serious side to him all the same. I raised my head and told the guy shut the fuck up or I will break his jaw with a box. The other guy came on with the "ahh come on now young McNally go away home to Loughshinny with ya", of course we were in Skerries, chippers right beside the church, and was known always as the central. The old lady the owner, of the family that owned it said, come on now lads there will be none of that or I will call the Garda. I went outside and munched down my burger there is a low set of steps right in front of the chippers, I was sitting there and out came the two fun makers on their own happy drunk buzz. I couldn't help it, Nicky said No, I said yes and I continued to kick the guy in the head three or four times while he stood there, I thought I was van dame those days and I walked step by step towards him kicking him up sides the head. With that the Garda were coming and so I started to walk away. I turned back while the Garda were there asking him what happened his face and why he was full of blood, the Garda were going to talk to lady from the chip shop. I walk right behind him and whispered , "you open your mouth and this is only half of what I will do to you, should have shut your mouth when you were told to" so the guard came back and the guy says he fell on the steps and that it was just an accident, "are you sure" asked the cop. Yes, yes he replied and then I piped up, now you heard the guy now piss off copper, stop trying to come around here making up bullshit. The guard told me directly, McNally you shut your mouth, I said hell no it is a free country I can say whatever I want, within seconds hand cuffs went on me, and he told me throwing me down on the front of Garda car, well then keep talking because I am taking you for a breach of the peace and maybe that will make you stay quiet.

Arrested again but lucky to get away without the assault charge. Off to the garda station in Balbriggan, this is another town about another 5 miles north along the coast in north county Dublin.

Because I was so young I guess they were obliged to call my parents and so my father came and got me, of course I did not want to see him either, so as soon as I got out of the police station I didn't go and get in his car either I jumped the high fence and took off down the streets, I knew balbriggan pretty well by this time in my life plenty of good session down the back streets of balbriggan too, my good friend Eddy who was ready to set the club on fire for me was from there, good few session in Balbriggan. My Dad didn't give up, he followed me and scoured the streets and caught up to me saying, I am not mad at you and don't have anything bad to say just get in the car come home and clean yourself up. I went for the bargaining and jumped in, all the way home my dad just went on and on about, look maybe you should just take up boxing, according to the police you are pretty good at it and I will drive you to a boxing club in the city for training if you want. We got to the house, I said hell no thanks, and I will never voluntarily stand there and allow someone hit me square in the nose, no way. That was what boxing was to me, my dad was pleading that it would be a great way to get it out and you might win at it. No not for me, too organized and allowing someone hit me in the nose, just not an option.

By these times turned sixteen, ready to head off and do my fishery school course and cannot wait, but drinking and drugging is not going to stop. With those were coming a weekly visit to the district court house for assault and breach of the peace and these petty things, the worst of it was the charges that the garda just made up to try and get me locked up in jail. For example I went a little nuts one night full of booze in a chippers, I was drunk waiting for a burger and some onion rings, the shop was crowded, I saw the girl I had ordered with take the onion rings out of the oil, bag em up and put them under the heat lamp while she tended to my burger, with that one of the other women working there, goes ahead and says something to her and decides to grab the onion rings and serve someone else quicker, to move the crowd through I guess. I jumped the counter and picked the lady up and held her up against the drinks fridge, what are you doing with my onion rings that's all I wanted to know. My friend who I had been out with for the night, his head appeared in front of my face between me and

the lady right up under my arms, well in between
my arms, WHAT ARE YOU DOING? I focused on
him and realized I had gone bonkers and had this
lady held up by the neck, I let go of her and left the
building. A couple of hundred meters up the road
walking towards my friend's house, the garda cars
were parked there on the street two of them, we
walked across the intersection and continued up the
street, when all of a sudden the two garda cars, were
pulling in at the pathway beside us, zoom zoom,
two cars pull up and all the garda jump out, I turn
around to see and the first guy jumping out of the
car is one of the Garda I have been having a terrible
time with, as I turn around I say "oh Duffy" I am
meet with a box to the head and a "oh McNally"
there is a little laneway just at that part of the street
and I got beat down that laneway by the Garda and
my friend is being pushed further up the street so as
not to see, there must have been five of them maybe
beating on me that night, now yes I did just come
from jumping over the counter in the fish and chips
shop and had been quite a scoundrel around the
town, but for no reason are these garda provoked by
me that night, they were punching and kicking and
beating pretty good, I curled up in a ball and held
my hands up around my head and just let them beat
away, I could take it.. As quickly as it started it had
stopped and they were gone, I tried to straighten out
my body and stand up I had a good few aches and

pains. I got up stretching out my shoulders and my back and walking out of the laneway, I really was sore and that didn't happen too often, I rounded the corner in the direction of going home and was still trying to stretch out the pains, like walking tall but not comfortably at all, as I rounded the corner, there is a bank and an atm machine there, there were a couple of people there and across the street one of the popular bars in the town. Standing outside that bar are a few guys and one starts shouting at me, oh great there he is you are gonna get it now he says, three of them are coming towards me, oh boy I thought another beating... I said fuck it and walked towards them here we go another fight, as soon as I was in the middle of the street, those guys coming towards me and me towards them, another garda car pulls up super-fast. The guard jumped out and put me in handcuffs and threw me into the back of the car, I am speaking all kinds of abuse at the Garda, they had no right who do they think they are etc. etc., they threw me into the Garda car so as my legs were across under the driver seat and my body was across the left behind the passenger seat and the other guard was sitting in the back behind the driver. I kept telling the driver to slow down as on the ad on TV, the person in the back goes out through the window first if we crash. The cop in the back had his hands on the head rests, right hand drivers head rest and left hand passenger head rest me strewn across the back seat, with that BOOM his elbow straight into my stomach, it hurt... so I tensed up my stomach which was still tense from the adrenaline of the beating I just took, shut up you little prick he said, I went ouch, ohhh, ahhh so he came again with the elbow, this continued the whole five mile journey, I was ready for each one so I pretended they hurt, but I could see him twitching his fingers on the head rest every time he was about to draw up the elbow for the blow to me, so I in between blows kept calling them assholes and that as soon as the cuffs come off I am going to beat the living shit out of the two of them…. When we got to the police station in balbriggan, the driver jumped out of the car and ran around to me and kicked me as hard as he could up in the centre of my ass, now that hurt he connected directly on the bone. And they pushed me forwards into the police station; the cop on duty for the night came with the book to write into it the entry I guess of my booking. He asked me my name, I guess somewhere in the protocol you have to be able to speak your own name to them to verify you are competent or something so me being the wise, guy felt an Eddy Murphy moment coming on and answered, my name is Johnny wishbone, and no let me guess you are Taggart…. the cops who had brought me in gave me a real good open handed slap across the back of my head catching the ear, a good hard clout as they would call it. Believe it or not the cop with the book, the night duty shouted at him immediately, not on my watch, there has never been any violence in my 22 years and there won't be any tonight. I thought great. With that he spoke to me directly and said look you are going into a cell until I figure out what to do but there will be no more of this kind of thing tonight, he made the cops who brought me in take the handcuffs off and then I unleashed smacking and beating on the two of them, with it we went spinning around the office I was smacking and punching and kicking what I could I remember a printer hit the floor falling from a desk as we were in a dance. I knew I was arrested and this was the police station but screw it, I was a man of my word, when I promised them I would beat them as soon as they took the handcuffs off, that is exactly what I started to do. I got wrestled down the hallway and into a cell. The night duty cop came and spoke with me and said, he did not agree with that no matter who was right or wrong and that my father would be down to pick me up soon. My charges came that week, assault on Garda threatening the life of a Garda and breach of the peace. Not a whisper about the mess in the police station, these were charges for when the cops had beat me in the laneway, they all said I started on them and that I was beating Duffy. I knew it was the other way around and my friend Jos and his cousin

Nicky who were there that night being pushed up the street, got visits from the Garda that week too, they told them you will have nothing to say about the other night or charges of breach of the peace and drunken and disorderly will be brought against them too. They told me that week sorry man, there is nothing we can do we cannot afford to be up in court too with fake charges, I said it doesn't matter. I had my day in court the following week and took the witness stand and when I was questioned, I said how could I beat anyone or threaten anyone when I was face down in the dirt in an alleyway with my hands up over my head getting beat by the Garda,,,, "No further questions" from the prosecutor. I forget the sentence exactly but it was bail by my dad and appeal to the higher court immediately. I walk out and go home with my dad.

All the way home my dad is giving me a real talking to, he is asking me when am I going to stop this behaviour, when is it all going to stop, he explains to me that someday there will be no appeal and there will be no bail and they are going to keep me. I explain what do you want me to do, yes some of the fights are real but all that this morning is lies, if you don't believe me ask Jos and Nicky if you want, they know but they cannot go witness because the Garda have threatened them, what do you want me to do. My dad started to believe me that I had taken a beating from them that night and so he was on my side by the time we reached home. My mam was home that day too, her day off I guess and we sat and had tea and a sandwich but my mother had a complete look of disgust on her face, we didn't talk about the court as mam was going to explode as she did not get involved in this court business but it was known she was disgusted, I think she was so disgusted she was willing me to choke on the sandwich by the look on her face.

Well the court and more like the casual attitude my dad had that day about the whole thing. My dad went about his business at that time and a couple of months later, I was visited by a Garda car at the home, my dad was there and in walked what they called the liaison officer who I had known and the super intendant at the time, My dad says, now tell them about the treatment from this Duffy fella. I began to explain how Healy and Duffy thought they were Starsky and Hutch etc. etc. within a week my dad told me if either of them ever have anything to say to me again I am to tell him immediately that their boss the superintendent had some words with them and they had been warned away from me. I didn't think it was true but sure enough, one night walking over the harbour Healy was in the Garda car by himself and he pulled up slowly on me and asked me hey, what you doing, I said heading over to the boat to go to work, he said ah yes a few joints and off to sleep. I laughed. Healy had the worst teeth you had ever seen so I started making fun of how rotten his teeth were, he laughed and then he said, "well I cannot do anything about you anymore, so have a good night" I figured at that point they really had been warned off me.

Chapter 9.

Easter had rolled around and I would be soon heading off to Greencastle in Donegal to fishery school, fishing is always poor in and around Easter, a lot of gales and wind and so not many days out fishing.

With Easter comes good Friday in holy week, well on good Friday in Ireland all the bars are officially shut and there is nowhere open to buy alcohol, so that week me and a few of the lads from the boats decided we should go and rob a keg of beer from somewhere, so off we went. We used to use ropes with hooks on the ends of them to pull boxes of fish up the harbour wall when the tide was out so we could load them into trucks when we are "landing the catch" so equipped with the hooks we headed up the town in the middle of the night. Two strong guys on the wall with the hooks, one on the street keeping watch and the smallest fella into the yard or shed of the pub, hook in the hooks and we pull it up and out over the wall set it down to the guy on the street and take off carrying the keg back over to the boats on the harbour. Now this way we had almost a hundred pints of beer to share for Good Friday. There was not much wages expected that week and so we were all trying to get a "sub" an advance on wages for next week because on Holy Thursday of Holy week is the last night to get into the pub for a few pints. We didn't need much because we had a plan and that is how the day went. Over to the boat around 4pm drinking away from the keg and 8pm or so head for the pub buy a couple of pints just to be on the scene "out for the night" and then back to the boat for more session and finish the keg all day Good Friday. Great plan.

The bar at the top of the harbour was really a no go for the fishermen, the second bar along the harbour road was more the traditional bar for the fishermen, and all the nice to do folks would be in the lounge and the fishermen in the bar, but the night club hotel bar at the very top of the harbour was not the place for the smelly fishermen.

One night when we were all having the usual session on the boats smoking joints and drinking tea one of the lads came down aboard the boats and say hey, blah blah blah is the manager in the pier house bar, he was a guy that used to work on the boats for his summer job so the guy used to fish with him, he said he invited me up for a few after hours drinks. The poor bar man; I do not think he thought his invitation out very well. About twenty of us showed up, the front bar two pool tables and drinks are a flowing nobody paying for anything or maybe some of the lads were giving him money directly for his pocket. We were drinking away free bar and playing pool. There was a boat from another part of the country had stopped into the harbour that night but one of the crew was originally from Skerries and he just hadn't been around in a while Dick was his name so he knew all the lads and was drinking away too. I was playing pool with Paddy, and Dick and somebody else were playing pool on the other table, I reached over to take the chalk to chalk my stick from there table and as I put it back, the guy Dick says with a weird kind of accent " it is a belt of a pool cue you need" I didn't think anything of it and leaned down to take my shot, with that, crack, the whole pool stick was broken across my back I stood up slowly stretching out my back and turned towards him, but I could see coming through the crowd Willie, remember my buddy Willie, well he caught dick with a punch to the side of the head and both dropped to the floor fighting. I was standing looking and I was picking up my pool stick to give Dick a good belt of it, when Paddy who I was playing pool with hit me across the arm with his pool stick, I said what the fuck and I dropped my stick and took off out the door. Paddy was Willies brother and paddy figured I was going to hit Willie with the stick, this is the sort of confusion that goes on when a large group of lunatics are all drunk in the same area.

Well Dick had been around more then and was one of the gang now and was always around but I never liked him, never obviously the guy broke a pool stick over my back for absolutely no reason, maybe he thought he could look tough in front of all his old friends.

Holy Thursday was here and I was over on the boat drinking away and there were only four of us because we promised, only us four because we had robbed the keg and it was ours to drink. The night rolled in and drinking was continuing nicely, a couple of extra lads came over they heard we had a keg and so the drinking and smoking was in full flight, then a couple of the lads decided they were going home for a shower and we would all meet in the pub later. I was left with Brian and Barry and Dick of all people, Dick. We had a laugh and the radio on listening to music chatting smoking a few joints and filling up our beer as we wished. It was time to head up the harbour road and head for the bar; I stood up and smashed Dick as hard as I could square in the nose with a solid fist. I said you thought you were tough breaking a pool cue across my back well now you are gonna pay for it. His head went down blood everywhere and he starts crying, leave me alone please I am sorry I am sorry. Brian had a hold of my arm saying leave him alone, look you are after smashing his nose to pieces, leave him alone, I ordered Dick to get off the boat and don't come back, he left. Smart guy really. I kept saying to Brian, fuck him, fuck him I should go after him and beat the living shit out of him. Brian convinced me let's roll a joint for the walk up the road and go to the pub. Off we went.

Easter time is wintery nights cold and windy usually dry but cold and windy so harsh conditions and the harbour road is a cold long road to walk on those wintery nights. The pub was crowded, traditionally of course good Friday everywhere is closed so the pubs are full on the holy Thursday night, we had settled in, me and my three buddies knew that we hadn't got much money so it was merely for show we were there, we had a table and Barry had been missing for a while, but all of a sudden this big fat man was carting Barry out the doorway and down the hallway of the pub, our table was right by the door and as soon as I saw Barry I jumped up and my buddy Gal beside me grabbed my leg and said, sit down, that is his dad. I said what? Who? It is his dad he explained Barry is over there drunk arguing with his dad and best not to get involved. A few minutes passed and his dad returned to the bar where he was drinking and after a few more minutes Barry slid in the door all quiet and sat at our table, I said are you alright, I mean I know it is your dad and all but if you want I will bust the fucker if he is out of line. Barry explained briefly that he had a horrible childhood experience with the guy sitting drinking with his dad and he was standing at the bar telling the guy to come outside and fight him, he didn't say to me in as many words that he was molested or anything but he said it was something bad and that that guy his dads friend was a piece of shit and deserved a beating. I said I will take care of it. At the end of the night the bar closed and we were outside and the old chaps came out, Barry's dad and his two friends, Barry was walking behind them and talking shit to the guy and then his dad turned around and start to let him have it verbally, they were off to the side arguing and I walked right between his dads two friends and smacked both of them with my head, they both dropped, of course and I kept on kicking them the two old fuckers, I didn't know why but this was for Barry and Barry is my friend since we were in cub scouts together. Gal came and pushed me on the down the street and so we left and started to walk back towards the harbour. As this was all happening the last bus had just pulled up and my buddies from

Loughshinny had showed up as another crew of the "lads" came from up the street, the word was out there was a keg over on the boat and everyone was going for a session.

I was a drunken mess that night, I had a quick smoke of the pipe on the way around the corner from the main street and on over the harbour road we went, I was stumbling and mumbling and falling off the foot path on to one of the lads girlfriends, well she was the sister of two brothers that hung out with us and she was going out with Mark so she was always around, same girl who took her brother home on mushrooms that one day, she was always around. I was falling and fell into her a couple of times and this one time she turned around and start to give me all kinds of abuse, I was a good for nothing useless prick and nobody even liked me and she hoped someday I get the living shit beat out of me, that was it. I hit the red zone again and unleashed on here I boxed her across the street and to where the beach side of the road was, I held the railings tight and just kept kicking her, my friend who I had known since I was four years of age Kenneth grabbed me by the shoulder to pull me off her, I came around with a punch I had no idea who it was, straight in the eye. One of the other guys was running down the road to find something to come back and beat me with. I walked on down to the harbour head slung low shoulders cocked, just a drunken mess, when I got there I stepped down onto the boat I had no clue at what I had just done or who was around. I stepped from the harbour to the boat and then when I was going from one boat to the next, I was jumped, I was being held down on the rail of the boat, that's the side. I don't know where I got the strength but I came upwards with a burst throwing my two hands up and all of them landed back off of me, I counted. 1,2,3,4 and Kenneth don't think you are getting away with as he was trying to scurry off, five of them were holding me down and I said which one of you lets go. Connor said I will fight ya, so I said lets go we walked up the harbour there is a patch of grass it is all known as red island, I said let's go Connor let's take a walk up to the grass. As we walked up he was psyching himself out for the fight and I was saying Connor I don't want to fight you, I don't want to do it. He kept his eyes front, face all in anger; you fucked up my sister now I am gonna fuck you up. We stood on the grass face to face the others on the road watching, I said Connor I don't want to fight you, he came at me and I knocked him out, I sat up across his chest as to hit him some more around the head and I saw he was just out cold, so I hopped over the little wall to walk back down the street to the boat and Liam was there with a stick of some kind coming towards me I pulled a few Van Dame kicks and a punch to him, I heard later I had broken his leg. I went down to the boat I worked on and took the keg and threw it onto another boat as I didn't want any of it any more.

There was a light on, on another boat where there was a couple of lads down below they had known nothing about any of what had happened and I started to tell them, they said go to sleep man, relax everything will sort itself out tomorrow. I guess they didn't understand the extent of what all had just happened. I said I felt so weak and wanted to just end it all, they were like no, no just get some sleep. I woke up the next morning with my buddy Kenneth whispering to me, hey man are you alright? I said yeah I feel weak as match sticks my bones ache. He said nobody knows you are here so don't get up for a while everyone is looking for you, it is not good. I slept some more and eventually got up and the harbour was bare nobody around, so I started to walk the long road home. When I got up the town all the lads from the boats were playing a game of soccer, one of the boat captains was in goals at one end and I walked towards him and chatted a little bit, one of the lads from the boats Deck, walked over and said, "If I was you I would go home right now before this soccer finishes" he didn't say anything else, I said fuck it and walked home. When I got there I took a nice hot shower put on a track suit sweat pants and took a nap in the sitting room. My mother woke me a little later saying your friend is on the phone, I went hello, "yeah its Bo, Listen the money you owe me forget about it he said, and I don't ever want to see your face again" and he hung up. I walked back into the sitting room to continue napping and watching TV with that a car pulled up outside the house, it was a neighbour of ours from a few fields up the road. An older man an ex-boxer, Kevin, he did not knock he walked straight into the house and straight into the sitting room, saying come here you, you little bollox. My mother came to the door of the sitting room, Kevin is there something I can help you with, and my mother was calling my Dad, Paddy! Kevin Cavanagh is in the house drunk talking crazy and My Dad came immediately. Kevin what's the problem, Kevin answered No Paddy he is a little bollox and someone has to sort him out. My dad walked Kevin to the front door, alright Kevin he is my problem, I don't appreciate you barging into my house all drunk and fired up now come, No paddy he has to be sorted, My dad yes Kevin I will sort him now come on, home with ya. I didn't know what was going on. I had no memory of anything I felt like shit and my bones felt weak. I telephoned Kenneth's house and he said yeah are you alright I said why. I said hey I have some hash but no papers to roll a joint meet me at the cross, the cross was about 500 meters from my house and 500 meters from his, so a halfway point. I walked up to meet him and when he was there, I seen his face, his whole eye was purple, purple and closed. Like the eyelid was as swollen as a golf ball and there was just a little slit looking where the eye lash would be, I said what happened to you man, that's terrible, he looked at me all red faced, you did this man, this was you last night. Man, he explained the whole story to me. Horrific, now everything was piecing together, Kevin from a few houses up the road from our house is the brother of one of the old-timers I smacked around outside the pub for Barry. Bo was done with me because I had mashed up Debbie's face and two of her teeth were missing. Deck had told me to get out of there because everyone was going to beat me up for beating up a girl. Kenneth forgave me immediately and said he had never seen me like that before and his eye would heal and he is not worried about it.

Me and Kenneth had a real closeness all our life, we started smoking cigarettes together when in national school, we used to smoke hash together, he used to fish for lobsters and I fished for prawns, later he became the captain of prawn fishing boats and was always or for a long time the one who always caught the most prawns.

When we were kids we were at a class mate's birthday party, she had a swimming pool in her house. Kenneth was in the pool and started to panic and felt he was drowning I got him out, so he always said to me "hey you saved my life once". But we had been friends since about 4 years of age as I had mentioned.

Chapter 10.

Off to fishery school I went that Easter Tuesday, a bus to Donegal and then picked up by the school bus and I was shown my family home and settled in. I was sharing a room with two guys one kid from Donegal and another guy from Wicklow and me from Dublin. There we were first week and Friday night came and we were all anxious to get to the local bars and check out the women scene. I was dancing in the night club with this girl and then I felt a tug on my shirt, my roommate from Wicklow was dragging on my shirt, he wanted her and was making an ass of himself and me in the middle of the dance floor all drunk.

The village in Greencastle Donegal where the fishery school is, is a small fishing village way up the northern tip of Ireland, nothing special a lot of the industry there is geared around the fishing industry, net making factories and the fishery college which trains engineers and captains and deck hands, like myself. The house we were staying in was a small family home, a development of about 15 or 20 houses all in line with a green play area between the houses and the road. The family seemed nice and they had a couple of small children. We would get up in the morning cereal; tea and toast were available to us. Then we would come home from the school for lunch and then in the evenings get a light meal. Nothing too fancy just enough.

Anyway first weekend this clown Seamus is pulling on my shirt in the night club, I said nothing; we got out from the minibus at the green in front of our house and walked towards the door. I grabbed him by the shirt and pulled him towards me and then by the head and twisted his head left and right and said ya see this grass here, this is the biggest boxing ring you will ever see. And you ever think to pull some bullshit like that again, with that he took a swing for me a box to the head so I started to give him a beating. The man of the house we were staying in was hanging out his bedroom window, "boys get in here before someone calls the police" In we went. The next day I felt terrible looking at Seamus with a black eye, he apologized to me for his behaviour and told me he is just a bad article when he is drunk. I apologized too and we seemed to have a good understanding then and we became good roommates and good drinking buddies up there in Donegal. In fishery school we learned about mending nets and splicing wires and basic stuff for fishing.

I had another outburst of madness up there. Because we were on such a small allowance it was hard to do any real drinking so what I would do on a Saturday morning I would get up with my allowance that we got for being on the course, I would hitchhike into the city of Derry must be 40 miles or more, might take me two or three lifts, when going from Donegal into Derry you have to go across the military border because you are leaving the republic of Ireland and entering into the north of Ireland which is governed by Britain, they use sterling pounds in there not Irish pounds but everything is a little cheaper. So for 15 pounds I could buy 6, 2 litre pack of cider, so I would do that on Saturday and have a 2 litre bottle every night for the week. Most of the time people would not give you a lift across the border because they didn't want to be having a stranger as a passenger and so I walked across mostly.

When you walk you realize how serious the border is because about a half a mile before the border in the fields and the ditches are military everywhere. Guns and the full brigade. There was one really long straight road and I would walk it approaching the boarder and in the middle of the road three military, British military stopping cars like any normal routine traffic stop. When walking, you see the stuff you miss when driving. On each side of the three military at the road about ten soldiers in the ditches. At the end of the straight where the road curved in the field and the ditch another ten soldiers. I mean what appeared a small basic traffic stop with three soldiers, had about 40 soldiers on standby. Scary stuff to walk past thinking what is this military zone I am in. But hey I needed and wanted my cider so that is how I spent my Saturday, hitch hiking into Derry and back to Greencastle.

There was one other guy from Skerries up in the fishery school at the time, Mark he was not on my course he was doing a captains course and would not look my direction because he was Debbie's boyfriend and I had just left Skerries and the whole Debbie situation behind me. So this one night I fell backwards while finishing off a bottle of vodka we had bought, me and this guy Owen, we all had taken to drinking whatever we could afford when we could. I fell flat on my back and when I came to my feet everyone was laughing at me so I fired off the way I do kicking and punching and go round and round with anyone who wants to try it. It was a melee, me back to my old tricks, somewhere through the whole punch up Mark heard about it and came and smashed me in the back of the head with a brick, it didn't knock me though I turned around and pleaded with him leave me alone I don't want to fight him and he said someone needed to stop me or we would end up with another problem like what I did to Debbie. The same drill I woke the next morning feeling weak and aching and a head ache, I blamed the vodka. I went to take a bath as that is how we could get a good wash in the house we were staying with, take a bath early in the morning because the lady would be washing her kids later in the evening and all the hot water would be gone, this bath was turning the colour of blood, my hair was matted together on the back, on the crown with dried blood. I had no idea why or what had happened. But I could tenderly touch the top of my head and feel this gaping hole type gash across the crown of my head. I was getting dressed and my roommate Seamus had gone to the little shop across the green and came back saying, the lads from the school are coming to talk with you. Then the man of the house while I was getting dressed called up the stairs, "boys some of the fishery school boys are here for ye" I grabbed my fisherman's knife and had a sweat pants and a hoody on and headed out onto the green where there were four guys sitting around. Mark from Skerries was one of them and then I approached all cocky "yes lads what can I do for ya" Nobody said anything I had my knife open in my pocket ready to start slicing and dicing, Mark said, man when is it going to stop. Two of the guys there had black eyes, and they all said they had no idea what was wrong with me and that Mark had explained I had always been like that. They said I had just caused destruction last night and it is not on. I apologized but said what do you want me to do the damage has been done. While I was standing there waiting for one of them to make a move, I knew I had this gaping crack in my head and was not feeling well at all but if you are gonna be tough, better be tough all the time wounded or not. We finished it in discussion and that was that, I went back inside and lay down, every time I took a step it was like I could feel the two sides of the gash in my head moving rubbing off each other.

The care taker of the school I met down the village that evening and asked him to look at it, he said it would be best to get a couple of stitches, I declined. I walked back for my house when passing one of the pubs in the village there were two old men sitting outside of it drinking and they called me, "hey you" "come here young man", I thought oh no what did I do to these, take that hood off they said, I pulled the hood down, bejaysus not a mark on you, well that was the greatest show we ever had in this town, because directly in front of that pub is the parking lot where I went Van dame on every body and I guess they saw the whole thing and were laughing and singing my praises for what a great show and a great fight I had put on for them that evening.

While up in green castle me and the guy Owen ventured into Derry and headed to a rave. At that time raves were spreading throughout England so the north of Ireland had a rave and we went, this was my first time to take ecstasy, but the people of the north and all the fighting of south and north and catholic and protestant didn't seem to matter at the rave, everybody was high. It was a great experience. High as kites, dancing like fools but a good night none the less.

I qualified the course and returned home to Dublin and started fishing again but the vibes were not good and the parties seemed to be people trying to get me wasted so they could take revenge for what I had done to Debbie and her two front teeth. I said screw it, I made contact with Owen from the fishery course he was from Galway and we made a plan to head to Cork and look for jobs on the fishing boats there.

The lovely town of Kinsale is where we landed and the pier had three boats, but someone had told us that yes the captain of one of the boats wanted crew. They told us where he lived and we went and knocked on his door. He was originally from Dublin and was said to be a bit of a stoner so we thought perfect, we will fit right in. He agreed to give us jobs and we were to show up to the boat on Monday morning. He wrote us out a check for 100 pounds and said go stay in the hotel up the road from the pier, I don't like people staying on the boat; he told us the local supermarket would cash the check. We left and Owen said screw that I saw an ad for a hostel out the road lets go stay there for 8 pound a night and drink the rest, so our first weekend in Kinsale Saturday night out with beer money in hand. We worked there for a couple of months and had a good summer working in Kinsale and enjoying acting the tourist on the weekends with our pay, great drinking town Kinsale. We were making our way, I then decided I would do better back in Donegal and so we hit the bus trail and made for Greencastle. I stopped off in Dublin on the way back and Owen headed straight to Donegal. By the middle of next week I headed for Greencastle, much bigger harbour with more boats. By the time I got there Owen already had a caravan rented from some guy and his girlfriend was coming up to visit him and the unfortunate thing was, they had mushrooms up in them fields too. We spent days out picking mushrooms and nights in the caravan getting high drinking mushroom tea. Jobs? We were in no state to be working we were just permanently high. A couple of the local girls we knew from the time doing the fishery course used to help us out, bring us a loaf of bread or a can of beans from their homes. We were two dead beat stoners for sure. I forget exactly what happened to that caravan I think the owner ran us out of it after we could not pay anymore around the fourth week. For us, we were high and we were happy. I returned down to Galway with Owen and I secured a job on another boat there. Owen just chilled out around his home. But the same pattern of events followed, I had broken into a car one night outside a nightclub and the owner had caught me and took me to the police and I made a whole story for the Garda that I was not stealing anything, a lady in the night club told me to wait for her in the car and then this guy showed up calling blue bloody murder and he was just the jealous husband or something. Turned out he did have a bit of a marriage problem at the time and so the Garda had to let me go.

I ended up one morning lying on the deck of the boat I worked on freezing my ass off and going to the porta toilets at the top of the harbour to wash my face, the water that came out of that tap could not be any colder, straight from the bogs, my face was a bloody mess, nose and lips all bust to pieces I had taken a serious beat down from a bunch of hillbillies the night before, I felt in a bad way. I made it to the pub Ti terry's and telephoned Owen please come and get me, he came and rescued me and I stayed in his house for a few days and then headed back to Dublin. Christmas was now upon us.

The New Year didn't bring anything different more court cases more lies from the Garda and more bail but my dad was for sure now, this would be the last time. More fights I was getting pretty sick of it too myself, I was out of control all I wanted was money for dope or booze whichever one. I was working as hard as I could, to get it. But there was no problem going missing for a day when there was drinking to be done and just miss the boat and pick up where you left off the next day.

The turning point, I am sure one could never imagine the turning point could come so soon, but for me something had to give, I was at the end of my road. There was not anyone left who even wanted to hang out with me, I was a time bomb, I would turn on anyone for anything if I thought I was right, might be my friend I had been drinking with all day and when it got ugly it just got ugly.

This particular evening was a summers evening we had come in from fishing early Saturday evening, I had kept some fish to sell to people so when I was in the pub I was selling off a bag of fish and in turn people were keeping me in drinks, until the bar was closing and myself and old time fisherman were the only two left. Big daddy and myself, he said hey lets go to the night club at the top of the harbour, I said he is not gonna let me in, big daddy said I will talk to him, we do not want to go into the night club just into the bar at the front for a drink. So he had a few words with him and came out to me and said now I gave him my word there would be no trouble so we are allowed in for a few quiet ones in the bar. We got in and were drinking away and laughing and the nightclub was going on up in the back, as people came from the night club to use the toilets, then we could see them as we were in the front bar where the toilets were. A few nice looking girls to look at would pass, and then this boat captain guy who I fished a few days with in the past came out to have a drink with big daddy and me, and he was a sloppy drunk anyway he went back into the night club and came back again, now whatever happened next was weird he either fell up a small step or he tripped on some carpet or he fully went for me, but his head hit me right smack in the top lip and below my nose and so I started to beat on him, all the floor security came rushing and gave me a few slaps and threw me out. I went down to the boat and grabbed a lump hammer and walked back up to the nightclub. I do not know where I passed out in the meantime but I got back to the nightclub which is literally 100 feet from the harbour and it had been all closed and every one had gone home, so I walked up the harbour road to the telephone box all drunk and phoned home and asked my mam would she come and pick me up. I had a lump hammer in one hand and a plastic bag with 6 or 8 haddock in the other. When my mam pulled up at the house there was a strange car in the driveway. I went to get out as I could see someone at the front door arguing with my dad. I was bringing the lump hammer with me and my mam grabbed my arm and so I left the lump hammer go. I could hear the guy saying where is he I know he is in there, good old basher, the guy who head butted me in the night club, he turned and walked towards me I said, you will get the fuck of this property right now or it will be the last breath you breathe. He said his teeth were missing and he is waiting for the Garda to come. I guess he had false teeth for some reason and he was blaming that me boxing him broke them or something. He ran past me and jumped into his car and I stood there kicking his car door, he locked the doors and moved himself to sit on the passenger side with his arms folded, I bet he didn't think what was coming next I put my foot through the window and unlocked the car door I pulled it all the way around flush with the bonnet, I had a hold of his leg as he was scampering to get out the other door. I pulled his whole body out of the car and just started beating the living shit out of him. My dad came out of the house and dived at me with a rugby tackle to stop me from killing the guy basher, I was roaring at basher how dare you come and wake up my family. I stood up square in the face with my dad, he was pleading with me to stop and I had a memory from when I was a child and I had been lighting fires on the beach which we were not allowed to do and my dad had come home and I was in trouble and he took me out of bed and was giving out to me and he head butted just a little saying I was a brazen pup.. Well that memory made me head butt my dad right then and there in the garden and I gave him a few punches, roaring at him how does it feel, huh how does it feel not so tough now and I am not so small anymore. My brother next to me John, came and grabbed me from behind wrapping his arms around me, saying I don't give a fuck you have to stop, I turned sharp and head butted him too, he walked back half crying I don't give a fuck what you do with your life, ruin it if you want. My ma was out in the driveway with towels trying to wrap bashers head as blood was coming from everywhere on him, my dad's nose was pumping bleeding he went back into the house, basher I guess my mother had called an ambulance for him, funny story about that was apparently the ambulance crashed on the way and then had to send another one, I was in the bathroom washing my face and my hands off from the blood and then I saw a Garda car pull in the driveway through the kitchen window. I looked into the kitchen at my mother and father and said, "oh yeah call the cops on me nice" I took off out of the house and around the side of the house, I picked up two red bricks one in each hand and as I made it around the corner of the house I walked right into one of the Garda and levelled him with a brick to the head, I then ran out the gate and jumped into the ditch across the street from my house.

The garden at our house is a big couple of acres and there are briars and trees all surrounding the garden and the ditches on both sides of the road. I had jumped into the ditch and made sure to grab all the branches to stop them shaking and the Garda car reversed out of the driveway in a hurry and took off down the road. I came out of the ditch and went to the back of our field, the garden and hid in another ditch so now I was positioned where they thought I went one way but I had doubled back and could see the whole house and the two driveway entrances, another Garda car had appeared. A different one I recognized this to be swords Garda another town about 8 miles away. They were walking around the house and the other Garda came back. My mother seemed to still be tending to basher in front of the house and I was hiding in the bushes towards the back of the field, the Garda were walking slowly my direction, so I was not sure should I sit tight could they see me or were they just scoping it out. I decided screw taking the chance and I ran through the neighbouring field hopped the ditch and made it to the roof of the shed where there had been old roof tiles and a few bits and pieces of hard-core stones from us throwing them up there over the years, I just keep abusing the cops about did they know that while they were out here wasting their time with me at 5 am in the morning that somebody was slipping it to their misses at home in their house, in their bed, they kept getting closer and trying to figure how they would get up on the roof to get me, as they came closer I would let rip a stone or two. A couple of times I connected square in the head knocking one cop out completely. I had run out of ammo to throw so I jumped up onto the roof of the house, there were a few more rocks and stones there. At this stage my boss from the boat had showed up, he had said someone pulled in to his driveway in the middle of the night looked like basher, he saw the cop cars flying around and just went for a drive to see and saw all the commotion at my house. And an ambulance for the cop that had his head split open an ambulance for basher. They had called for a fire truck to get them to use the pressure of a hose pipe and blast me off the roof with water. I kept saying I was not coming down so the Garda could beat me like they do and I am not coming down. Eventually I got bored so I got down off the roof, and came around the corner and smacked another guard in the head with a brick, I had to make a run for the fields was my thinking and I could escape them by tracking my way to Skerries through the fields. As I ran past the front of the house, two cops stepped out of the way, my boss stepped out of the way and my dad made a diving rugby tackle and took me to the ground, within seconds the cops had their foot on my neck and I was in handcuffs. It was just outside the front of the house near to the bedroom window, my two younger brothers were at the window of the bedroom screaming, yelling at the cops "you leave our brother alone" I was on the ground with smelly shoes on my neck and my jaw. Cops, ambulances, bloody heads with towels soaked in blood. It was a mess.

They took me to the Garda station house in Balbriggan, mind you along the way the two cops in the car kept threatening to bring me somewhere quiet and really mash me up but the cop on the radio was waiting for them at the station and so they were under the clock and they discussed they wouldn't get away with it as the boss was at the station waiting. We got there and straight to a cell and then I wanted to sleep it off, a doctor visited me asking me my name, I refused my name, I kept saying to them you know who I am so fucking write it down, the doctor came in the jail cell and said, Hi I am doctor such and such, what is your name, I said it is written in the book outside now go fuck yourself. The only place to get a judge on Sunday was in the city Dublin, the Bridewell and so I was transferred into a cell in there that afternoon, when leaving balbriggan the Sargent there whispered to me, you should have played ball with the doctor, he could have got you two weeks in the mental hospital and all this could have went away, but you are too hard headed he said. In the Bridewell were me and three junkies on Sunday evening awaiting a judge. For me it felt like about 11 o clock at night but it could easily have been 4pm who knew it all seemed a little dark, I got my time in front of the judge and the judge said "remand to custody", "bail set at 350 pounds". My father and mother were there in the court and my father was shaking his head from side to side NO to the judge. No bail for me. Off to jail I go. From a cell in the Bridewell to north circular road Dublin, St. Pats institution, prison.

Chapter 11

There are two or even three prisons there, for youths is St. Pats and same building cut off is adults mount joy. Big old military barracks type stone buildings, thick walls and barred windows, the bars had a piece of Perspex, flexi glass making it like a window. The walls must be two feet thick and so the window openings were about two or even three feet thick with the bars embedded in the stone walls. I do not know the full history of the building but an old castle type military jail or something. It has been there a long time. I was brought there, they then strip you and search you and process you, and they did not have a uniform to fit me as you must wear the prison clothes and they gave me some tighty whitey under wear and a vest and sent me into another holding cell with 6 other guys. Now here I was in prison finally fucked, no escape now and all the stories about prison I was put in a cell with 6 guys and me in a pair of jocks and a vest. I had a pack of cigarettes my mother had given me earlier, they let me keep those and that was it. I climbed up onto a top bunk that was available and I remember being scared and weak from all the episode and just wanting to sleep, but no way I was going to sleep with these guys around me, I didn't know who they were. One of the guys sitting on the floor kept asking me for a cigarette but he was so strung out or still high from heroin I could not make out exactly what he was saying, to which I just kept saying I don't understand you, now leave me alone, I was weak and needed more sleep but was also ready to start beating heads if needed be, the 6 of them if it was going to be what was needed. The next morning I was taken for a shower and processed in and given the rules and some clothes and taken to a cell, this was a three man cell for holding people on remand just like me waiting for the courts to process them and release them usually, so short term type of cell, I didn't have to do any work like the sentenced prisoners because I was just on hold, so it was breakfast, yard time, then dinner and cell time then recreation in the evening and then lights out. By the next day or two the hangover had lifted and the reality of I am here for a while was sinking in. I received my first visit, from my mam and dad, dad was wearing a pair of sunglasses, foolish of me I asked him why and he pulled them down he had two deep black eyes and answered, because of this is what you did. I gritted my teeth and told both of them, if you don't go bail and get me out of here don't be wasting my time with visits, someone useful could visit me and bring me some hash, "if you don't get me out of here, I will get out eventually and I am coming for the both of you".

I had to visit with the Chaplin of the prison and pretend to be scared and afraid of small spaces and I might kill myself, he said is there no way to get the bail, he allowed me to use the phone. I called my boss and said, hey I think I have about 400 coming to me in wages, go ahead and use that and go bail for me. The boss's wife I was talking with, she said, your father came and visited with us and asked me not to, it is for your own good and so denied me. Same day in the Chaplin's office I got a visit from a social worker, turned out to be the same councillor that had kicked me out of his office a month or so before for walking into his place high. Jimmy was his name. He was cool he made a few jokes and we chatted a bit. Then it was back to the cell and this was my new life. I had to go to court about once a week to keep getting my remand extended, so it was beginning to look like I was never getting out. The good thing was there were more drugs in the prison than were outside so smoking joints at night to fall asleep was a great time. On a visit with my parents one day who updated me that the psychiatrist that we had seen as a younger chap for the reason of the school was going to do an evaluation to try and explain to the judge that you were not worthy of prison, my dad had been in touch with her but she didn't want to visit me in prison. Walking back from that visit waiting for the prison guard to open the door, my old cell mate had passed me a lump of hash, he was returning from a visit with his mom. She had brought him in some hash, as we walked through the door with the guard another came running hold on stop, I put the hash in my mouth, they choked me up against the wall to look in my mouth and they stripped all three of us returning from the visit, they kept telling the other guy they saw him getting the something now where is it, the other guard saying he saw me put something in my mouth. They locked the other guy up for 24 hour lock up, that was the punishment for breaking the rules. I think he got three nights, that's 24 hour lock up for 3 days, no out, no yard time no recreation. I had the hash and hid it in my cell which was still the three man cell and when they brought the other guy from 24 hour lock up that week they housed him in the same cell as me, which we thought was a trap to catch us so we sat on the hash for another couple of days, but it seemed like there just was no other room for him and one spot left in our three man cell. Because it looked like I was not going to be getting out soon, they went ahead and housed me in a one man cell up with the rest of the sentenced guys and that was my spot, c block. I used to hide all the needles in my cell as I didn't have track marks, needle marks, on my arms and so was less likely to have my cell searched for heroin. So at night I would receive a lump of hash and all needed to roll joints and I would pass out all the syringes and the heroin, they would all get high on heroin and I would pass along the joints as I rolled them light them and got my good smoke off them first, things weren't bad, my neighbour was so grateful he loaned me his Walkman to listen to music at nights and even would get me breakfast in the morning, so I would sleep a little later and get my jug of hot milk and corn flakes delivered to my cell by my neighbour. For me, it was not a bad deal just for hiding some needles and a bit of heroin.

The in and out to court continued, sometimes to the district court in Balbriggan and sometimes to the circuit court in the forecourts in the city centre, Nothing seemed to be moving. The councillor, Jimmy visited again and was pretty hopeful he was gonna get me out of there, just stay good and have patience.

There was this one shy little junkie guy who used to be my cell mate, he just stayed high all the time and this other clown had taken his sweater one night at recreation and thrown it out the window, as a some type of stupid joke. Ya see when we get our uniform if you do not bring it back every week you only get replaced what you bring back so now he would be minus a sweater and you will get 24 hour lock up for that too. So I walked over to grab his shoe, he and two of his mates were sitting atop a pool table that had a big sheet of timber over it so it was more like a table, with their feet up I grabbed his shoe and tried to pull it off so I could throw that out the window. With the struggle and him pulling his leg back I let it go and he burst himself in the nose with his own knee. From the way he was sitting on the table top feet up knees bent, it was like a spring loaded knee because of me pulling on his shoe. He jumped up to try and fight with me and the prison Garda jumped in everybody back to their cell and the guy even tried grabbing the pool stick off the prison guard to fight me, they just sent him to go see the medic because his nose was gushing blood. I went back to my cell. For this little altercation I received nights, 4 of them 24 hours lock up for 4 days. But I was not worried about it, why? I had a Walkman with music, my crossword books and plenty of hash to smoke every night courtesy of the junkies on my block.

A week or so later the same guy tried to take revenge and started a fight with me in the yard but before I could get any kind of slap at the guy the prison Garda were in breaking everything up, at least he felt he got his revenge my vest got ripped in the scuffle and I had to go see the warden again and get more nights, he warned if I was in any more fights it was going to be very serious. As this was my second and I had a report of smuggling drugs in too. Jimmy the councillor was not too happy to read all this. It appeared or seemed that my probation officer had re-entered my entire case load of everything ever as all my urine test had come up dirty and I had not been keeping to the terms of staying clean for probation and so now all my cases were being accumulated into one file in the higher court in the city to be all dealt with against me at once. I would love to find a record of that; it is a list of paper as long as ones arm. They have this thing grievous bodily harm GBH, actual bodily harm ABH, assault. Assault and battery, assault and terrorizing the lady from the fish and chip shop. Assault and battery and actual bodily harm three counts on Police while in the line of duty. Possession of cannabis, they had gotten less than a gram of hash one time in a search that was like a crumb in the lining of my denim jacket on the pocket, a charge none the less, these are to name but a few another couple of trumped up charges about breaking the fish and chip shop window where the owner says he saw me do it, I was nowhere near the place when it happened. The assault and the threatening of the Garda on the night they beat me up, a few breach of the peace and a few drunk and disorderly charges.

There had been a night before all that where I was in a fight after a nightclub and beat this guy up he actually was the guy I started this with after another disco but it got broken up and the night it got broken up was the very same night the chip shop window was broken, but even though the Garda were at that fight figuring out what was going on they still wouldn't say that they knew I was nowhere near the fish and chip shop the night the entire store front was smashed all the glass, floor to ceiling glass store front, it wasn't me, but I had the charge. So the night I met with that guy again on the streets I said let's do it now, my buddy's gal and Barry said do you want us to help I said no you guys go and walk on down the street I will catch up, last thing I am gonna let him say is a gang of us beat him. The guy wanted me to walk down a lane which I knew was really close to his house instead we walked up the driveway of another house beside the laneway and I beat him senseless in doing so I remember I had such a firm grip of the skin of his neck while I was punching him in the head, I let go a little to try and re grip and hold only his clothes, at that exact time he saw it as opportunity and tried to swing for me, that is when I really let him have it, I was not going to stop punching him in the head I just was not going to stop, his girlfriend was there screaming and crying. I let go of him and walked off, as I was walking off she tried to hit me with a branch of a tree and came running at me as if to claw my eyes out, so I head butted her straight in the nose and knocked her out too. Violent is an understatement of the highest degree when it came to me and my fists and my head or my Van dame kicks.

I walked on down the town, when I caught up to my buddies that night they were in the garden of the police station pulling up the flowers, ya see there is this tidy towns competition throughout the whole country of Ireland and this one Garda in particular took great pride in the garden of the Garda station and so he had won a prize or three over the years for best looking garden of a police station or best kept garden or something, well my buddies were making sure it wasn't going to happen this year. There is a bout a 25 foot long garden path up to the front door of the Garda station so when I caught up I made a run and threw my leg up and kicked in the door of the station. Why not there was nobody around. I fully understand the idea is to break out of a police station, but hey I broke in. We wandered around in there for a laugh, we found all the alcohol that had been confiscated from underage drinkers and so that was a score, none of the file cabinets were open and there was no money, so we grabbed a few papers and set them alight. We headed out the door and away up to gal's house to drink a bit, later we would be heading to the boats anyway. We never looked back to see was the station a blaze or never even gave it a second thought. This was another charge as about four hours later we were arrested walking back down to the harbour that morning and Barry spilled his guts. Breaking and entering, attempted arson, the list of charges went on and on.

I had many dates in court at this stage where I would be taken from my cell, remove my prison uniform, put on my own original clothes that I came into the prison originally wearing, go to court wait in holding cells under the courts, attend court go back to the holding cell and go back to jail. This was all done under escort of prison Garda and so the holding cells and the transportation was for all criminals from St. Pats and mount joy together. Finally came the day where my case was going to be heard.

It turned out the councillor Jimmy had been on a work assignment in a house down the country for teens with drug problems but he was not sure the judge would go for it. The psychiatrist who had seen me as a child when requested by the school took the stand and gave a full description and details of why I was not prison material, I was handcuffed to the prison guard from the holding cell and sitting in the court, my mother and father were seated close but not in the prisoner section, they were mumbling to each other, I grunted to my dad can you shut up please, It is not good court etiquette to be causing any disruption in the court that might get the attention of the judge, it is really a way to turn the judge against you from the beginning. My dad whispers to me, your mam says she knows the judge from somewhere but cannot think where. I reply tell her hurry up and think then. On my way into the court that morning the doors of the court room, they have double doors to the foyer area and then a little area and then double doors into the court room itself, my barrister wanted to speak with me in that little entrance way and two other guys, I was cuffed so five of us were standing blocking the entranceway really. The two other guys were introduced to me by my barrister; these are the Garda that you caused injury to that night. They would like to speak with you. Of course being fresh from prison I had nothing but the "fuck the police" attitude, my barrister said, please hear them out. The Garda explained to me, look, we need you to plead guilty to these charges of assault and harm to us in the line of duty, I said I am "not guilty!" for every charge they bring, not guilty not guilty not guilty! The cop said you are not dumb just wise up for a minute, if you do not plead guilty we are screwed; if you do plead guilty we will speak on your behalf to help get you out of prison. I said "fuck you" they left me my handcuffed buddy the prison guard and the barrister remained, the barrister said. They want to sue their boss as they received significant injuries and one will never work again and they can make a claim against the state to receive compensation for their injuries, they will speak for you as you will open an easy path for them to make their claim. You should do it. You are looking at somewhere around 8 to 15 years in prison at the moment, I went and sat in the prisoners section of the courtroom with the prison guard handcuffed to me and other cases went on. Then I was called, I was allowed to be uncuffed and went to stand in front of the judge, I listened to the doctor give her testimony, the judge said I will leave it to you doctor to make a recommendation of where we could send this young man, this doctor had high respect from the judge as she was a very well-known top psychologist/psychiatrist in the country and she was seriously telling the judge there is no such place in the country for Aidan, but prison is definitely the wrong option.

We listened to the sergeant from Skerries give his testimony of how in 17 years on the Garda force he never felt fear until the night he came up against Mr McNally and his violent rage, that I was a ticking time bomb with no warning when I would go off and so they request that I be removed from the streets of Skerries. The judge informed the other witnesses that he had read their statements and he did not wish to put them through a traumatic experience again by making them give evidence or testify, I did not realize there were so many victims, but I did see the lady from the fish and chip shop and I felt bad for her as I saw her to be just a normal mid-fifties woman. The Garda who were injured spoke as to how they felt I should be given every chance the court could extend me as they viewed me as confused and misunderstood and perhaps prison would only create a master criminal rather reform me. Jimmy the councillor introduced a house in Cork as ideal for me and it required a 2 year suspended sentence or they would not receive me there. My barrister spoke immediately,

"on your say so your honour, the parents are here ready to drive Aidan to this facility in Cork as there is full support of a loving family behind this young man" the barrister beckoned for my mother and father to stand up. The judge asked the prosecution did they have objection to this treatment facility?

I was standing there trying so hard to look as innocent and as apologetic as I could through facial expression to the judge, before the prosecution could answer, my mam and dad were standing and the judge said, "Mommy, I know you" my mother nodded her head with yes your honour, "mommy I always knew this was hard for you, please sit down"

He turned his head to me, "You, you do not deserve this chance, but your parents do," he looked down to the clerk of the court "clerk I want it noted that wherever I am seated in the country he is to be brought before me if he breaks this chance" he starred at me hard and he said I am giving you a chance do you understand this? I nodded yes, they went on then to say two year suspended and the burden of transit to this facility should not and will not lie with the parents, the state, he called upon the sergeant from Skerries again, informing him there are to be no fireworks, you are to provide an escort to Cork with Garda that have no history with this young man and that was that, I was taken back to holding cell awaiting the court paperwork and told I would be driven to this place in Cork by the police. I had a suspended sentence over my head and all would come back at me two fold if I screw this up. I was taken back to the prison before lunch time and the prison Garda explained to me go and get your lunch and by this evening you will be processed out of here. I went in the yard and everybody in the yard was cheering when I got called to the warden's office you're finally getting out, what a joke to be on bail this long. In the wardens office, the warden explained to me that he was going to allow a special visit to me from my father as there were some paper work that needed to be done and it is best my father explain. I went for a visit in the visiting room and my dad explained to me that due to jurisdiction of the judge and the courts, we needed another signature to get me out of the prison and that judge will not be available as they only realized it when it was already 5pm. And so for the night I remain in prison and will be out tomorrow. I packed up my puzzle books, crossword books gave away my couple of bars of chocolate, funny thing, back then a yorkie bar used to come in a foiled wrapped bar in a paper sleeve, it has all changed now, but the junkies loved the yorkie, they didn't care for the chocolate they just loved the foil. Next morning I was processed out and the cuffs of the prison came off and the cuffs of the Gardai went on and into the back of a taxi. Escorted by two cops and a taxi driver we left north circular road for the Cork road. Half way along the Naas dual carriageway the cops were doing the daily crossword in the Irish times newspaper and they were stuck I said let me see, I had been sitting handcuffed in the back seat, the cop in the front passed the newspaper back and all I needed to see was the number of the crossword, crossword# 293 when I saw that I knew I knew it because I had just spent a while sitting in a jail cell doing them all from the crossword book of the Irish times. I toyed with them a bit and said, try 6 down as an I and an E, then 18 across should be reindeer, try 23 down to be steam boat etc. etc. The cop started filing in the blanks and they were convinced, this kid is a genius he is doing it by just glancing at it and closing his eyes, I completed the crossword for them along the route.

We stopped midway maybe Cashel I think for their lunch break, typical government employees have to stop for lunch break, but anyway, they decided to leave me handcuffed to the arm rest while one of them stood outside my window and the other went in and ordered some fish and chips, what idiots leave the Skerries/rush/balbriggan area where the fish is fresh caught daily and order fish and chips in the middle of the country, but sure there you go, they would not even let me out of the car to have a cigarette for fear I would run away. It must have been written across my face because all I could think of was get to this open prison type facility and take a few nights sleep eat up some grub and as soon as I have my bearings I will head for the fishing boats, why because the summer previous I spent fishing in Kinsale and so it should not be hard to hook up with some of the fishing community and be on the run, and they will never find me. That was my plan no more going back to St. Pats or mount joy I had made myself that promise. But doing a runner from this new facility was high on the agenda on my way there. We got there around 7 in the evening it was summer so still good and bright around 7pm, one of those nice summer evenings where it looks like the weather will stay great forever, bright purple and red sky, The place was in east Cork, Ladysbridge, well half way between Ladysbridge and Garryvoe beach, which is on the Ballycotton road out from the main cork city to Youghal/Waterford road. About a mile and half from the beach Garryvoe, so as far east as you could go in east cork really although Ballycotton fishing village was about 5 miles further east, well south east really.

Chapter 12.

People have often asked me how I know my way around the country so well, I can tell you from busses, Cork to Donegal and Dublin to Galway when chasing down jobs on fishing boats and Donegal fishery school and now police escort to east Cork from the north circular road, I can say it comes natural. Of course the travels are only getting started at this stage.

The cops handed me over and some registration type book was written into and the cops left, I was handed over to a young lady, girl really called Anne, she was the head honcho for the night, she said they were expecting me. When the cops left and had cleared the gateway down the lane of the driveway, Anne laughed and said in about as strong of a Cork accent as you can imagine, "I didn't know which of you was the new addition to the house and which was the cops, are you sure you are only 17, you are huge" needless to say Anne was a little on the shorter side. I honestly want to say it was a Thursday evening, yes that's right Thursday early June 1993 I have to figure. There was a group of about 8 lads in the house all said hello and welcome, and they were off to the shops, the shops I thought, I had spent nights in my jail cell wishing I could just walk across the street and get an ice pop. These guys had just got paid and were off to the shops. The smallest funny smiley face of the group Timmy came back from the shop and had bought me a mars bar and a can of coke and gave it to me. Saying I know you didn't get paid this week so here I bought you this. We get paid 9 pound every week so we can buy what we want. They had jumped into a nice fiat minibus type van and headed off to the shops somewhere I did not ride along. I was shown my bed in a converted attic with six beds laid out. It was an old cottage that had the attic converted and staff bedrooms were down stairs and a nice kitchen and dining area with three long tables and benches. There was a greenhouse type tunnel with vegetables growing in it and a dog run with 5 or 6 greyhounds in it. All we were missing was chickens walking around the place. But they would not have made it too far as the grey hounds seemed to be savages. That Friday everybody had to wake up at 7.30 am and be at the breakfast table by 8 am, first was a meet at the gate of the house and run to the local cross roads and back about a mile or a mile and a quarter, round trip. (I remember thinking what is this summer camp?) Then it was breakfast and then house duties. This meant whatever was your duty, mopping the floors, washing the dishes whatever it was and then 9.am more staff showed up and it was school time. I was not placed in school as they didn't process me yet to see was I dumb or what? So I was put on work detail which was mending and staining a picket fence which ran the length of the driveway. I remember thinking how is this one staff member going to stop me from walking out the gate and taking off running? Oh well maybe they are testing me, put the new guy right by the gateway and see will he run, so for that reason I kept painting and working all day. One o'clock lunch / dinner, a big fine lash up of grub, roast beef and potatoes mashed and veg, all the milk ice cold you could drink. prison milk always had a creamy sour taste to it but this was the bees knees this, best of food, turned out the lady who volunteered was a local lady and came every day to cook for us, and she was a chef of the highest degree, but she loved cooking for us, good old Pat, she brought her friend along to help every day too Eileen, two nicer women you couldn't meet.

Every day it was some ones turn to help them in the kitchen but the dinners were restaurant style every day. Another local man drove the bus, the van for us to go out places when we needed and the rest of the time he would give me jobs to do around the grounds to keep me busy when the lads had school. Good old Dick, I was fond of that old timer because he didn't judge neither did Pat and Eileen they were just good salt of the earth people who enjoyed helping us out. And me and Dick would spend the day mixing concrete or making a fence or digging the ground in the tunnel for the vegetables or whatever, he would make me laugh, him and I would spend a lot of fun times talking about the female staff and which one looked best or was fat in the behind.. Good laughs with old Dicky boy.

So that first weekend I am becoming acclimatized and the weekend staff come on Friday evening and we hang out on the patio outside the kitchen after the tea and it is all a good laugh, the staff mostly were on placement courses for some sociology degree or other from college and so there were shift changes all the time as they were college students, not much older than ourselves but it seemed to be working. Saturday came and this staff member seemed a cool dude, Wayne is his name, he said I heard you are a fisherman, I said yup that's me; he said lets break out the bikes and take a cycle over to the local fishing pier Ballycotton. It is about 5 miles, "sure we'll be grand" I soon learned the Cork people say "sure we'll be grand" for everything. Off we went me and Wayne on the bicycles and I was just sitting on the harbour wall looking out to sea and Wayne was hanging out and we smoked a couple of cigarettes and chatted about nothing in particular, fishing and boats and the ocean and headed back to the house for tea. Now I had just come from, lights out and locked up to cycling around the country side in east Cork, something seemed a little dreamy about the whole thing, I had explained to Wayne, drink and hash and cocaine or whatever, I was not specific to pills or sniffing glue or anything I just worked hard and partied even harder and it has caused a ball of trouble, he said ah "sure you'll be grand". Sunday we all piled into the van for activities as they called it and we headed back roads around Cork and into north Cork close to Fermoy, we ended up at this riding stables where the lady kitted us all out in hats and whips and boots and gave us a horse each to ride, we had free reign of the farm lands and rode the shit out of them horses, galloping and jumping ditches for hours. Then back to the van and home to Ladysbridge for the supper and bed, well before bed every night was a house meeting and everyone was being asked how they did for their day and it was an answer of responsible or not responsible and if not responsible, a consequence was handed out. I had not got a clue what they were saying. The whole house was talking in Cork accents and it was hard to understand. I figured it out soon enough though, basically the routine was this, up in the morning 7.30, run to the cross and back, take breakfast 8.am do household chores, be present for class or work for 9 am. Lunch 1pm, class or work again until 4pm then house chores, group meeting with a counsellor and then in the evening a meeting of Narcotics anonymous or Alcoholics anonymous, or an activity, bed and lights out 10pm. So before bed the house meeting would be when you were asked if you completed all your chores, did you get up on time, did you make the run, did you say grace before your meal did you attend work, did you do your household chores. If you answered responsible no big deal if you didn't, then everyone else in the group of lads got to decide a consequence for you. So for example if you didn't do the run in the morning, next morning do two runs. If you were ten minutes late out of bed, then get up ten minutes earlier the next morning. If you were late to breakfast five minutes, then wait at the table for five minutes extra before eating tomorrow. If you didn't do your chores you would have do it again tomorrow and then something extra, so that is why they were answering responsible, but some of them would rat on each other, a guy would say responsible and then one of the others would cut across and say I believe you were not responsible and you should receive a consequence, you did not do the run today and so would get an extra consequence for lying. I had a pass for my first week because I was new and needed to learn the system. The only two rules in the house, NO drugs or alcohol, No fighting everything else were guidelines and carried consequences, if you broke the RULES you were probably getting kicked out and that for most meant prison. I do not know why that first weekend, was it little Timmy buying me the can of coke, was it the cycle with Wayne, the freedom of it all, the rest of the lads the staff, the laid back nature of things or what, but I decided I was not going to be running and I was gonna stay and be responsible and get this clean they were all talking about.

There was Keith, Ger, Damien, Timmy, Alan they were all from cork, then Jason and James they were from Mayo and me from Dublin. That was the group I landed in the middle of and we were in a house for recovery from drug and alcohol abuse run by and established by the mighty Father Roch (rock).

There were many other guys who came and left and many staff who came and left, the main ones at the time were, Lorraine, Sharon the teacher, Wayne

who I had mentioned, Anne who met me first day,
Jean and Brenda who were cousins, Pat and Eileen
in the kitchen, Dick driving the bus and the foreman
there were many other staff too who came and went,
big John, Terrence stuck around for a long time, but
on weekends some of the staff would invite us to
their homes and we might have tea and a snack.
But we were like almost free really, into shops and
walks to the beach and runs and 10k road races and
horse riding and squash in the local courts and
indoor football in the local boarding school
facilities, some of the lads belonged to the local
boxing club, I ended up being allowed to train and
play with the local rugby team so pretty soon my
schedule was up early run, do the daily necessities,
train for rugby Tuesday and Thursdays, indoor
soccer on Friday nights, horse riding or road races
on Saturday, play squash Sunday nights with a
morning run every day too. That was the system for
the next 13 months approx... the key to the whole
thing was no substance abuse any more, and when
you really felt the urge there was group therapy and
one on ones with councillors to try and talk you
through it. Many guys came and couldn't hack it
and left. Many times there were bad attitudes and
disputes between boys in the house and staff, but it
seemed to function along. Father Roch would come
and visit and he was a class act for sure, he would
brink cigarettes for us and sweets, he was a cool

dude to be honest, he wanted to see us all working or studying and playing sports and just not feel the need for drink or drugs. He was and had a genuine vision. We had many fun times and events, we even had a trip on the ferry to England for a week all organized by Roch, as he always put it, due to his vows of poverty taken to be in the monastery as he was a monk and as a priest he was "a professional beggar" and he asked for donations all his life. The house we now lived in donated to him. The vans the trip to England the food all donated to him for his hard work "begging" Mobile phones were becoming a thing at the time we were not allowed to have them anyway so I took to writing letters to many people and saying Hi and I was well and a few pen pals developed, my bosses wife, the wan that said no to my bail, I used to look forward to her letters so much to fill me in on what was going on with the harbour and the fishing, I wrote to some older friends and some wrote back and some didn't. Our parents were allowed to come to visit once a month and we were given the task of running a family day where all our family could visit. On family day we were allowed to be taken out for a drive with our families for Sunday lunch somewhere if we wanted, we could go to the mall and do some shopping whatever we wanted, we were free. Just be back before tea time.

I wrote to my friend Donna when I was there and one time when I had to take a train trip and an escort had to come with me I got to visit with Donna and catch up, I was escorted to the court that day on the train to Dublin and out to the courts and a quick lunch at home with my parents and a visit with Donna and back to cork, escorted by Wayne and the probation officer Timmy. Timmy was a big woolly headed dude who would remind anyone of the character George from Glenroe, a ringer for him with the heavy Cork accent though. He was corks answer to the big Lebowski. I visited with Donna she was settling down with her boyfriend sharing a house in swords with one of her uncles and his gay partner, I remember going to the bathroom and all the candles in there was funny as this is what a gay house looks like. Donna is like my sister, we were babies together because our mothers were friends so there is a photo somewhere of me and Donna in the wash basin, baby bath tub together, I remember Donna was growing up quick too with her daisy duke shorts and miniskirts, one night down the town of Skerries one of the lads oh look over there Donna now she is fine, of course with her long legs and her big boobs, many a lad had an eye for Donna but she was madly and deeply in love with an older fella Keith, I said to him, my friend that night, must have been around 16 at the time, oh yeah Donna, I was a little pissed off to hear a guy one of my group from the harbour ogling her as she was the closest thing I ever had as a sister, but anyway I remarked, yeah eyes off, I had a bath with her, he said yeah right I said yeah I even have photographs to prove it I will show you someday, completely naked in the bath me and Donna. Of course he didn't know I was talking about when we were both less than 1 year old.

Donna and her sister had spent a good bit of time up in our house in Loughshinny, they lived down the road a bit in Loughshinny and her mam didn't drive so her dad and my dad were friends and my mam and her mam were friends so during the week my mam would drive us all to the supermarket for the weekly messages and for many different reasons they would be in our house and I used to love when Donna was there because I would terrorize her, I would close the door of the sitting room for example and tell her, her mammy was leaving and without hesitation she would burst into tears, then I would run out and say I didn't do anything , we were about 5 years at the time, and we were in the same class in national school.

I remember when I was 7 one of the local fisherman another friend of my dad's, sheriff and his brother Fred came to our house one evening and then mam came into the room and said Joe is dead and I have to go with these men to go sit with Marian while they tell her the news, Joe was the biggest man you had ever seen, not fat, not skinny just fit and healthy and big tall man I used to love when he would come to our house as he would hide money above the doors to the rooms and put me on his shoulders and walk around collecting the coins and I would have a pocket full of money for sweets, Joe was Donnas daddy and he died when she was 7. From that point on Donna and her sister Melissa spent a lot of time with our family, we went on family holidays in the summer together and our lives were just more intertwined. Many evenings after school there was us five boys and Donna and Melissa around the dinner table. I tried my best to keep in touch with Donna through the time I was in the house in Ladysbridge.

After the 13 months there, we were given another option was to move to another house this time in west Cork halfway between Bandon and Clonakilty. The house was a big old farm house on about 10 or so acres of land in a village of Ahiohill *ath ee o hill. This was our new halfway house; we were accepted to attend the school in Rosscarberry which lies about ten miles west of the house through the town of Clonakilty on the Skibbereen road.

Chapter 13.

If you have never visited this part of the world Rosscarberry is one of the most picturesque places as there is a lake from the ocean between the road a via duct and the convent /secondary school sits on the hill to the north and sand dunes to the beach to the south. Three of us, me, Keith and James had been accepted to the school as regular students to do 6th year the final year and try and prep for exams and gain a place in one of the colleges if we could.

This was another house donated to Father Roch and the same rules and daily routines applied except this time every day we were attending Mt. Saint Michel's secondary school in Rosscarberry. I was 18 Keith was 18 and James was maybe touching 19 but the class mates there were all around the 17 and 18 mark so we fit right in. They call it a school year but really it is September to June with exams in June and so with all the breaks and holidays it is a very short 6 months of school that we had to use to the best of our ability and try and sit the national exam the leaving cert. If there ever were genuine good honest vocational people, Sr. Angela and all the sisters of mercy in that school were them, along with every staff member who did everything to make us feel welcome, comfortable and aid us in our plight to become something of ourselves. I mean we had a math teacher who would come to our house as many evenings as we could let her as she worked so hard to make us pass our math. I had a biology teacher who allowed me to go to her house on weekends Saturdays to take extra biology and I would sit in on 5th year the class below us on their biology classes when I had free periods and I would do the same with fifth year French. We had to write to the government explaining the circumstances of who we were and what we were doing to gain an exemption from studying the IRISH language as it is very complex language and it did not seem enough time to take on the whole 6 years of Irish in one short year, so when our class had periods for Irish we would go sit in on different 5th year classes and we took history through a correspondence class as there were no students taking history in the 6th year that year. All of these teachers worked hard on helping each of us to get as much information into us into our once burned out from drugs minds to help us get to the leaving certificate. It was a struggle but any struggle is a tough road but a much easier one when you have dedicated people helping. We were not in a position to pay these people they just said they admired our efforts and would help all the way. They did exactly that help and go beyond help to get us to the leaving certificate, what do you know we passed, I passed Keith passed and James passed. All three, I took up civil engineering in RTC (*regional technical college) Cork and Keith took up architecture. James was happier to be working with a local mechanic.

If ever there was a movie where you watch the guy and the girl having a high school romance, well it happened to me, I gained a pen pal, we were not allowed as one of the rules of being accepted into the school, not to chase the girls, the parents had a meeting with the teachers before we were accepted and this was one of the conditions. We didn't like it but we agreed, girls were off limits, and so the school year rolled along with us continuing living the program of NA and AA going to local meetings, staying active, I continued my rugby in east Cork, and we studied our asses off on the weekends with grinds from our teachers.

My pen pal was the one taking my eye in school every day, when she wouldn't come to school some days I would feel grumpy, when I would see her in my English and math and geography class I would be so happy, we shared stories and we sent each other letters in the mail. In the beginning we did not even pretend to know each other in front of all the other class mates, we would take smoke breaks at break time I would be with James and she with be with some other friend but it was all under the cover of being just friends hanging out at break time, sometimes I wanted to kiss her so much it was unbearable to be around her, especially after I spent all night reading her letters over and over again. At times maybe I didn't have any stamps and I couldn't tell the guys in the house so I would have to wait until got a chance to go to the post office to send her another letter, and I knew by her look the way she might ignore me that she was waiting on a letter, as it was my turn to reply. I would pass her in the hall ways fast and mumble "sorry I dint have stamps but I do now" I would see her light up and I wanted her. Our letters were not love letters but they were, they were not sexual we just chatted and became two people falling for each other. By the time the leaving cert came nobody really knew but they had their suspicions. I thought she was so marvellous and a singer to boot a beautiful voice, we even gave a talk on drugs to the whole school after we had been there for a few months and she did the singing for us at like an interval. The whole school now knew why we were there and none of them treated us any different, the whole school was behind us. I remember the last week of school for us 6th years and then it was a little break and return in two weeks to take the exams, Clare the love of my life right then at that time, used to be allowed to drive her mom's car to school on some days and this particular day we were cutting out early and me and her headed to the beach down the road of the sand dunes to the beach and we snuggled in along the dunes and we made out, kissed violently, passionately and softly, it was amazing. I felt so in love with this girl I don't know why it was so intense, I understand, it had been building for months. The good thing was it was kissing and groping. Because to confess a truth I got off from her smell her touch and her kisses, I kept thinking, "please do not drop the hand" I had "came" in my shorts like a 14 yr. old kid on his first time, now granted it had been almost two years, but this girl did it for me. I am not embarrassed to admit that I had a sticky mess in my shorts and was terrified that if she found out, she would have nothing to do with me, but it worked out perfect, we went back to school and I was picked up by the van and went home and sang love songs all night. The exams came and we took them in the school big hall /room and it was hard and I answered what I could and did what I could, I remember seeing Clare sitting up ahead in the math exams and all I wanted to do was do it for her. Once the exams were done the house and the suspended sentence were over and I was free to do whatever was meant to be next in my life. I went immediately back to the fishing boats to earn some money that summer and when I came ashore I would come and spend the weekend with Clare, her parents were so the nicest and they made me so comfortable as I was Clare's boyfriend.

Father Roch had another house in the city a nice 4 bedroom house in Douglas part of the suburbs of Cork city which was there for us to live rent free if we needed it. I had always been hitch hiking everywhere, from east Cork to west Cork for rugby, from west Cork to the city and back for Clare, after one month of fishing I had seen this car in a garage and I said to hell with it I need to buy it, fishing helped me do that. I remember the leaving cert results night when we all went and got our results and there was a big night out for everybody and every one was getting drunk, but not us of course. At the night club me and Clare were kissing and dancing and all over each other and now all the class mates knew and things clicked that, that is how and why things made sense to them all as they reflected the class year, everyone was so happy for us that night like we had got married or something and I was truly in love with this girl. Clare started college that year in Tralee and I continued fishing until college started for me in the RTC Cork, but I lasted only a few months I lost interest and the fishing had me hooked again, I moved and rented a house near Roscarberry and fished in Baltimore in west Cork and soon moved to fishing in union hall also west Cork. I would travel to Tralee to spend nights with Clare and I would spend the weekends with her always, I always went on Sundays to play rugby. We were dating and we were serious, she would take the bus to Cork city when I was in college and me to her in Kerry and we would go out and eat at restaurants and we were boyfriend and girlfriend, we got to take in the big Slane concert, REM that summer after the leaving cert and another time I remember holding her at a Michael Jackson concert that her brother had invited us to. We were in love I guess, high school sweethearts. I had turned twenty that next year January and Clare was 19 I can remember the specifics exactly but for respect let us leave them out but I remember my first son being conceived and all the pregnancy that year. 1996 Clare would turn 20 in September and she would give birth to our son Darra. It was like a dream, I recall the night she phoned me and said her dad had found out. Her mom knew for a while she was pregnant but her dad had found out now too. I came over to their house and her dad could not look my direction and left the kitchen, her mom asked her older brother to come and sit with me as the situation was tense, Clare was upset, her dad was furious and the tension was real. I remember thinking if her dad Chris wants to slap me around then I am open to it, if he wants to talk about it I will try and talk like an adult, if he wants to ignore me he has every right to do so. It took about a month of avoiding him really and then it all just became the part of life and we all grew extra anxious to have this new baby, Darra.

Darra was born 16th of November 1996. A whopping big child, tall, long and absolutely gorgeous. Clare's Dad was one of the first to visit, he was over the moon, and this was the first grandchild on both my folk's side and on Clare's. The day he was born well that night actually after being in the hospital from early am the morning before, Clare had phoned me and said her water broke about 1.30 am her mom was driving her to the hospital, I drove behind them, when we got there and they put Clare in a gown and a bed and her mom was so nervous wondering are they doing everything right and treating her right. She had been a nurse in her younger years too. We were in the hospital all day and Clare's mom went home and said she would be back later, Clare in a worried look said to me, I don't want my mom in the delivery it is me and you, I said for sure, ok absolutely. I had no idea where my nerves were, but it was happening. The exact minute he was born. Close to midnight if I am not mistaken, I had a feeling come over me I never experienced before, something warm came slowly and gently from the tips of my feet up through my body to the crown of my head and out, I had a sensation of complete and utter serenity and magic come over me, I heard the nurses whispering behind me, we better tell the parents, I was ready to explode and swing the doctor around the delivery room. Hearing the nurses whispering was causing some panic to set in. Clare was on the bed exhausted, I mean she just gave birth to an 11 pound baby, they brought him over for a couple of seconds while they explained, that due to him birthing face up they fear some mucus may have been in his first breath and it can lead to jaundice so they will take him to the emergency care unit just as a precaution. They then wheeled Clare in the bed into another room and offered her some tea and toast, the nurse asked us in the funniest accent did we want the nurse to ray heaster the baby, we said what? She said ray heaster, the baby, you know like ray heaster, Clare figured it out and bursts out laughing register, yeah that's fine we can do it no problem, I said to Clare enjoy your tea and toast I am going to see where he is. I followed the yellow tiles like the nurse had told me to over to the emergency care unit, and there he was laying there a beast of a baby. All snug in an incubator type glass covered thing. Amazing was the feeling, I had a top of the moon smile that would not subside. I walked back over to Clare to tell her he was fine and she was out cold, the midwife nurse, said in all her years delivering babies he had the longest spine she ever saw and that means he will be a very, very tall man. Clare was fast asleep and the nurse said this would be a great time for me to go and get some sleep too. So I headed home the road west singing and beaming and just the highest I could ever be on life, Now it all made sense, I don't need drugs to be high I don't need alcohol everything everyone had been telling me for the past two and half years or more had been true, life gives the best highs ever.

Clare had gotten a thousand pounds from her grandmother as an inheritance and she signed it over to me in the credit union so I could get a loan to buy a car, that very morning I was at the mechanic shop buying that car and over to Clare's house to get some underwear and stuff for her and away to the hospital. I got to the hospital at about 9 am with flowers and her things but she was not there, the nurse said oh that's a beast of a woman, I told her wait while I get her a wheel chair and I will wheel her to the emergency care unit, but by the time the nurse came back Clare had gone walking. I followed over and there she was with Darra our new baby. A proud mommy and I could never have been so proud of someone else at that time, to see her give birth and see her sitting with this child she was the most amazing woman ever to me at that time in my life, that specific moment was simply put, amazing. There was another couple who came for regular feedings of their baby in the emergency unit their target weight was 5 pounds and they could take the baby home, their baby was born at only 5 months in the pregnancy and they had been feeding and visiting for months to keep their little fella alive, that couple stood in awe of Darra as the two lay next to each other in their separate little incubators, Darra, he was like a giant next to that little baby. Clare and myself soon brought Darra home to Clare's parents' house, my mother and my brother had come to visit the day Darra was born and what do you know that exact week my mother hit 5 numbers in the lottery again and so she was delighted to take the train to Cork and stay in a hotel and buy us a car seat and a buggy for the new born grandchild. We were over the moon with our new baby.

For the next while we tried to figure out if we could get a crèche and could Clare return to college after the Christmas holidays and somewhere to do baby minding near the college so Clare could study and be a mom, I continued fishing and in January 6th or 7th the weekend of my 21st birthday we christened Darra, Darra Patrick O Donovan.

Chapter 14.

We had driven to Dublin that Christmas with the new born baby to spend Christmas in Dublin and funny as it may be the evening we arrived, we were met by my nana who lived in a granny flat at the end of our family home, oh she said there has been a terrible accident, your father was trying to fix the satellite dish and he fell off the roof, he is in the hospital, Clare and the baby stayed with my nana and I went rushing to the hospital to see what's up with my dad. When I got there he was strapped to a bed on mild pain killers and waiting for a surgeon to take a look as he had damage to his spine, I could see him through the hallway on the hospital bed and hear him groaning every so often, I thought, man, this is the rock that never gave up on me and never stopped fighting for to win me back as a son and help drag me out of the pits of despair, don't let anything happen to him. My mother was in shock and waiting for doctors, there was nothing anyone could do and we had to go home that night and leave him there in his pain as it seemed like the hospital kept saying yes a doctor will be around to see him but we knew that meant tomorrow morning. Christmas passed with a few hospital visits and the day of new year's eve we decided to head for west Cork again, I just made one quick stop at the hospital and brought Darra in it was getting cold and the forecast said snow was coming for Dublin, I dashed through the corridors of the hospital I got to dads hospital room and said dad here is your grandson, everyone had said the hospital due to germs is no place for a new-born baby so here he is I held him up on his chest and my dad couldn't hold him, dad had crushed two vertebrae broken another and cracked another, the doctors had said, in the case of one vertebrae damaged some paralysis might occur in the hands or feet, two damaged usually one side or the other, with three or more they fear the pelvis down might be paralyzed so he was in a restriction type brace where he could not move from the neck down, we headed back to the car and made for Cork, once we got clear of the Naas dual carriage way there was no more snow or slushy conditions and we drove our way to west Cork for new year's eve. When we woke up new year's day that year the whole outside of Clare's house was covered in snow, it is very rare to get snow in west Cork, but there it was and all news reports were about the power outages and the horrible conditions throughout the country, it was as if we drove to west Cork on the lip of the snow storm as we didn't experience any of it yet we would never be able to make that journey new year's day as the country was completely white. A week later the gang from Dublin came down and we had the christening like I said that was my 21st birthday weekend and I was chuffed to pieces to be having Darra's christening.

With the return of the college year myself and Clare's mom drove down to Tralee with all the baby stuff and prepared Clare's college house with the cot and the buggy and everything and then Clare decided, there is no way, I want to be with my baby all the time and so she dropped out cause she could pick it back up in a year or two. Clare's dad was an accountant in the local town, a turf accountant and so she could work with him and I went with him to the track to clerk for him many Thursdays, Listowel, Tralee, Tipperary town, Clonmel and Sundays to point to points in Cork, I was doing what fishing I could through the winter months and I even packed in the fishing to go work as a helping hand in a hardware store which had a lumber yard. It was 125 pounds a week but it meant I could be around the baby every evening.

I would take Thursday off so I could go racing with Chris, Clare's dad and that was extra money and so we were doing what we could. Me and Clare and Darra all were living in a house together in the centre of town Clonakilty. There was a guy the next generation of father Roch's crew coming thru the same route I had come and he was doing an apprenticeship in one of the local garages in Clonakilty and so we gave him the other room in the house so we had help for the rent.

That lasted a while and life was ticking along just fine. There was a neighbour of ours who I had known for a while now around the Clonakilty area. She loved to see Darra but for some reason always called him Darren... She was a nice giving lady but she suffered from some kind of depressions and liked to booze a little too. In this new house in Clonakilty we had held Darra's 1st birthday party I will always remember how great and big he looked and was only one, but he loved the attention that day.

Anne down the street had been suffering this depression and I had said to Clare I feel sorry for her I wish I could help her, I used to make sure she would get up in the morning and offered to help her with whatever she needed, light a fire or make tea, she had given me a key to her house as she knew some days she just might not get out of bed at all and I could come in and roust her up and get her motivated. She had checked herself into hospitals a couple of times for this depression and they always let her out with a pill or two and that was it. I mean when she was clear and normal she was great fun and laughs. It was around St. Patrick's weekend my friends Keith and Noel and John and Neilus had come to visit, these were the lads that had gone before me and with me in Father Roch's. I had come from working with Clare's dad for the day and Clare had told me she thought she heard the alarm on Anne's house going beep beep a few times, I said but no because she is in the hospital in Bantry. With that the lads came to visit and Keith had said to me looks like there is some guy on the street throwing pebbles up at your friend's window.

I stuck my head out and walked down by Anne's
house and asked him who he was and what he
wanted, he said oh you must be Aidan, Anne told
me about you. I think she is getting out of the
hospital today he said, Anne told me you have a
key, I said yes but her car is not here so maybe she
will be home tomorrow, he gave me his name and
said he would call back tomorrow. I went back to
my house and the lads were there having tea, and I
said let's wait a minute for that guy to leave and
check it out. She was like four doors down along a
town house street where all the houses were side by
side. A real nice two bedroom town house, I went
down with Keith and put the key in the door, it
opened but the chain was on, on the inside, I yelled
in the gap Anne its Aidan, where are you is
everything alright. Keith says ah no, she is sleeping
leave her alone, I said no, let's get something from
the house, I went back and jimmied the chain and
opened the door, I said Anne, Anne it is Aidan are
you awake, I kept calling but no answer, I walked
up the stairs announcing myself all the way up
because I dint want to startle her Keith waited at the
bottom, I saw her lying in the bed but I didn't see
any movement, I went shooting down the stairs and
said Keith she is dead, The lads were freaked out
and Clare too, I said look you guys get out of here I
will talk with yous during the week I have to do this

right. There was one other man lived about 300 meters around the corner, John was his name.

The lads left and I went straight to Johns house told him what I had seen and we needed to go check it out, together we went in the house shoulder to shoulder up the stairs calling out her name, we walked into the bedroom telling each other, no there is no movement, wait I think she is breathing, we pulled back the covers and Anne was there lifeless. We scurried to the bottom of the stairs and I said man that sucks, John had also been someone who was a caring neighbour and used to pop in on Anne every now again. Anne was a divorced woman who lived in the town house and her husband and two grown children late teens lived in the family home on the outskirts of town.

I composed myself for a second and John was freaked out and me too, I called the emergency number to explain to them where I was my name the address and where we were and how and why I found this woman dead in her bed. I asked them to send a priest too. We waited and the Garda showed up and the coroner and the rest was all process from then on. It was a hard weekend to sit there in their family home after a funeral and have no answer when a teenage daughter eyes full of tears is asking me what did she say last, what were her last words and her teenage son asking me did she speak about me much. The police had told me to stay local for there will be an inquiry and I may need to testify in court or give a statement at least. That was it, Anne was gone and the only real death I could remember was my granny my dad's mom when I was about 15,

I remember that funeral in the church with my granny, I remember the cemetery and my uncles and then my dad taking us, the family, to the local bar in Rialto where my grandmother's house was and the first time my dad bought me a pint. He got himself a pint and asked me and my older brother if we wanted a pint, we said yes, three pints in, my brother bowed out and one time in the toilets he said to me, he is going to bury you under the table, he is testing you he drinks like a fish and now he just buried his mom our granny, watch out. We had another couple and then back to my grandmother's house where all the relatives were, I continued drinking and I got stocious drunk. I could see my dad sitting with his aunts and the table next to him had about 30 empty bottles of stout and he was calling for more, I slipped out and went on down the street in rialto I had remembered a friend used to rent a flat there and it was a good smoking house for hash, so off I went. I do not know how or what bus I took but I did make it home that night. That was the only thing I knew about funerals and the afters, but now in my twenties and a sober living man, Anne dying was a real moment and the funeral afterwards too.

We moved off that street, Ahiohill house was vacant and they wanted a care taker to keep the place lived in and would put me on a course as care taker officially and we could live there rent free. Me and Clare moved and we were now living in this big old farm house that was having an addition built on to it so it could be brought up to health board standards and could eventually be used as a fully recognized treatment centre for adolescents. At the time it was almost complete from the remodel we lived in the main house which was an 8 bedroom farm house. The additional part they were building had a class room, another 6 or 8 bedrooms, a canteen type area for eating and our part of the house had a large sun room area and large living room, big dining room and toilets everywhere. The work men would be there during the week and on the weekend nothing, I gave up the hardware store job and went back fishing as it was summer again and there is more money to be made out on the porcupine bank in the summer.

There was a big field with a horse and a stables for three horses as she later had a foal. Darra turned 2 in that house and I had seen an ad in the newspaper for thorough bred Labrador dogs and the lady that bred the dogs was very near to the harbour where I was working at the time, Castletown berehaven is its rightful name Castletown to the fishermen. The lady lived in Allihies a village west of Castletown, I went out and bought the puppy and brought him home to Darra, Rigby they called him. What a great friend Darra had, this little puppy was adorable. Every one used to ask, are you not afraid with a young baby and a dog, we used to laugh oh no if you could see them together it is Rigby who has to run and hide from Darra as Darra is the one doing the biting. It was the right time to buy Darra a pup 2 turning three why not a little friend. It was not looking like me and Clare were going to have another baby anytime soon so why not.

There had been a few heated arguments but we were still doing our thing. I was fishing; Clare was working part time with her Dad and taking care of Darra. I was working sometimes with Clare's dad during the winter months when fishing was scarce and I was betting on the horses too, sometimes win sometimes lose. Looking back now spending the extra 50 pounds here and there was not a good idea, but we were never broke or anything bad like that. The Ahiohill house came to an end as the construction was complete and it was time to look for a house and we found a nice one that looked out over Clonakilty bay a smaller older farm cottage type house, it had two bedrooms upstairs a nice back yard garden and down stairs little kitchen little front room and a TV room. This house is where Darra turned three; this house is also where I and Clare split up. She moved back with her parents and I lived in the cottage about a mile or two over the road. I was devastated at the time to not be with Darra, I could see myself and Clare had fallen out of love just as we had fallen in love and we could be poisonous to each other for ever or we could split. I tried living in that cottage and doing some fishing and then go and visit Darra and then take him for a day or a night and we would hang out together and he was the life of me, it was difficult not to have him all day every day but he was used to daddy going fishing and I was used to missing him.

Coincidence as are coincidences, right around that time fishing was quiet and the nuns from the school in Roscarberry hired me to clean all the windows in the school over midterm break which put money in my pocket, which helped, I still did some work with Clare's Dad and I got a message from my mom one time when I called to say Hi, that doctor Marie Murray had called the house looking for me, who is this doctor. Well this is the doctor who spoke very highly for me in courts a few years ago when I needed it and helped me in the court, the same doctor who I had seen when I was 11 and been told the school would not accept me unless I had a psychological evaluation, yes the very same doctor had looked me up, I made contact with her and spoke with her and she was seeking advice from me, as she had a new case and was a little uncomfortable to discuss due to confidentiality issue but she had come across a young man that reminded her so much of me that would I be willing to take some time and chat with the young man, of course I said in a heartbeat yes. And then I continued and spilled my guts to the trained professional as to my situation having to walk away so to speak from my son and how hard it was that I had grown up with my dad always there and I could not understand or get the grasp of what do I do now with Darra, I was clear I was not pining for Clare it was Darra. The doctor's advice was simple, stay in contact with him make as much time as you can available and when it is time he will want to be with his daddy, she advised be prepared for until he is 18 as it will be a long road, that the child development happens in the first three years and he will not forget daddy and just try and live and, she said that she was confident that in my tone I will never deny Darra and she was sure that from what she knows of me and my history everything will work out for me in the end as I was a good person. These at that time were great words to my ears and boosted me up. I had had an on-going interaction with this doctor over the years from the school thing and the court and the jail, once doctor Marie had contacted me to do a radio interview. She had been writing a book and when she was at the chapter of adolescents and abuse of substances in her book and she was working hand in hand with the national radio station program where she had a segment once a week in the evenings which involved her book chapter by chapter and she had said to me that she really had me in mind when writing her book and if I didn't have any objections would I do the interview to go along with her book. Of course I always felt in debt to her for her kind efforts in my life and I said yes, she explained to me that RTE would pay me for the interview and just to discuss some of my story with the interviewer. Darra was not long born at the time of that interview; of course in the book and the radio interview my name was changed to hide my true Identity. I had explained to the nun up at the school as I had been living close to Roscarberry and fishing in union hall that this interviewer from RTE was coming and would it possible to use a quiet room in the school to conduct the interview. I cannot remember the interviewers name but when I met with him I knew who he was, not by face but by voice, I had heard him on the radio before for sure. He explained to me that the machine we were using to record the interview was his favourite and he had used it for like 18 years it was one of his first, he had the newer version but they now made the newer ones to break so to speak and the older one gave him much more happy years. I was chuffed when he told me he had interviewed people like Mandela and Jeffrey Dahmer in prison or some weird crazy serial killer and now me with the same device and numerous other big time interview names. I will never forget getting the check from RTE, I got a copy of the program too that aired with my section.

A little while later the doctor had made contact and said that the parents were going a different route with their son but thank you for being willing. I had gotten my advice and was thinking of how I will deal with Darra. I decided to move back to Dublin for the first time properly in about 6 years and fish from Howth as there was always good money to be made fishing in the smalls of the southeast corner of Ireland on the run up to Christmas, it was either that or try and get a job on a boat that was going to fish for herrings as there is god money in that through the winter months also, but that involves being anywhere on the south coast as the herrings come to spawn at different parts of the coast at different weeks through the winter. Either or both are hard cold work that time of year. I joined a crew of a boat from Clogherhead which fished out of Howth and we used to keep to a similar routine as all the prawn boats work about two weeks to two and half weeks, do some clean up and repairs to the nets and get paid. Our check that time for the two weeks was in and around 2 thousand so it was good money, I would finish up on the boat in Howth, have my check in the bank and have a plane to Cork from Dublin booked or a car hired for the weekend and off to Clonakilty to hang out with Darra, we would go stay in a hotel and eat in restaurants and play wherever, we would just spend the weekend together. I would sometimes fly and maybe a friend Keith or Noel or Neilus would pick me up and drive me around or loan me a car either way I had good friends and I could count on them. They were all Cork lads and they were my friends, I would spend the weekend with Darra and love every minute of it when I would drop him home maybe on a Saturday evening I would go hang out with my friends in the city, go out to night clubs or whatever we were all sober living young guys so the party scene wasn't there but going out and living was and we did that for a while. I would visit with my rugby buddies in Midleton and maybe do a night out with them or sometimes myself and Darra would go and visit with Wayne, the staff member who used to chaperone me to the local rugby matches when I was living in the treatment facility house in Ladysbridge, we had remained good friends also. One night when I dropped Darra home he asked me to sleep with him like I always used to and this evening was different because I had to say no but I didn't know how to explain to him that I could not sleep over anymore, I am sure if I had asked Clare's parents could I stay they would not have given it a second thought for Darra's sake, but I tried to explain to him in a little man way that I could not sleep together in nanas house as I had to go back to my hotel that I was paying for and I would see him tomorrow, Darra had a very understanding mind at a young age. I lay with him until he fell asleep and went off about my night with the lads and came and saw him the next day, then all he knew was daddy was going fishing and would see him in a couple of weeks. It used to break my heart leaving him those nights. But what was I to do it was the way it was and just keep doing what I was doing.

Darra had been used to me going fishing for a week or two so that was how the story stayed, I would telephone to him sometimes from the boat if we had come ashore midweek to offload fish and some evenings I would be talking down the phone and no answer from Darra but his Na-Na would say, he is listening alright he is just acting upset and not talking.

Chapter 15.

I had been in communications with a number of companies about commercial fishing jobs in Alaska at the time and most of the responses I had been receiving were good as I was what would have been called a qualified professional fisherman at the time, with the ability to take the wheel, find fish, mend nets splice ropes and generally had a good understanding of the engine room and engines and hydraulics and different equipment on the boats. There were three job offers for me to go to Alaska and fish and take a job there and from when I was back 14 and 15 I always had the idea, that my profession is as a fisherman and I might as well go and get paid for it where they make the big money.

I flew back to Dublin that weekend after Darra pulled my heart strings about stay and sleep with me daddy, as I was walking through the airport I went up to departures to wait for my brother to pick me up from the airport. As I walked through the terminal at Dublin airport I looked up at the departing flights and I walked up to the counter and asked the lady, how much was it to fly to Los Angeles and back, she quoted me a figure and said how long for I said well a couple of months. What time of year I wanted to calculate with the salmon fishing in the summer months in Alaska it was possible to earn 18 or 20 grand in a couple of months with the right kind of season fishing, so I said May of this year. I had picked Los Angeles because I always wanted to see Hollywood and Beverly hills so I figured secure a job head out there ten days earlier take a holiday in LA and then off to Alaska. So I paid the lady the 1,400 on the spot and booked my ticket. With that kind of pressure on I would have to make a deal and secure a job sometime between now and the fishing season and my holiday. So I booked it for May of that year. I didn't really know what I was doing if I think about it maybe it was the big escape but my intentions were to try and earn more and then take the off season at home so I could maybe be with Darra every day. And afford a much easier life maybe who knew. I secured the job and in the meantime fished away from Howth and spent the weekends with Darra. I had told my crewman I was going to LA and he didn't believe me at the time I said watch come may I am out of here, I am going to fish in Alaska. I had spoken with Clare on the telephone and told her I was going to go to the states and fish and would only be home every so often, if she had said don't go I would have stayed, but she had her life going on too so she wished me well. So it was set I told my mam and dad about it and they were a little shocked, a lot of people said to me how you can get a visa after all your criminal record, how can you who have a ban for 196 years in total from driving and have a driver's license. The key to all that was everything I had ever done had no record it all happened while I was a minor and so once I did not break the 2 year suspended sentence and satisfied the probation officer by staying in Father Roch's everything had been wiped clear. I was a minor and so a visa for the states was not a problem. A lawyer friend of my father had his two children born in the states and his son was about my age, he said here use my sons social security number he will not be going to live in the states it will not matter and they will not match two and two because the computer systems are not interlinked. And that was that a fool proof way to act like I was born in the states and grew up in Ireland. I got my fishing license for Alaska using the fake social security number and I was set. In the year 2000 I headed for Los Angeles.

Bags checked in and nervous about this immigration deal but immigration was in Los Angeles so I was on the flight, we were delayed at Dublin terminal for some reason or other, the p.a. system said there was some migration delays and we were waiting for clearance and all passengers would soon be boarded. I had been on many planes before as my dad had the good fortune to take us on family vacations when we were kids to Spain and France and Italy, I had visited Paris and Spain a few times myself, but I had no idea what a 12 hour flight was going to be like. I had been given a seat with a window and everybody had seemed to be boarded and the seat next to me was empty so I was set for a nice snooze.

Chapter 16.

I was in say 19e or 21f or something I cannot remember, but we were delayed a little and waiting and waiting, then I saw this guy get on the plane and he was the last passenger we were waiting for and I was trying to lip read the air hostess, I could have sworn she said 19f or whatever the seat next to me was. Here he came, a big fat and just like the movie I mean orca fat. He came clambering down the aisle, banging of every bodies shoulders and head rests they were closing the doors for take-off and he arrives right beside me, "hey you goin mate", an Aussie he had looked more like a Mauri but Aussie he was. He was a funny character, Jimmy is the name he said, I shook his hand, Aidan, oh your Irish great, I am Aussie, No shit Sherlock, he began to explain he had flown in from England and was heading to the states and they were giving him hell about his baggage and he thought he was going to miss his flight and I could tell the whole plane could hear him, loud voice this guy, his voice was as big as him, I had the giggles to his stories and his ways and he explained to me once we take off he will walk around looking for empty rows of seats to get a sleep and that he did. We chatted I told him how I was heading out there and why and he said maybe we can share a place when we get there keep the cost down. I thought yeah sure but I am planning to stay in this hostel type hotel in Venice beach when I get there it is only $35 a night so it will do me fine for my time there. We eventually landed and now for the immigration part, look serious but casual and relaxed this is the United States border and sometimes they turn people back. I breezed through welcome to the U S OF A said the guy, I had made a plan with Jimmy, Jimmy Barnes that I would wait for him outside I must have smoked three to four cigarettes and eventually jimmy comes out with sandwich boards and signs and two wheelie suit cases, He is explaining to me that these are prototypes and he will be showing prototypes for marketing purposes and the customs were giving him some hassle, I said come on man let's get a taxi. Into the taxi and I have my travellers friend handbook and tell the guy where to take us what street on Venice beach, but when we get there the taxi says I cannot drive down there, they are shooting a movie and the streets are closed, if you get out here you can walk back two blocks and you will be right there. As all good Irish travellers when we travel I am of the belief that the taxi driver from the airport, is always lying and trying to rip me off, the sun is starting to go down and this taxis driver is kicking us out cause Jimmy Barnes won't shut up, what the heck is happening, I did see the truck trailers with the sound equipment just like any music concert type truck with all the equipment as the taxi went around the block trying to get us closer. We had no choice but to get out I had a simple back pack and another suit case easy, Jimmy two wheelie bags, and these sandwich boards for advertising or whatever he called it. The back pack I had with me my mother gave me for luck she said, she had always used it on her travels as she used to go off on these charity walks for the Irish heart foundation and walk 100 miles in some foreign country as a way to raise money and get a holiday while she was at it, but she always said the walks were hard, this back pack had been everywhere, the great wall of china and many other places and so that was my luggage.

We could see the bright lights of the movie thing and trucks and people all around and we finally reached the destination. We looked at the hostel, Jimmy turned and looked at me and I turned and looked at him, the only thing in my mind was this place for sure has one of those chalk lines of a body from the night before in the rooms, this looked like a shit hole of shit holes, no wonder $35 was the price. Jimmy before I could say it, says, I am not staying here, this is the beach I am going looking for a hotel. I agreed and we walked on up the street, around the corner and there is a lovely looking hotel front the marina Del Rey beach hotel. Perfect I said let's try here, there was a little Russian or Bulgarian guy body builder guy pumped with muscles behind the reception he says it is $140 for the night. I am thinking dam I only have 2 grand budget for this part of the trip, this is going to kill me for my holiday, at least he will be sharing half so maybe not too bad. On the reception counter is a pile of printed up sheets of paper, "sorry to our clients for the interruptions from the movie filming going on at night". I said hey man give me a room right at the street where they are shooting the movie, we will stay there in the noisiest room you have but we want a discount, ok, ok, he answers let me call my boss, He makes a quick phone call and says room number xyz $80 a night, but they will be shooting movie all night. We answered that's great cause we are so tired from flying that it doesn't matter. We parked our bags and jimmy shows me the Australian bird caller whistle. A piece of bamboo with a stick that you blow into and pull the little stick up and down and it changes the noise, like a little plunger stick inside the bamboo whistle. He explains to me he is going to sell these and make his fortunes in the states. He has two suit cases full of the things and a sandwich board with a US flag and an Australian flag on them. I am blown away, this guy is a character of characters, and he said that is why the customs gave him such a hard time. Being that Jimmy is overweight by a couple of hundred pounds he is huffing and puffing and wants to take a break I say "let's go walk around and sleep later" alright he says.

We left the hotel and headed back down through the movie area to the board walk of Venice beach. Store fronts and people buzzing bright lights but you could see a bunch of places closing, we are approached by some of the street hustlers asking for money, this one guy with a long stick over his shoulder with a red bandanna tied at the end of it with his belongings in it, he had a cowboy hat and cowboy boots on and a biker type looking guy with a beard, wants to walk with us, he had a thing like tom sawyer would have when he is going to run away or the stick with the bandanna ball at the end of it. Jimmy won't stop talking to him, Jimmy says "I want information" the guy says well information is my specialty, I am the mayor of Venice beach, I will be happy to accommodate you for a small fee, I said yeah man I do not have any cash on me, he went to put his arm around me and said, "well there is an atm machine right over there" yeah maybe tomorrow good luck.

Jimmy sits down because his big fat swollen feet are killing him we now have reached the Santa Monica pier, everyone has seen this in movies, it is the long wooden pier with the merry go round type of rides on it down the end. I say come on Jimmy let's go, we walk to the end and straight away there are girls there who want to chat with us and know who we are and what we are doing and maybe we should all hang out. Me being the sceptic at the time thought, yup more thieves let's forget about them Jimmy and walk back. Jimmy was just interested to know where he could set up camp and sell these bird caller whistles.

The board walk along Venice beach actually has little markings on the concrete slabs that mark out each street vendor's spots and those are the lots that you have to have a city permit to sell from, at night it is all bare because there is not too many people. But a few of people still selling paintings and jewellery and sculptures explain this to Jimmy as we wander back to the hotel. Jimmy is beat and wants to rest his feet, I say yeah it is cool I am gonna hang out and watch this movie making for a bit I am buzzed, really tired from the flight but I just landed in LA and they are making a movie. I angle my way to an area that has a good view of things and I stand there watching under a tent like gazebo thing, and then a couple of black guys come and stand around me and I am thinking again here we are, LA and I am about to be robbed, they are cracking yo momma jokes and give me the what's up? With a look to include me when they crack the jokes, they are really funny, the one guy has the biggest whitest eyes I have ever seen and he keeps almost including me in their joke fest and open his eyes even wider. Then this big huge huge dude walks up I mean super tall, it is all slap hands from everybody and even me and we all just are standing there watching them shoot a scene from the movie.

Let me tell you what the movie was it was called Double take, and it starred Orlando Jones and Eddie Griffin. These are just two black actors, I knew this when I went purposely to see it in the cinemas when it came out around Christmas time later that year, it was then, then I knew, the black guys I thought were maybe going to rob me and were making all the jokes that night, were indeed, Orlando jones was the big white eyed guy and the smaller dude with all the yo momma jokes was Eddie griffin, and make matters worse the tall black dude who walked up slapping hands was Kobe Bryant of the LA Lakers, I had been standing in the actors chill out area while they were shooting the movie, never knew it til months later, but that was my first night in LA. Back to the marina hotel and sleep like a baby.

Day two LA, I say to Jimmy, I want to explore a bit he says let me get some information on this board walk and then I will go with you, so we take a breakfast right there by the beach and a few of the vendors explain to Jimmy the only way to get a spot on the board walk is to go to the city department but it will take months he will have to try and do it illegal, Jimmy didn't like that. We head to this guy who has bicycles for rent and he wants $40 for the day and we have to give him our passports, I said no way I am giving up my passport, give him yours Jimmy, eventually the guy says ok, Javier was his name, bike rentals right there on Venice beach. Off we go cycling the winding pathway through the sand along Venice and Santa Monica but Jimmy just has had enough, he cannot take the heat and he is out of breath. He says just go ahead I will see you later; I had my Walkman on and was ready to go adventure. I did not know it then but at the time I was cycling towards Malibu and then cut up some other road, Blvd. it is a famous one they made an entire movie about its name. I cannot remember now, maybe it was place. That's it Mulholland drive. I was cycling for miles it seemed, I managed to cycle my way through Beverly Hills and then was looking for Hollywood. I stopped a guy walking along the street a black dude, I said hey, could you help me how do I get to Hollywood, he stopped with three dudes sitting on the corner sipping beers the big beers out of brown paper bags, he said where you from I said Ireland then he was all helpful and said you will be easier to take the freeway but the cops will get you for cycling on the freeway, he said man this is California he gave me directions and sent me on my way with a piece of advice, do not stop and ask for any more directions until you get to Hollywood not everybody is as friendly as us, this is mother fucking California man. I took his advice and kept cycling and eventually hit the surrounding area and when I was close by I figured because I saw the street with all the stars on the ground, how cool is that. I did not have a camera with me just me the bicycle and my Walkman, and of course my back pack that had been on the Great Wall of China was now on sunset Blvd., Mulholland drive and Hollywood Blvd. It was here I ran into some problems I was cycling along and a police officer beckoned me, get off the bicycle sir and cross the street, I said excuse me; I had picked that up from Jimmy. He was saying it since I met him, in a high pitched voice of Australian accent, "excuse me sir"

Get off the bicycle sir and walk across the street, ok I went to walk away from the police officer, he said sir, NO! This way sir! I thought man these Americans have a real attitude problem, I walked towards him then and said why what's the problem, what is going on. He said sir please walk your bike that way, there is a movie premiere. I said I am sorry I just flew in from Ireland, as soon as I said that the cop was real nice, and explained me the street was closed as the stars would be arriving shortly. I walked the bike along the foot path/ sidewalk to where there were a crowd of people and red carpet and cameras everywhere. A lady with a headset and a clip board, said OK the official crowd we are crossing the street in five minutes, I locked the bicycle to a pole and walked into a shop and bought a Kodak disposable camera and now I was being ushered across the street as part of the official crowd to sit in the bench style seating that was set up. I had bought a bottle of water too as the lady with the head set explained there is no coming back until all the stars have arrived. They gave us mission impossible 2 baseball caps and that was it. I was listening to the people in the crowd talking about a writer's strike that was coming up and all the stars gossip and it appeared I was in a crowd of true Hollywood star stalkers more or less. I stood there, snapping my camera and all the stars came to say hello and walk the red carpet, what I now know is I was directly in front of Mans Chinese theatre where the premiere was about to take place. I never saw such a pasty white girl not even from back home in Ireland as Nicole Kidman when she showed up really, really white. Tom cruise obviously with her, and you name it Metallica, Tim the tool man, Ving Rhames John Coffey from the green mile the list was endless I thought wow this is amazing this stuff really goes on. They then offered 25 tickets to sit in the theatre and watch the movie. It was a class time.

I could not believe it I was star struck and in the centre of movies and stars and actors and famous people, I thought I could get used to this. I climbed on the bicycle as it was late and dark I asked a bicycle messenger guy the quickest way back to Venice beach he told me the quickest route and off I went, dark of night no lights no reflectors just me my back pack and the bike. When I got back to the hotel Jimmy was upstairs with serious sunburn he had been on the beach for the day and was roasted, he was like a beached whale in his bed, yelping because the little sheet was too heavy on his skin, I helped him out and went and got some after sun aloe vera from the chemist and rubbed it on his back for him the poor fucker was roasted. On the television was this show e Hollywood where they were showing and talking about the premiere of the movie I was like Jimmy I just was there, I spent the last couple of hours there he could not believe me but it was the truth. Look it up mission impossible 2 somewhere mid to end of May 2000.

Jimmy began to explain his day and he had me in knots upon knots of laughing, ya see in the morning when we rented the bicycles from the guy Javier he didn't want to give us two bikes with only one passport, and he said he didn't have a bike strong enough to hold Jimmy as Jimmy was big and fat, well Jimmy's story of that day had him looking to open a bank account and he explained to me that he was in the parking lot of the bank but couldn't figure out how he could secure the bike somewhere while he went in so he had his hand in the air calling the security guard with his "excuse me sir" and then he heard poof poof he had cycled the bike across the metal spikes to stop cars exiting that way and put two big gaping holes in the tires of his bike. He had to walk all the way back. When he got back Javier was laughing thinking it was because of his size but when he saw two holes the size of fifty pence pieces he wanted Jimmy to pay for two new tires and they had a big argument. As he was telling me the story he would try and sit up or move and then yelp some more with the pain from the sun burn because after his long day of exercise and walking he went and lay on the beach and fell asleep, he was literally scorched like a beet root all on one side of his body only. I was almost pissing myself with laughter at the state of him and every so often he would laugh too but could not because of the pain and he would keep saying tomorrow I am going to sell 1 thousand dollars' worth of bird callers.

To give you an idea we were staying very close to the wall that has the big mural of Jim Morrison on it, the beach and the boulevard of Venice beach is where the guy in the roller skates goes around playing the guitar. It is all real they are out there. The next day the boardwalk was full and Jimmy was set up. I hung around with him for a while and then walked along the beach, met this girl from Germany who was on holidays and hung out with her for a while. It was hot they kept saying like 85 degrees I had no idea what 85 degrees translates back into when doing Celsius, as that's all us Irish knew, but it was hot. No bicycle for me this day, Javier got my bike back gave Jimmy back his passport for a $20 bill and everything was good again with him. I got a phone card and phoned home to say Hi to my parents and speak with Darra two phone calls chewed up $10 of a phone card but at least I had checked in to say hi.

The following day the street around the corner, where the movie was being shot was a like a construction zone, they were restoring the street to its original style; they had bread boards with pictures and architect drawings and photographs as they had decorated the street for the movie. When they restored the street the hostel hotel didn't look half bad at all, we had been fooled, we arrived into a movie set when we got there the first day. Turns out that scene in the movie is supposed to be a little village in Mexico and so what we thought looked absolutely horrible was only a movie set, setting the scene for a poor village in Mexico. The hotel wanted full rate now because the movie crew were gone and we said alright we are moving out and around the corner to the hostel it was. Jimmy was hustling making a few sales and I was hanging out enjoying the beach.

My friend Wayne back in /cork Ireland had married a girl from California that year and on one of my weekend visits to Cork to visit with Darra I had stayed over the night with Wayne and his wife Deni. While we were eating dinner that evening after I had dropped Darra off at his granny's house Wayne's wife who I hardly knew at all but was the whole purpose to stay over and have dinner was to get to know her, she had called a friend of hers up in Arizona and told me I was perfect for her and we chatted on the phone, I said if I ever get out that way I will give you a call and come and visit she said in an all-out sexy American accent, oh please do. So that day in LA while Jimmy was selling whistles I called her up and she said come and visit and told me about south west airlines how you can get a ticket cheap, so I went out the airport and flew to phoenix Arizona, said good bye to Jimmy and the German girl who had spent the night, she didn't want me to leave but I had to keep things moving and so off I went. When I got to the airport in phoenix all the taxis did not seem to want to take me to the address, thunderbird way or thunder valley road or something, they were acting like they didn't know where it was, so I had to call the girl Julie, my friend Wayne's, wife's friend and have her explain to the taxi driver, they negotiated with me $60 for the trip and I thought another airport taxi cab that is ripping me off. He got lost but then eventually we found it. Now because of the long journey I guess she left to go to work and I had missed her, the administrator at the gate of the condo complex was waiting for me and then she took me to where Julie worked to get a key and drove me back again, it was a bit of a mix up, especially when I walked into a stripper bar to find her as this is where she worked and nobody knew a girl called Julie that worked there, and now the administrators of where she lived knew she works at a strip club now too. What a mix up Aidan what a mix up.

One of the waitress girls came by and said oh I know you mean Jennifer. Yes, she said yes you are the Irish guy, out came Jennifer/Julie and gave me a hug and a hello and a key to her apartment she was clothed by the way. Sweat pants and sweat shirt, cute too. It was so kind of the admin lady to drive me back and see me safe and sound in the apartment. Let me tell you though this phoenix Arizona is a sweat box of a place, I mean you have to be indoors with air conditioning, there is just no two ways about it. It is a must. Big digital signs outside shopping centres were reading numbers like 96 and 98 degrees. I still didn't know what they were in Celsius but could tell you it felt twice as a hot as LA. I was thinking because the beach and the breeze there maybe it just seemed cooler, but this Arizona, Phoenix was no breeze. Warm wind when you walked out the door or opened a car window it was like opening an oven door the way the heat hits you.

Julie came home that evening and we got to meet and chat properly. Nice girl, she wanted to treat me here and there and everywhere, there was an attraction but something about me knowing she was stripping just stopped me, and something in her knowing I knew she was stripping stopped her. We hung out and chatted into the morning and slept and cooked together and hung out together.

From phoenix I called the boat captain the boss, big problem, he said I have not heard from you in a couple of weeks and I gave the job to someone else, I said what? I am on my way there this coming Monday, he said sorry but I expected you to call and keep me up to date, sorry. I was in the middle of the desert and worried how far my money would get me and what now. My plane ticket home was for a few months from now hmmm. I explained to Julie and she said great hang out here for an extra week. I was the Irish guy the new guy on the block, Julie would go out to work in the evening I would watch TV and then at about 2 am Julie and all her friends from work would come over and we would all go and hang out in the pool and the hot tub till 4 or 5 am. The Irish guy was in town. Seriously one cannot make this stuff up.

In true Irish fashion ten girls straight from the strip club all wanted to hang on my arm and get close to me just because I don't know they all thought I spoke funny with a funny accent.

These girls were all living pretty rich though and having a fun time making big money. On the weekend I believe called Memorial Day weekend we headed to a lake, with their boss and all the crew from the bar they worked at. Two lake boats a speed boat and a cruiser type party boat. These people were making major big money doing what they do.

The Lake I believe was called lake pleasant and it was at the end of or along the freeway known as the "feel good freeway" I thought it was all a joke but no, there is a big huge lake in the middle of the desert. We went not skiing but what do you call it oh yeah tubing, a big yellow rubber tube, where you hold on for dear life while the speed boat tries to go as fast as possible and watch you splash it was a lot of fun though and the girls were all very very hot and it was a fun time, that evening when we got home I could not lift a slice of pizza, my arms were hanging from the tubing. Julie had a friend who had an ex-boyfriend packing a U-Haul truck and driving to Seattle Washington, I said I will split the cost of the petrol if I can ride along and he said sure!

The end of that week I headed off in a truck, up through the desert in the night time because it is cooler then. We had to make a stop in San Francisco and pick up a bed from some friend of his so off we went thru the night. The drivers name was Caleb, he was a mullet hair cut blonde guy about my age early to mid-twenties and away we went. I paid for the first fill of petrol $100 then we stopped for a coffee and a quick snack alongside the freeway and I paid again and now I could see the pattern, if I had not have asked for the ride this guy was going nowhere because he didn't have two pennies to rub together. I thought maybe I will just get out in San Francisco and leave him stranded. We got to San Francisco the next morning and we made it to the destination where to pick up the bed, the story got even better, we were picking up a girl and her bed because she was moving home to Seattle and all the rest of her stuff was being shipped already, she lived in the Haight Ashbury area of San Francisco. She let us sleep for a while and take a shower, and then wanted to take us like tourists around the city, to Haight Ashbury, then fisherman's wharf by the ball park, ride the cable car it was fun really one sunny day in San Francisco.

We hit the road that evening again for Seattle Washington. What a beautiful drive, I 5 is the freeway and it goes up through mountains and forests and it looks like real grizzly Adams territory amazing views all the way along. The girl kept pretending to fall asleep and was trying to put her head in my lap the whole entire journey, I even told Caleb one time we stopped for petrol and he said, dam I have known her my whole life and never knew her to be like that. I was honest with him, I said at first it seemed like a fun idea but now it is just annoying. Oh and as it turned out the girl's mother had paid for the truck and the girl was paying for all the petrol from here on out. This guy was something else really.

Chapter 17.

We arrived in Bremerton, Washington and that was the end of the road, the mother lived in a half-finished house in the woods, there was no shower, so I was given a bath to take but there was no door to the bathroom so it was a little weird, the girl came in and sat beside me while I was in the bath, she was half hanging over the side of the tub and asked me, why don't I bathe you and make you feel good, I thought what is going on with these people her mother is walking back and forth right there and everything seems a little too hippy like, but they had money and were snobbish I could not understand. I got out of the uncomfortable bath and said okay I thought you said we had to return this u haul truck to Seattle let's get going.

There is a ferry from Bremerton to Seattle across Puget sound and we boarded it and went to Seattle, the girl had some of her college friends meet us in Seattle and there I meet her friend Renay and her husband Chris, very cool cool people, a young couple both working Chris an electrician and Renay some corporate office type, we hung with them and towards the end of the evening Chris said, hey man I need a brother like you to hang out with, why not come and stay with us until you find a job and there it was I was now staying with Chris and Renay in Kirkland Washington which is a suburb of Seattle.

Chris was cool he could not loan me his work truck obviously he needed it for work, but he did the next best thing, he loaned me his mountain bike and with that I could take the bicycle path to down town Seattle. Believe it or not Seattle has this great map of bike paths all the way around and thru the city, I never was somewhere so amazing, special tunnels for bikes near freeways and paths along road ways, the whole city is designed very well to get around on a bicycle without ever having to encounter too much traffic.

Chris and I would hang out on the back porch and smoke cigarettes and shoot the breeze as they say, chit chat, then on a few evenings go to the local pool hall and hang out shooting pool, we had good laughs and fun and his wife Renay was cool she was the active type, actually they both were they enjoyed snowboarding and extreme mountain biking. Chris had this thing as a pet that just freaked me out, a bearded dragon, a lizard to me. I said man if that thing gets out at night and is running around I am liable to stomp on it, us Irish are not used to any form of lizard, roaches, bugs nothing, please make sure the lid is firmly on every night please, He got a great laugh out of the Irish guy afraid of a little lizard. Chris was a tanned looking character, I being new in the United States had no real understanding or concept of what the "melting pot" was how a whole bunch of different races and creeds live within the United States. So I asked Chris where are you really from cause you have this exotic look or something, his wife took great fun and laughs in that one, she said he was her little slave boy she adopted from indo china. He explained me something about an island called Saipan was where he was from and I cannot remember if he said his mom moved here to Seattle when he was a young kid or he had been adopted here as a young kid, either way he grew up in America and so was American like everybody else in the united states.

Saipan I used to joke "is that where they legally eat dog" from then on if were out walking around the town of Kirkland or neighbouring suburbs and someone was out walking there dog, I would ask Chris if he was hungry. After a few times he caught on and then eventually if someone passed walking their dog, he would start to lick his lips and smile. Renay thought this was cruel & disgusting, but yet she could not help from laughing about it.

I used the bicycle to go to Ballard every day to fisherman's terminal, it is the harbour area of Seattle where all the boats were preparing nets to head north to Alaska for the salmon season, a bunch of small fifty foot boats seiners, it is a type of fishing where the boat goes around in a circle laying out a net and comes back and picks up the end of the net again where it started. So when the boat has both ends they start to haul back the net, at this time they have a tall wall of netting in the water, as the boat slowly hauls back the net one person will be hauling a rope, this rope is attached close to the bottom of the wall of net all the way around so it begins to close the bottom of the net like a purse string, and so the style of fishing is called purse seine netting or pursing or purse seining. So eventually you will have the bottom of the wall of the net all crumpled up and so no escape downwards for fish. All the floats floating still in somewhat of a circle, where they are closer to the boat now and would have metal rings attached all along the top line of the wall of netting, when they are secured to a hook that hauls them up in the air so no fish now can escape out over the top. The fish will be all within the net and the hauling continues of the wall of net until there is only fish visible now. This is called drying up the catch, when dried up it is time to roll the netting into the boat and waves and waves of fish all come into the boat with each new segment of net hauled or rolled or continued to be dried up until there are no more fish in the net. The process of fishing for the most part is who can catch the most each haul cutting time at sea into the shortest possible and so the speed and efficiency of any crew always help keep the costs down and the catch profit margins higher, meaning everyone gets paid more. This is the basics of fishing of any kind in the commercial fishing world. Like any business, keep expenses as low as possible and gain as much profits as possible.

At fisherman's terminal there were a bunch of boats and I walked the docks looking for a berth, that's what we call a job basically. I had a few people of interest and I was honest with most that I didn't have a work visa because that is what they wanted to see, unfortunately I didn't have one and many a captain said they would love to take me but they might end up arrested for taking an illegal immigrant. What I did do was secure a couple of boats who needed their nets fixed and overhauled before they went fishing. I was standing there in my shorts no t-shirt sun beating down on me while I mended the nets for $15 per hour, I would work a full 8 hours and get $120 with lunch thrown in by them and however many cans of coke it took for me to continue working. Not a bad deal for me at least I was earning and I was in the heart of the fishing buzz. There were some bigger boats which were crab boats but because it was summer months they were preparing to head to Alaska as tenders for the salmon fleet, basically a tender is a boat who will take the catch from the smaller boat and bring it to the factory for them so the smaller boat can stay fishing, so the bigger boat drives around the fleet of small boats offloading their catch and the little boats stay catching. Those jobs were not that hard and so crew positions on them were not really available. In Ballard there was an Irish bar and so in the evening on a few occasions I headed up there to eat some potatoes and Seattle's version of Irish food. I hung out there and let the barman know if he heard or knew any fishermen looking for a crewman I was around and available, I bought a cell phone and gave the number out to a few people around the pier. The area has boat yards where boats were getting repairs done prior to their next season in Alaska and I asked about some of them too. It was not looking hopeful for a job and the 20 mile bike ride was getting old fast too as I was on my feet all day each day for a couple of weeks mending nets, but at least I was earning. I had found this one little bar like a neighbourhood bar close to the harbour where there was a group that used to come and have a few drinks and shoot pool in the evenings so I had found myself hanging out there a few evenings too. They were a young trendy crowd; the ferryman maybe was the name of the bar, very close to Ballard oil which was a docking station for boats to fuel up at. Right at Ballard oil was a great little diner, café place that served a great breakfast, pork chops and eggs and fried potatoes. I was enjoying Seattle and the food and the work and the hanging out very much.

At the ferryman pub I had become one of the folks who got some respect as I could shoot a game of pool with ease, brings me back to my dad and my first holy communion.

Tradition back then in Ireland when I was seven was we made out like bandits for our holy communion and got kitted out and took loads of photographs, like for example Myself and Donna were seven together and there are many photographs of us that day in front of the church, actually one of her children recently, we dug up an old photograph of our holy communion day and her little girl wanted to know we were getting married then, because we were at the front of the church railings and Donna was kitted out in a white dress and I had a suit on. So the tradition was to go visit all your relatives and they would hand you a card in an envelope and there would be money inside.

I had amassed 170 pounds or something close to it and so my dad commandeered the money and said he would build me a pool table with the money I said cool. He built a counter top to sit on this long rectangle table we had with a proper slate base and real green felt and rubber cushions a nice pool size snooker table, me and my older brother enjoyed having arguments over the pool table and breaking pool cues off each other's backs in the midst of a fight so a bar fight with a broken pool cue across my back was nothing new to me had been doing that since I was 8 years of age. For this simple reason I could hold my own on the pool table plus the size of the pockets on a table in the states, they are much larger than what we had back in the bars in Ireland.

I didn't win every match or game but could take a few challengers one after the other. I would buy a coke and play pool for the evening. Everyone would have the big laugh, the Irish guy who doesn't drink, well alcohol. The true stigma of being an Irish man and a drunk I was letting the home side down on that front, because a can of coke was my limit.

They laughed at me a lot about no alcohol, I met this guy Chuck there, he used to love a few drinks in the evening and shoot pool. One Friday he said hey I am going to do a party on my boat and everyone is invited, but it is a work party, he had a yacht in a local marina and he said the work party was free beer and pizza for anyone all day, whoever showed up to help sand and varnish his yacht. I told him I will show up and help I had nothing else to do now the salmon fleet had left. I went and hung out with chuck that day and had explained to Chris and Renay that this guy Chuck from the bar had offered that I could stay on his yacht and call it my home base as the marina allowed people live aboard the boats, as they were paying rent anyway. Renay and

Chris said cool they actually were genuinely worried and wanted to check out this Chuck guy and make sure I was going to be ok.

I headed over to Chuck's yacht Saturday and we started sanding and varnishing and having fun and laughs, some people showed up an old girlfriend of his and a few of the folks from the bar, those who were dead beats and wanted a free beer, but myself and chuck put in a great days work, that evening he said no way dude, I have to buy you dinner you really worked hard today and we accomplished a lot, I said no problem you have allowed me to make this my home and I appreciate that. Chuck had explained to me he was in the military when he was younger, a marine and he knew what it was like to travel because he had explained when he got out of the marines, he was not ready to settle down and take a normal job so he did a little travelling. He said he had a full understanding and people were good to him when he travelled so the yacht was mine to stay as long as I needed.

We drove off in his car, both of us big red sun tanned faces from the day's hard work and off to a bar for some food and a few drinks. We ended up at an English bar, where they had a couple of pool tables and so we took up our normal positions, I go first beat the guy holding the table and then me and Chuck get to play. Two lovely young girls wanted to play us and so we doubled up me and the blonde and Chuck and the brunette, chuck wanted kisses so the deal was every time they win they kiss if we win we kiss, I let him win all the games so he could get it on with the brunette, they were twins believe it or not. They had the most striking resemblance to Meg Ryan you have ever seen, really look alike for the actress, so we continued playing and they invited us to their place oh yeah and one of the dead beats who showed up for beer that day and did very little work, he tagged along. We headed back to their apartment and they were drinking away, chuck said he was getting some competition from the dead beat guy with the brunette but I said oh well, I am fine the blonde wants me all the way. I had to go out and interrupt Chuck and whisper to him hey do you have any condoms, he said I think in the car I went out of the apartment balls naked looking for his car and search everywhere, none to be found. The funny thing was I had to say no sorry girl, just not gonna happen. She was furious who was this Irish guy? Who does not drink and won't take the offerings condom or no condom. I was not into this whole polluted idea of the states and aids and diseases so No was the answer, she tried getting smart about it, saying "oh well, just as well I would kill you with sex, I am that good" she laughed I said sure, I am sure I can say the same but not gonna happen, she also kept on saying "you Irish would not be able to keep up, I am a sex machine" I laughed, Chuck finished trying and trying with the sister but was getting nowhere and we left & headed back for the boat.

I laughed all the way back to the marina, because he was super upset, that he picked the brunette and he was getting all the kisses and groping in the bar and then when we got back to their place, he was the one getting none and I was the one denying the blonde, I laughed, that is how it goes my friend, good old murphy at work. Murphy's Law, that is. Chuck said we have to go out more often, this Irish accent thing draws the girls without any effort, you are a stud with the accent, I said hey man come on I am a good looking guy too, he laughed, Nah it is just the accent.

Chapter 18.

Before I had left Ireland I had signed up to a few dating sites and seeing as I was going to be in America I thought well maybe I could meet someone along my travels as they might be in the same area as me, while in Seattle I had checked into one of the sites from an internet café one of the days and there was a message from a girl in and near Seattle, because I had put something like current city or something like that. I messaged her back and gave her my cell phone number and within seconds she was calling. I thought ok, her user name was Puerto Rico girl something or other, I never put two and three together, she was American born and bred but was Porto Rican descent like her folks came from there, again not too familiar with the whole melting pot concept. I met with her we hung out and had dinner with like six of her friends, I got the feeling they do this a lot and all come along to see if the guy is cool or not, we went bowling and had a good laugh and finished the night with a kiss and that was that. She texted me all the next day she wanted to meet me again but this time without her friends and she wanted to go further, I had nothing going on, was lazing around the yacht and so invited her over. She came to the marina and walked down the dock to where I had explained to her where the berth for the boat was and she came aboard, within seconds of her entering the boat, she was on me, violently madly passionately kissing me and stripping my shorts off, I thought why not. And we spent the day humping like jack rabbits until Chuck came to pick me up that evening. The girl left and texted me all that evening saying she was not crazy but she was into me and that she wants more and more Irish.. She would not bother me with bullshit but wanted me to say I was hers. I was showing Chuck the texts as they were coming in to my phone and he and I were laughing, but it was funny and cute but crazy too. Chucks advice when I told him she was Porto Rican, he said stay away! Her and her family might kill you, jokingly but serious dude already she is being a nut job. I said but she doesn't seem nuts in person, maybe you should meet her.

Chuck was a martini cocktail guy who likes to hit the jazz bars and sip a martini and this buzz was cool on an evening or two as he knew all the good spots. Chuck would tell me I was his wing man, but his whole pick up line was let me introduce you to my Irish friend, he is fresh off the boat and the girls love the Irish accent, so they sit and giggle and drink their drinks and want to go further every evening, Chuck was stupid laughing many evenings, I don't know what it is he said "the girls love it and they flock to you". I always insisted it was the good looks, he always disputed it is the accent because you are ugly LAUGH OUT LOUD. On another evening we sailed the yacht well powered by engine really through the lake, Seattle has water everywhere, the sound and then there are lakes and so there were bars with docks, you could drive the boat across the lake to west lake and tie up the boat and get out and be right at the bar. This was a fun time, hanging out with Chuck picking up girls for him and laughing the days away. He had a serious job by day sometimes I would go and visit with him, he was a mortgage broker and so he was hustling deals as much as he could. That following Saturday he was off from work and I did not realize that he had given his number to the twins and had been chatting with them, he had invited them sailing out on Puget sound and so Saturday morning I wake up on the yacht with the blonde there, Laura and chuck saying we are going sailing. Laura had a daisy duke shorts on and a light see through hemp type material top no bathing suit the bare nipples clear on view. Out through the locks we headed and out into the ocean well Puget Sound at least we hoisted the sails and were cruising along. I was up on the bow laying on the deck it was so peaceful I had never been sailing before, I was used to the ocean but usually with the roar of a diesel engine from a fishing boat but never on the ocean so peaceful just the water lapping against the boat. Laura had her top off sun bathing and she was a very nice perky c cup, she nudged me to look back, Chuck was at the wheel with a beer in his hand he always loved a Tecate and a lime and was stark naked, when I looked back at him with a look of disgust, he smiled and said get them off nodding his head towards Laura, I knew chuck wanted some of that Laura girl because from the night we met them last week he was upset he got the prudish sister. Laura had turned over to sun her back and asked me to rub lotion, she said in my bag the lotion and plenty of supplies, I grabbed the bag and there was a lip gloss, a pack of Marlboro lights a cigarette lighter, sun tan lotion and a pack of condoms, I laughed this girl is relentless. With that she was lying on her belly and I know, was sticking her ass up on purpose, there definitely was not any underwear and the thinnest strip of denim between the ass and the crotch, nothing left to the imagination. I didn't know what to think. I didn't know where to look I thought these Americans are sex starved lunatics, I got captain Chuck down there steering rockin out with his **** out and this one practically naked telling me there are plenty of condoms, I was so into the peace of the ocean as I had never been sailing before, what the hell is going on. We headed back ashore after a while and Chuck headed to the store to grab some food and some more beer and me and Laura got it on down below in the cabin. When Chuck came back he didn't really know and so he was trying to work his charm to see would she go for it as he knew or believed she was dying for some sexual action and the big stupid Irish was too modest to go for it. We ate watching the sun go down and chuck was ready for some martinis. I said I was going to hang out with Laura some more and back to her apartment we went. It was bedroom the rest of the night all day Sunday and I drove her to work on Monday morning and had strict instructions to pick her up after work at 6pm. I said hey cool I have a car to tour the city today and enjoyed driving around in what she said was "my girlfriend's car" if anyone asks. I thought ok cool. My phone at this time was receiving Porto Rican text messages where are you what are you doing, how was your weekend, I want to see you, I said sure come on let's take coffee, I met her by the locks and we hung out I made sure to park where I could see the car but where miss Porto Rico could not see me getting out of it, by the locks you can watch the salmon jumping up stream. They made them a stair stepping area so the salmon could still get up to the lake even if the locks were closed, While I was hanging out with Maritza, Laura started texting me, Maritza said oh you have someone else, well I wanted to talk to you about that, I was thinking maybe we could be dating and be exclusive to each other, I said I just met you last week or so, she said well it makes her jealous that someone else might be texting and she wanted a relationship. Maritza then wanted to go back to the boat for some loving I said, nah Chuck and I had an argument I am back staying in my friends in Kirkland, she said that's great I live near there, come on I will give you a ride. Now I had to really start lying, I said well my friends are coming to the city after work and are supposed to meet me for dinner and so I am just going to be hanging out here for them for a while longer. She said she wanted to meet them and introduce herself as my girlfriend, she said everything I have explained about them made them seem real nice and cool people. I said yeah maybe later in the week because I need to ask them if I can stay with them again on account of not having the yacht and they might say no if you are here, because if your my girlfriend why I cannot stay with you. Maritza started with "oh hell no, my mami and papi will not go for that" At least now I knew she lived with her parents. It was pushing for 5pm and I was trying to nicely get rid of Maritza because I knew I had to drive to the far side of town to pick up Laura with her texts of don't be late and we are going to take dinner in bed tonight and all kinds of other texts. At that exact moment I was been driven nuts by just the two of them, so Maritza left finally and I jumped in the car not too sure of the route but I remembered the exit from the freeway to get to Laura's office but how did I get to that freeway? I made it 6.15 not bad and seeing as we were close to Chris and Renay's house I said lets go and meet them.

We went to visit and Chris and Renay made some food and Laura had a few drinks and was proclaiming her undying love for the Irish guy, on a quick smoke break on the patio, Chris is busting his ass laughing at me, saying I thought you said you had been seeing a Porto Rican chick, Oh man I explained to him the afternoon I had and he laughed and laughed some more all the while telling Renay, I will tell you later. We headed home to Laura's and fell asleep, what a day.

The next day same thing up early Drive to the office and keep the car for the day, I headed to the bar in Ballard, the Irish bar and see if any news or any guys from the fishing fleet had been in, the barman told me he had one guy might be interested, I left my cell number again as the barman says he didn't have it. I visited a few other big fishing companies in the area and filled out job applications. I was walking back the street in Ballard about 11 am and decided to stop for a hot chocolate as I have always loved chocolate, basically at that time in Seattle the joke was, you were nobody unless you had a coffee cup in one hand your shades on and your cell phone in the other, so I took a hot chocolate at a coffee shop. Sitting there talking to Chuck on the phone about the laugh I had yesterday. It was the year 2000 Starbucks had been born, Seattle best was in full flight and cell phones were all the rage, Seattle was a centre of it, a mecca with Microsoft and technology also in full flight. While I sat there this blonde girl tall not too slim asked if she could join me I said sure, she was waiting for a friend of hers to discuss some things, I thought ok sure, she sat we discussed the fact that I am Irish and we were there at a table chatting and laughing when her friend showed up, he was from Iraq it turned out the girls recent ex-husband was from Iraq also and they were trying to communicate some differences and the guy was a middle man between the ex-husband and the girl. We chatted and then he left after a half an hour. I got the feeling I was being used as if I was the new boyfriend so I said to her, did you just use me to get at your ex-husband, she answered kind of. I said I guess I have no problem with that as long as I do not get into any trouble, she looked me straight in the eye and said, "I live three blocks from here and my daughter is with the nanny. I have not been laid since my divorce 8 months ago, If I am going to make you my "pretend" new lover, why not test drive" being in the united states and sewing the wild oats, why not. She was cute off we went. We got to her house and she said wait I have to put the dogs away, she went in first I imagined a little handbag poodle or something. We headed for the bedroom and it was on! Humping and grinding and sex full on. I was standing behind her, she laying on the bed me standing on the floor as always proud to be Irish and creating a memory when I felt something weird, I thought that's a new sensation, the dog was standing behind me licking my balls while the sex was happening, I shrieked a little as I saw one very large Rottweiler dog behind me and another standing at the door of the bedroom, she looked back and said oh its ok they won't bite, they are just intimidating. All I could think of at that exact moment was if this dog bites down I will be minus one ball, not a good moment and time to finish ASAP. I got my clothes on and out of there all in about five minutes; I did not exchange numbers and a quick hug to her and legged it.

I headed back to the boat, while I was sitting on the back deck of the yacht in the marina, I was approached by a guy, said he had a motor boat in a different berth and loved the way this yacht was shining maybe if I wanted a little extra work I could sand and varnish the wood work on his boat and polish the brass and the fittings. He asked how much I would Like I said $15 an hour because I remembered that seemed a good deal when mending the nets, he jumped at it he said he was afraid that I would say too high a price. Now I had a job again. This guy's boat was up by the front of the marina almost like berth #1, he said he had the boat so long it was a classic and it was, a beautiful boat, I forget the make and model but it was one of those old style motor boats that was like a luxury car on the water. He had the good berth because he had the boat in the marina through the entire time and was good friends with the owner of the marina through family ties.

Now this work was getting me recognition, people were coming and going all the time in the marina, now I was seeing tons and tons of people who lived aboard their boats. Many were stopping by and asking me for my card as the work was making the boat look superb. I didn't have a card obviously but I did offer Saturdays to people for $20 an hour and they were happy to pay. I finished his boat and moved on to the next one, now anyone who wanted to hire me it was $20 and hour. I stayed busy those weeks, with sanding and varnishing yachts by day Laura picking me up in the evenings to eat and sleep at her place and Maritza would come by at lunch times for some action. The guy from the luxury type motor boat Darrell I believe his name was, came by one Friday afternoon and said, hey the owner of the marina asked me to do her a favour, she said her daughter has been divorced for a while and she wants me to take her out on a date, she is bringing a friend though and I thought if you are not doing anything maybe you want to come along for the night out just to keep her friend company. I said sure why not he was to pick me up at 8. I made my excuses to Laura that I was going to be working late as the owner wanted the boat ready for Saturday morning and away we went out to meet these girls. We are waiting at this bar where they serve food in a booth and along comes the two girls, my date is this really skinny boy looking girl who is so into mountain climbing and veganism it is not even funny, and then Darrel's date is the buxom blonde who owns the Rottweiler's, what do you know. We smile and act like this is the first time we have met. The night went on and we went to a night club dancing, Darrel was getting drunk and pressing up on blondey and the vegan was sipping on iced water and burnt out about telling me how red meat was bad for me. The blonde took her opportunity when Darrell headed for the toilets and the vegan went to the bar for more drinks for everyone, the blondey, says come dance with me, I said I do not know how and I would be no good at it, she was a bit tipsy too she leaned in to me and said, "dancing is like fucking, if you can do one you can do the other, and you know how to fuck" I thought holy shit, Darrel was returning and I tried to act like she was drunk and falling around, but he had seen her leaning in whispering to me, now he was upset with me and he said it is time to go. As we walked to the car, she said here is my number I am gonna let him drop me home and call me in ten minutes you know where I live. I was dropped off at the marina and Darrel and the two girls headed off in his car, instead of walking into the marina I headed up town for her house, why not… she was pretty good at it herself. We got to her house and she said no dogs tonight. We jumped in her car and headed to the tip of the coast out past the locks to this mansion house on the hill, "I don't want Darrel coming back after he drops off my friend" Ok I said but what is this house, oh this is my moms, she owns all three marinas you see below you and has another three in Florida, she is in Florida right now so the house is empty. We got it on that night three times, on the third time I had to fake it because I was worn out, I ran to the bathroom to flush the condom before she could see. Took a shower and passed out.

I continued working on the boats in the marina and every so often walked around the commercial boats but nothing was doing. I knew my plane ticket to go back home was coming up in a few weeks well four more weeks and it was looking like it was gonna just be one fun filled holiday after all.

Chris and Renay had called to let me know their friend the "jewess" they called her had moved out from her mom's house in Bremerton and moved to the city as she had landed a great job and was moving into Queen Anne district. Renay asked would I be able to help with some of the heavy furniture and is it ok to give her my Phone number, I said sure why not, Renay said be sure to charge her, her family are loaded and her dad pays for everything anyway since their divorce. I received the call and she explained me her address and that she had an armoire that needed moving and she would happily pay me a hundred dollars to help.

Sure, why not. I finished up the day early varnishing the boat as the evening seemed to me maybe it might get a little damp anyway so it worked out, I headed for queen Anne 104th street north or 14th street north, I remember I got lost because the streets north and west in queen Anne seemed confusing, anyone that has been there can understand this, I made it finally. She had a great apartment looking out over the bay almost or sound I guess you call it. It was up on the hill. The armoire I was dreading this as they can be very heavy, it was very heavy but all she needed was to slide it along the floor from the hallway by the front door and into her bedroom, she said the movers had just left it there. I moved it for her and she handed me $100 as agreed, I said thank you very much, I felt bad taking the money it was all but ten minutes work, but I needed cash now always for my survival plan to stay going. She poured me a glass of juice and poured herself a wine and I sat there on a lounge seat looking out the window at the view, she very straight forwardly, said, "I was trying to blow you in the u haul van on the way up here, you resisted. I would love to offer you the same great experience" I said "wow I am flattered, that's about as blunt as anyone has ever been with me". She said, "I know you needed the money for moving the furniture, why don't I give you $200 more and you lie back and relax" Now there is an offer you don't get every day, I said show me the money and she went to work. Later I left and all was well. On the way home on the bus I received a call from Renay and she half knew the story and wanted all the details, so I told her the truth, Renay laughed like crazy saying I know her since kindergarten and there is no way you are telling the truth, I said believe it, it just happened, Renay from now on was sniggering at me and calling me gigolo or deuce bigalo.

That evening Chuck said lets head out for a few cocktails I said sure why not; it was only 9pm. Chuck had membership at the local gym and I used to use the sauna and the showers there as a guest on his membership card. It was one dollar every time I used it and it was 24 hours. I said to chuck let me go take a shower and I will be back in one hour meet you then he said sure that was fine he would pick me up at ten. I headed up to the gym and took a long shower and then went into the sauna for a nice chill out relax, I was almost falling asleep in there it was rejuvenating, while I was in the sauna some people came in and went out and came in and went out, it was men's only and the other locker room had a women's only so it was a fully naked ordeal. I was lying back in the sauna and I could hear this noise while I was relaxing, my eyes were shut and I was not taking notice of who or how many people were actually in the sauna, it was a big sauna hold about 12 or 15 people. I was trying to hear the noise and I thought it sounds like people kissing, then I really didn't want to open my eyes, I could hear this smacking type nose, slight like two people exchanging spit or something now I was not so relaxed and was figuring my exit, I opened my eyes, to see this guy sitting across from me his manly parts all full attention he was stroking himself and sucking his finger looking at me, I blinked immediately and no, it was true he was there and it was happening, I stood up put my towel around me immediately and told him his was a sick faggot pervert, he tried to cover himself and said in a girly voice oh I am sorry, I thought you were gay… I took a quick shower and high tailed it out of there to meet chuck, we headed to a jazz bar and then a pool bar to shoot a few games and I told him about the gym, he said I should have complained, he told me he thinks he knows the guy as he one time put a guy in check for sitting in the Jacuzzi and playing with himself, Chuck got a great laugh that now I could start charging the guys, he was getting hammered and I was having a good laugh too as he was taking the piss out of me directly but the way he was putting it was extremely laughable.

Maritza had told me how her step dad lived over in Bremerton and had a boat and she had been explaining to him about me and the work I did in

Seattle and he said he would love to have some help and would pay $200 a day for a Saturday and Sunday if I came out there to work on his boat, I said sure sounds like a great deal I was making about 7 to 800 at the marina and an extra 400 on the weekend, this is good money. I was staying with Laura now almost permanent and she was a crazy thing, she tried to even get her twin to come to bed with us, but here sister would have none of it. I needed a break from her and so the weekend to go and work was the perfect excuse. I had to go to Bremerton to work. Maritza picked me up Friday evening and we spent the night at the step fathers, he and his girlfriend made dinner and we went to bed, I told Maritza there is absolutely no way we are having sex with her step father listening, no way I was going for that, she said I made a good point and sleep is what we did. The next morning the step father had some rental properties and said, look change of plan I would like some help laying tiles in one of the rental properties and I will pay you the same $400 if that is ok. I said sure and all day into the evening we laid tiles. Sunday we got up and went to check out the boat, the step father said, take a look and give me a price for the entire renovation job and let me know, here is the 400 and if you give me a good price for the boat you can start on it and take your time. The boat was in bits. I figured it would take me 2 months straight to work on it and if I only charge $160 a day the whole thing would be like $12,000. Maritza said tell him, he is rich he won't mind. He said ok let me think about it and I will be in touch.

We hit the road back to Seattle, it was dusk around 5 or 6 in the evening and I was driving. Light sprinkles of raining were coming, I had been making jokes with Maritza that I was not used to driving on what seemed to be the wrong side of the road and keep an eye on me because at any moment maybe I end up on the other lanes, she leaned over to turn on the windscreen wipers because of the rain and I swerved a little saying, gosh don't distract me I am already nervous enough.

Distract you! she replied, I know how to distract you, with that she opened my pants and put her head between my legs, I remember that evening driving into Seattle all mellow and cool with what was going on, I 5 splits the downtown buildings and has a great view when it is dark driving on the freeway between the buildings and I was leaned back thinking automatic cars are great just one foot and cruise and Maritza was busy with her mouth. I had come to the marina out by Ballard, right around the time when Maritza was finishing up and she wanted to spend the night with me on the boat, I said no way we had just spent all weekend together and she should go home and call me tomorrow, she said I was so weird and left. I texted Laura, I am back at the marina, she was there in under ten minutes and back to her place.

Laura ran in the door and threw herself on the bed; she had very sexy underwear on and was laying belly down with a pillow under her belly perking her ass up with this lacy black outfit on. I said allow me to shower and throw my clothes in the laundry, I put the money where we hid money at the time in the bedroom; she said oh you were working unless someone is paying you for sex, I laughed, she laughed. I said no there is no one like that but she could if she wanted to, we laughed together. I headed for the shower and now knew it was time to perform but it had been like only 15 minutes ago Maritza was on me and so I just straddled her from behind and she was wriggling and I tried and she was all sorry and said "I told you when we met I would wear you out" I said Laura to be honest we have not been together since Thursday and because I was away all weekend I was afraid I might not last and be done too quick so I took care of myself in the shower so as not to disappoint you, in the hope that in about thirty minutes or so we could do it and I could really rock your world for you, she turned over all loving and hugged me and kissed my forehead, with these words, "Oh my god you are so thoughtful , I love you"

Tuesday night was pool night at the ferryman bar, I had been at the gym and showered and was all tan looking fresh from the shower in a pair of black track suit pants and a t shirt, I walked into the ferryman pub and walked straight past everyone at the pool table area as I needed to wash my hands in the toilets, they felt a little sweaty. When I returned Chuck was keeling over laughing, I thought what is wrong with him now, he was standing in front of this girl who was dark haired big chested, nice looking girl, she was shooting pool against chuck, I stopped a little back and looked on, the girl looked at me and chuck continued bellowing this laughter, I really thought, man this guy is this drunk already, it is too early, he must have closed a big deal today at the office or something. I walked closer, the girl grinned a half smile and turned on her heels to a stool at the bar where her drink was, chuck was one hand on the pool table the other holding himself up with the pool cue, laughing hard, I said what's up man, what's the laughing about, do I have a hole in my pants or what? He explained,

Dude, this girl I do not know her but I was shooting pool with her and you walked in, as you walked through the bar she said to me directly, oh yeah I would like to take him home and tie him up for a few hours. He said the funny thing is she had no idea you were coming to play pool and that I know you because the way you just walked right past, I said you were a friend of mine and she said she would be mortified if he knows me for real when I came out of the bathrooms she said, oh shit do you really know him and you walked up with your red tanned Irish ass. He found this most amusing, I was seeing the fun in it for him, he said I do not know how you do it, he said it is amazing, the girl was sitting by the bar and trying not to look and chatting with her friend. Through the night I thought I have to break the ice with her, I walked up to her and said, Hi I heard a rumour, she replied with her chest out oh yeah what kind of rumour, I said something my friend said about something you had said, she said straight to my face yes I said it. I replied to her, well if the invitation is still open, with that her false confidence dropped and she didn't know which way to look, I said it is ok if you live close we could head there right now if you want, I live in the marina in a yacht, if you like boats. She said it is ok my car is outside, let's go. I jumped into her car and we drove off. I wasn't quite sure what part of town we were in because I never been here before but she had a very nice large house all to herself. She had a computer in her room at a desk and she insisted on making some tea for her Irish guest, I asked to make some emails and she turned on the computer, I checked the fishing jobs to see if anyone had put in any new ads for jobs online, I sent a couple of hello how ya doing emails to friends back home and we went at it. I texted Laura that I would have to drive Chuck home as he was really drunk tonight and that was coast clear for an all-nighter. We were going at it like animals and then we were kitty corner across the bed, every upward motion I could see the floor over the corner of the bed, and I noticed a lot of bullet shells on the floor. She noticed, because she asked what's wrong. I said nothing. We kept the motion going then between the mattress and the box spring of the bed was a handgun, I was having very weird James bond movie killing scenes visions of what might happen next. I kept my eye on where that gun was and finished out the act. When we were finished, I would not let her hug me or put her hand near where the gun was tactfully of course. We chatted for a while and through this conversation she explained to me she works for the FBI and that's when the ice broke about the gun and we laughed silly about the weirdness I felt when I saw it first, she insisted that it was not fair and she should have explained before, now she owed me the favour of taking care of me again to relax me and make me enjoy it this time, She dropped me back to the marina around 6 am and I never ever saw her again.

Chapter 19.

The very next evening about 5pm I got a call from a guy that said there were two boats heading for Alaska tonight and one of them needed crew, they were heading up for the Pollock fishing season if I wanted to go be at Ballard oil at 7pm. I was in a panic I was calling Laura to bring my stuff and Chuck that I was taking everything off the yacht and Chris and Renay, I was so excited I was heading to Alaska finally.

I met the crew off the boat a big tall 6ft6 Scottish guy and the skipper (captain) the owner of the boat said come with me to get you your stuff and a fishing license, we headed over to the supply store, I was kitted out with hoodies and warm clothes and a box of knives and oil skins and boots and a survival suit and all the necessaries, the owner said don't worry get what you need it will come out of your first check. For the fishing license I needed to use the social security number, the fake one from my dad's friend the lawyer's son, I blurted it out no problem I had it memorized and off to the boat we went another crew man joined us and then another, we were fuelling and the boat was ready to go two big chest freezers full of meat frozen and a whole pantry room full of everything you could imagine we were heading to Alaska for three months. The boat was about 115 or 120 feet long trawler with a wide open deck two net drums which had nets on them but they had big blue tarps covering them, the skipper explained to me while he was showing me to my cabin that the tarps cannot come off until we clear past Canadian waters otherwise they can accuse of us fishing in there waters without permits. We headed north and in the day time after clearing Canadian waters we did some work on the back deck to the nets and other gear, sonars, the crane the net drums the doors etc. all fishing gear, I was on my way. We worked and ate and slept and I think it took us four days maybe five to get to our destination Dutch Harbour Alaska, I was so excited I could not wait, all this trip and past few months this is all I could dream about and now it was finally happening, AMAZING what dreams can come true in a lifetime. Me from little old village of Loughshinny north county Dublin, now in the north pacific heading for the Bering sea, Alaska. God knows I enjoyed my sleep on the boat steaming north, I had needed a break from all these girls, and I was acting crazy having "relations" three and four times a day. Sleep was like a baby.

We arrived to "Dutch" in the early hours of the morning it was foggy more like a fine close morning as they would say, low wet clouds. There was one boat offloading fish next to the harbour, big pumps, pumping the fish directly into the factory; the harbour is basically part of the factory. This boat looked like any pelagic boat from Ireland, Killybegs Ireland. It was built in the states to the same design and we really could have been pulling into the harbour in Donegal for all I knew it had taken us so long. We tied up the boat and all went below to sleep. When I awoke the next morning we were going to have breakfast and take on some fishing supplies and straighten out the nets. I walked up the steps and could see it was a dull kind of day, typical weather like Ireland really, dull not dry a dampness to the day, I opened the door out on to the deck and very quickly ducked back inside and closed it. I stood there looking up at the rigging and the wires above on the back deck, all along them were not seagulls like you might get in Skerries, oh no! There stood perched along all the rigging and wires, bald eagles would you believe, I mean not little gulls big chesty bald eagles, with the heads of wisdom peering at me. The captain came behind me and said, what's wrong smiling he didn't know what to make of me yet, I said look at all the eagles, oh yes he replied, they are the typical scavengers here just like gulls they want fish, they are not interested in you, I said are you sure because they sure are looking directly at me, he laughed and opened the door, come on look they fly away. I knew we were in Alaska alright.

We worked that day taking aboard some extra cod ends and the bag for the nets, big nets they were, and the chaffing gear, which is to help protect the net from getting worn out while it drags along the bottom was all chains and the heaviest ropes you have ever seen, everything was handled by using the crane on the deck as it is all too heavy for man power. We put ropes along the sides of the bag of the net, they were called zippers, so basically everything was as heavy and hard core as you can imagine for fishing gear. We were ready to head out fishing that night to the Bering Sea. Myself two other crewmen an engineer and a captain and away we went.

All signals on deck are hand signals, to the crane operator and to the wheel house that operates the net drums. We shot out the nets and started fishing. We had a little machine called a transducer, which basically sends a signal from the net to the boat, the net was equipped with what are called eggs, when the mesh of the net expands to a certain width it will pull a little pine and the egg will transmit to the transducer which picks up the signal and alerts the wheelhouse that the egg has gone off, we had four of them on the net but as it turned out we always hauled our nets when the third one went off, each egg gives us a signal that 100 tons of fish were in the net, so when 3 went off we had 300 tons of fish. And that was it for the next three months; I basically had not slept in a bed for 89 days straight only the bunk. We got advances on money when we came ashore to offload usually $300 to buy cigarettes and whatever we wanted for going back fishing, I used phone cards like crazy every time I came ashore, calling to Darra at his grandmother's house. Same routine, sometimes he was all chatty and sometimes he would grunt and his granny would tell me no Aidan he is not in the mood. I would have to calculate the hours as Ireland was 7 or 8 hours ahead of us. When we would get our check for fishing I would stick it straight into the post and send it to my dad, where he had instructions to put something in the bank for Darra take something for himself and put some in my bank. That was the system in place. Alaska, Dutch harbour Alaska the most expensive place in the world, a burger king meal was like $17 or something ridiculous. Everything was blamed on being an island and the cost of importing everything. They were a few different harbours because each factory had a different harbour, in the town were a bank, shops and a few bars and the main hotel. All of the factory worker's accommodations were the buildings around and fishing equipment strewn everywhere. Here there and everywhere. There were taxis buzzing everywhere, giving people rides to and from harbours and bars and boats.

I walked to town one evening nice evening and when I came to a part in the road that crossed a river, there must have been five million salmon in the river; you could walk across them, all on the last part of their spawning journey. Amazing to see, there was one big eagle sitting perched on a rock as I walked past, he was watching me but I can assure you I was watching him much more closely, I past him and he swivelled his head watching me and I kept on walking, then I heard his cry, at this stage I could tell the difference and what their screech was like, I was walking into town and the road hugged the shoreline at this piece, I turned to see him and he was flying my direction, down he swooped and snatched a salmon right out of the water in his claws, about maybe ten feet from me and flew off across the water into the distance. I will admit at that moment there was not another sound anywhere and I was as close to nature as I ever felt, I had been through many storms out on the ocean and seen many wonderful things but that eagle was very impressive that day.

I bought some paintings of Alaska and sent them home to Ireland along with my checks and back then, even thinking back to it I was having one of the greatest times of my life, all I was doing was fishing. I loved Dutch Harbour Alaska.

89 days later it was off season we had filled our quota and it was time to head south to the lower 48 is how people referred to the states the mainland states. We were not staying up in Alaska for the crabbing we were heading to the pacific for our crabbing. Off we went again this time with an estimated 11 days ahead of us. We had taken off all kinds of equipment and left it in Dutch harbour and we were steaming again. We headed south and made a stop off in Oregon to fuel the boat, there are no taxes in Oregon and so fuel is that much cheaper and when you have a boat that is taking a few hundred thousand gallons of fuel, always good to not pay tax on the fuel. We then continued south for Half moon bay California. There awaiting us was 1000 crab pots to load onto the boat and get ready for the crab season that starts November 15th every year, they have a big run to a market supply for the "thanks giving" holiday in the states and then another run to the Christmas market. The season stays open until almost May I think but the big fishing is in November December. All the local fisherman of the area are in protest they will not fish while this monstrous boat of ours is permitted to fish, because what they can catch in their maybe two hundred pots in a week, we can catch in a day

so it makes it very hard for them along with that every year this season of crab fishing has a strike for the price of the crab to increase. Our boss said screw the strike and we went fishing. So people had painted scab on the side of our boat in the middle of the night and a few times some of our pots went missing people just cut the floats off so the pots ended up untraceable on the ocean floor. I was pissed about the start of the season and thought about quitting because Darra's birthday is the 16th of November and I will have to call him on the 15th to wish him happy birthday, I could tell he didn't understand when I said I was not coming home for his birthday because I was fishing but I would see him soon. I had come out here to fish and fishing is what I was doing.

The thanks giving holiday rolled up really quickly we had fished for ten days or so and it was time to take a two day break well a day and half it is like a mini Christmas, everybody has to get home to their families for thanks giving. Thanksgiving is always the third Thursday in November I believe and so it is usually around the 25th of November but it can change here and there by a few days.

Chapter 20.

The captain was driving north and I had an
overnight bag with me, the faithful back pack and I
was dropped off in the centre of San Francisco
California. I had been there once before, I had been
emailing my brother back home recently and when I
went to a café, internet café in San Francisco, I
caught up on some emails and one from my brother
with details of his college friend Ed, who was living
in San Francisco and a contact phone number for
him. I made contact with Ed and he was living in a
hostel on the cheap with a few other international
straifs or waifs. I met another Irish guy there who
was from Galway Martin, pronounced Marteeen, he
was cool he was just working away a bit of
construction and having a good time in San Fran. I
struck off with him for a bit of grub, as we chatted
over the spuds and a feed, we had headed to an Irish
bar he said had good food just like home, Martin
Macs on Haight Street. Anyway there was a full
Irish crowd in the bar a good happening spot. As we
were eating the spuds, he explained to me where he
was from in Galway and I said that sounds very like
where I went to the Gaeltacht when I was a kid he
said, yes collaiste Lurgan which means college
Lurgan, yes he said all his life growing up his
mother was taking students from that college every
year. Martin was fluent in the Irish language. It was

great to chat and hang out with Martin and have the feed, when the grub was done he was off for beer at the bar. I joined him for a coke and met a few people a good crowd from Cork, west Cork but not Clonakilty further west, Skibbereen but we did know many of the same fishing people from all my days down that part of Ireland. This girl had walked in and was sitting with another girl I could tell the other girl was Irish alright, but not this one, she was like an Indian princess, the native American type Indian princess, or something exotic, I could see Martin and a few of the other yobos in the bar checking her out, she seemed right at home with the Irish crew and they were swigging away the beers,

I walked right over to this most beautiful woman I had ever seen in my life, and asked her. Your parents must be something else, she said excuse me, I said your parents must be stunning to have created you, she gave me the canned response oh why thank you, full American accent. I said I am sorry to be rude and try and "chat you up" but you took my eye and I have been watching you and trying not to let you catch me looking, but you are absolutely beautiful. She smiled and was really cheerful and did not want to let my hopes down or anything but did not encourage me much either. Her name was Irene, what a beautiful looking woman, to me a close resemblance to Selma Hayek if you know her, not always but definitely similar colouring and very good looking girl, nice clothes straight white perfect teeth and an all-round cute cute package.

One of the Cork guys followed me into the toilets one time and said to me, Oh yeah the fisherman from barley cove, which is a spot down in west Cork, I laughed he shook my hand, he was well oiled and he started to squeeze my hand. He said "that girl out there Irene is protected by all of us here and especially me, so don't try any funny business alright" I said sure man, no problem. We finished up the night and I was able to get Irene's email address because I simply explained I do not have a phone that works on the boat and I won't be back until around Christmas but if it is ok I would like to email her when I do get back, she gave me her email and that was that. At four am I was picked up by the boat captain at the same spot, on Van ness in downtown San Francisco and away we went crabbing again.

I never said anything for about a week on the boat, we just went day and night hauling and stacking pots and hauling and shooting and counting crabs and stacking and hauling day and night for about the next 15 or 16 days. Eventually I told my crew man I had met the most beautiful woman in San Francisco. He laughed oh yeah a girl with equipment, a he-she maybe, they all look beautiful.

I started to think is it possible this woman looked so good because she is a sex change from a guy and he had me convinced. For a day or two, I said hell no this girl is all woman. I am going to find her and ask her out when we go ashore. San Francisco is known to be the gay capital of the world and so yes there are many guys walking around where it is hard to tell if they are women or men, but I had only given that a thought for a sleepless moment on the back deck one day after being on the go for 36 or 48 hours.

We came ashore around the 18th of December and we were finished for the year until heading back to Alaska in the New Year. We got paid; I had two checks from the boss man, one for $12,000 and another for $7,000 I believe it was, that was for our crab fishing for the month and half. There was another crab fisherman in the harbour who had a smaller boat called Paddy, of course, big Paddy from west of Ireland Galway. A nicer fella you could not meet, a gentleman he had said a couple of his friends were coming his way and would give me a ride up the city, San Francisco. Two brothers from Dublin, one of them was living in the bay area and his brother was out to visit him for the holidays, I said sure Paddy that would be great maybe you could help me find a place to get these checks cashed. One of the Dublin guys the guy who lived there, said I live very close to that exact bank it is the head office, we can take you by there to get the money and then where ever you need to go, I thought awe this is great everybody so helpful.

My friend Wayne from east Cork who had his new wife who was Californian was now out here living in the states again and through emails it was arranged I was going to come and spend the holidays with them in northern California, they lived about 100 miles maybe away from the harbour, where I had come into on the boat and so in the grand scheme of things not too far away really, a town of Healdsburg, northern California. I left the harbour with my gear bag and left the boat behind and headed for this place to go and cash checks, I got to the bank and the bank said they could cash the 7 thousand check but there were insufficient funds to cash the other check. I was furious, I called this little prick Dooley and told him and called him every kind of asshole, he said it was his business account with 1 million dollar overdraft and they can cash, but not for me they were not going to do it, he gave me the name of the finance manager in the corporate headquarters up in Seattle and I made the branch manager from the branch call them to verify the funds. I was furious and very rude with the bank tellers and manager in that bank. The corporate manger asked to speak with me and he explained. The funds are there but they are not there it is going to take 24hours. I had walked outside to explain to the Irish guys outside, I am looking like I am getting royally screwed over here. Those lads offered here I will give you a loan of 500 or a thousand and you can pay me when they get it straightened out, I had walked back into the bank and spoke with the corporate manager over the phone. I explained I am heading to Healdsburg and I need my money, he explained this is from a corporate business account and then can only see what is in the daily cash available account. If you came into my branch I could cash them immediately for you. I said well click a button and make this lady cash it now. He said it appears you were very rude and they are not even trying to help you, they are a smaller branch and I do not have authority to tell that manager what to do. I said find someone who does. He said walk into a different branch tomorrow and have them call me first I will put the funds in the account to clear your checks at the exact time. The guys gave me a lift to San Francisco and I headed for Healdsburg I took the 500 dollar loan from the guy and was very, very annoyed at my situation. The next morning I got up and looked for a branch of the bank on the internet, the nearest one was Napa California The wine country Napa. Roughly 30 miles away. Wayne and his wife Deni had a dodge van as a vehicle and so with them going to work I got the run down on how the van worked and all the little quirks and dropped them to work and headed for Napa. Following the road signs it was not that hard to find. I found the bank too I believe it was US Bank, I walked into a lovely old bank building one like from a western movie on the outside but inside was all modern, I walked up to the teller and handed her the contact information of the branch manager in corporate headquarters and began to explain to her, I could see she was very confused like it was her first day on the job or something. The other teller was trying to listen as she saw me pass the note and I think to this day they thought I was trying to rob them. She called her manager and I explained again about corporate and the manager up there and, this manager just said show me the checks. I handed them to him and he said but they have already been indorsed and have a stamp, yes I had to explain the whole ordeal of yesterday. When he took the details he said he would call the branch I was at yesterday. I had to strongly explain please don't call them they do not like me in that branch, can you please just call the guy in Seattle. The nice lady the teller whispered to me, it shows insufficient funds in that account, I said I know please just call the guy in Seattle fair play to her she walked into her manager's office and made the phone call to Seattle. When she returned quickly I thought we are in business, but no, the reply from Seattle office was the corporate manager was on training for the day and would not be available until tomorrow. I said no, I have given you strict instruction as ordered by the corporate branch manager to call him and disturb him no matter what he is doing to come and deal with this matter. The nice lady went back into her manager's office and I sat on sofa chair in the bank waiting area and waited. The lady came back after about ten minutes and explained to me that she did indeed speak with the manager and please allow 30 more minutes and she should be able to help me. I walked out into the square with my bogus checks in my pocket and thought what a horrible mess. I went and took a burger and fries at this restaurant around the corner, nice place the whole restaurant is on a river, it actually looks like the place could wash down the river any moment. The boat captain was from Napa he had given me his numbers cell phone and home phone, he said contact me if you get into any trouble.

I sat eating my burger and said to myself I will call him alright and give him a piece of mind about these checks. I returned to the bank about 40mins later and the lady opened her window and cashed my checks for me and away I went with my back pack and whole heap of dollars in there, Now I was happy. I had time off it is going to be Christmas I have dollars and I am in a new land. I went to one of the stores and bought a box of chocolates and brought them back to the bank lady and said they are few and far between; people who actually help and thank you very much, sorry for being rude to you earlier, she was delighted. I drove the van back to Healdsburg and got back to Wayne and Deni's house. They were living with her sister in a big old beautiful house in Healdsburg with a full apartment out the back that was their apartment, I was on the floor on a mattress but I was happy to visit with them. I had made it back to Denis work and dropped off the van and took the bus back to Healdsburg actually.

I met this girl on the bus who actually was Native American, we chatted from Santa Rosa to Healdsburg, she told me she was living with her granny and if I wanted later she could borrow her granny's car and show me around. She said there is not much to see but kicking it with the Irish guy would be cool. I went back on the internet and made some emails and sent Irene an email and she didn't reply, so I thought ah to hell with her, I thought if someone worked in an office they would be on email all day seeing as how they are sitting in front of the computer. Anyway I called the Native American girl and told her where my house was it was about 7pm, she came in her granny's car to pick me up. I had told Wayne when he got home what I was planning but I forget to tell Deni, so when the girl came I said I am off out for a while. Wayne and Deni had been home for about a half an hour from work and Deni was like, what? You're going where? With who? A date? What the? You just got here. I said I know it just happened. I went out and we drove around for a while, she brought me to a place near Santa Rosa it was a park type spot up high Buena Vista, it looked down over the valley. She had explained to me what it was like being Native American and how she knew the Irish seemed different than the white Americans. We were parked I guess in the lovers spot and she leaned over and started kissing me, it was a winters night and nobody else was around so we got it on, her granny's car was this big old Lincoln and had loads of room but I was interested in really going full swing, so I made her come around and lay across the front seats while I stood at the passenger door giving her one for Ireland, by this time I had developed this idea that I was doing it for my country right smack bang at crunch time the fifteen seconds of darkness she turned her head back to me and smile and said, now you have been with a real American. I laughed and she laughed and it we clothed up and drove home. She was a cute girl a bit chubby but beautiful skin and nice and tan and a cute girl. I said can we do this again and she said

sure, just call me. I got home and Deni was all
questions and I had to lie through my teeth of
course because I just wasn't comfortable talking
about things like that. Wayne made some tea and I
sat chatting about the whales in the Bering Sea and
how sometimes you could see what seemed like
hundreds of them all at once. I checked my emails
before going to bed, they had a computer in the
apartment so it did not disturb her sister or any of
the main house folks, and boom there was a reply
from Irene. "Yes Aidan I am available Tuesday
night I have a work do to go to but nobody likes
them, it is the Christmas work night out, so I would
love to meet with you it will give me an excuse to
leave the work thing early, here is my cell phone
number call me or let's just meet at Macs around
9pm"

I had totally forgotten about my Indian girl and
went to sleep that night dreaming about this new
girl Irene. I kept thinking will I recognize her, what
if she looks different, will she recognize me? Oh
sweet dreams. Tuesday came along fast and I was in
the city, with my little back pack and a few new
clothes I had bought with Wayne and Deni we did a
bit of shopping the night before at the mall, I had
money burning a hole in my pocket I wanted to
spend it. I made it to Martin Macs bar on Haight
street and was there waiting for Irene to show up I

didn't know anyone in the bar and was standing around the centre of the bar. I ordered a coke and drank that down and then said ah fuck it can I have another coke please. It was 9.20 I thought fuck maybe she is not coming, I could see her girlfriend down the end of the bar with a couple of other girls having a few drinks but they did not recognize me. With that the door of the bar swung open and in walked the beautiful Irene just exactly how I remembered her, I mean the most beautiful hair and face and the way she walked. I looked at the mirror behind the bar to see how I looked and as I stood to turn around and say hi, she was head down and kept walking to where her friends were, I thought what the fuck?? She just walked right past me. I watched her taking off her coat and getting comfortable on her stool with her friends and was kind of hoping for a little hey or acknowledgement of any kind. Now it was like, what do I do? bow down my head and slide out the door or walk up into the middle of 5 girls now and 4 of them Irish, oh I am screwed here on this one, I plucked up the courage and walked up and Irene when she saw me came down off the stool and said Oh hey, you made it with a hug and a kiss to the cheek. Relief, embarrassment thwarted, she said Oh you remember Bridget and this is blah and blah, these are my Irish friends, this is Aidan from IRELAND. We chatted, they drank and really I will hand it to the Irish girls they gave me and Irene space to chat and hang out together; I thought they would be all in my business, but they helped a brother out. Irene started telling me how her and Bridget were soon to be heading off to Vegas for 4 days for Christmas and they were gonna have a blast and everything was going to be so great and how she was glad I could make it to hang out with her, and I basically was like oh dam, what now she is giving me the nice meeting you bit. We had talked about how it was snowing up in the mountains in Tahoe and that I had never been snowboarding I would love to go, Irene said she had never been snowboarding before either, and the Irish girls were drunk and saying just go, just do it go to Tahoe and snow board. I didn't know but Tahoe is a 3 hour drive away up into the mountains. Now before the Irish girls were going to let their friend go to Tahoe with a stranger came the grilling. What's your shtory? Who are ya? Where ya from? Who are your people? It was coming heavy now, the funniest thing. Bridget has a brother married back in the west of Cork a farmer, and he is married to my old rugby coach's sister. Isn't that a small world now for ya, my old buddy J C. John Colbert, has a sister married in west Cork to Bridget Cullinanes brother and I am standing in San Francisco hoping to get a vote of confidence from these friends of Irene's to go snowboarding. Full approval and we left Macs. The plan was we would go tomorrow after the morning traffic Irene didn't have to go to work because of the office party the night before, so perfect, but where now? I walked Irene home and it was not clear what was happening exactly, she had had a few drinks and I was sober and she was walking home and when we got to the door of the apartment building she said I don't usually do this but Bridget seemed convinced you are ok. We went in and then Irene said I am beat you can have the coach or the bed, and she went to get into her pyjamas in the bathroom, I said well she should not have offered I have been on the boat so long now any chance I get I am taking the bed. Irene came out from the bathroom and was definitely shocked that I had taken the bed and she went and got a blanket for herself for the couch. A few minutes passed and she was a little drunk and she said good night with the TV on, I said, Irene I told you I am real man, I do not have to fuck just because I sleep next to someone, come and share the bed I promise I will not bite or there will be no funny business. Irene jumped up from the couched and scurried to the bed like a little school girl. Jumped in and went to sleep. I spent the whole night making sure I did not even tip my toes off her toes, I hardly even slept. The next morning we went up on Haight Street and had a nice breakfast pork chops and eggs for me and then we drove out to the sports authority store in Daly City to get some snowboarding clothes. We were now ready for the road ahead. We hit Tahoe around 4pm that evening and we needed a room, one place we asked, well first off unless it is the Hilton or one of the casino big high rise hotels Tahoe is full of motels. One we asked said yes we have a room with a hot tub, would you like to see it, they let you view the room before you commit. The tub was pink and heart shaped, Irene looked at me and said if we stay here and you ever tell anyone I stayed in a room with a heart shaped tub I will kill you. We didn't take it, we found another one down the street that had a tub like a half of a swimming pool long and deep perfect just what I wanted to soak in. We had bought some salads and some mashed potatoes and some other items from the deli to have a nice meal in the room and Irene had gotten a bottle of wine, but we had no cork screw in the room, so Irene went to go and ask the front desk if they could open it for her. She had been gone a while and so I started digging into the beetroot salad while I was waiting for her. The room was nice, it had a log cabin type feel to it all wooden on the roof exposed and a high ceiling it was nice, TV mounted on the wall so it could be swung round if you were sitting at the table the way I was or turn it back to be right at the end of the bed.

Irene came in the door all keeled over, hanging on the door knob, she said I was calling you, you are useless I said what happened, she walked slowly towards the bedside all crunched over, I just broke myself she said, I fell on the ice outside, I almost stabbed myself with the bloody cork screw and broke myself on the ice. I was laying there calling out for help and your name Aidan, Aidan help. Dam I am really sorry, I didn't hear you. Oh she said she fell straight on her ass and she thinks she broke the bone in the middle in two, she was hurt. I said you want to go to a hospital? No, she replied, if she wanted me to pick her up, she said I will be alright in a few just let me lay here, what was I to do offer to rub her ass and make it better? I did and she laughed and once she started laughing we laughed together and she laughed hard making herself hurt a bit saying she broke herself. We ate and lay in bed and watched TV, this bed was bigger than Irene's bed and so I was not a scared to make sure I didn't bump of her in the night, I did wake up however holding her. We didn't talk about that we headed for the slopes and purchased our day ticket which included a lesson first and rented our snow boards. I watched her fall a bunch of times in the class and she got a great laugh at me falling, if there is one thing that is the most awkward of all is when you fall while strapped into a snowboard, There is no way for me to impress her now I thought. We hit the lifts and had a great day, she had the hang of it and I had the hang of it and then we both fell in a heap and I held her and she held me and all in all we had a fun day snowboarding. When we were finished, we headed back to the hotel Irene had said, thank god that is over, I was terrified to break my ass again, but we rock! So we turned the tub on and I soaked in it and Irene waited and gave me privacy and then I got out to dry myself off and she got in I her panties and bra, so I was pretty sure this might be all it will be for us. We lay there watching TV and falling asleep after a long fun day. As we lay there probably ten o clock the TV down low and tired, a little voice came from Irene with her head half pressed in the pillow, "you know you can kiss me if you want" I didn't hesitate and we made out all night long, I loved her smell and her hair and her lips, these were kissing lips. How soft and perfect she felt. We made out a lot. And fell asleep holding each other. The next morning back to San Francisco and I headed back to Healdsburg, we kissed and said thanks for a wonderful time and we will hang out after Christmas when she gets back from Las Vegas. I was on cloud nine, "pepe le pew" I was thinking in over drive I should go to Vegas, yes fly in the flight before her and be waiting when she gets off the plane. Yes I should be in the room next to hers and just open my door when I hear her arrive, all kinds of crazy stuff going through my Head. I finally felt on the bus riding back to Healdsburg, that day, I had fallen in love. I did not know what this was before, I thought I was deeply in love with Clare, Darra's Mom, but this was different. I got back and told Wayne and Deni about the weekend and I would say they got a little tired of hearing me say the name Irene.

I jumped on the mighty internet again in Wayne's house and I knew the hotel she was going to be staying at in Vegas, I telephoned to them and I ordered a huge hamper with flowers and chocolates and all kinds of goodies from the hotel concierge to be delivered to her room on Christmas morning. The concierge I spoke to was a woman and so when I explained to her I wanted something wonderful but not over the top, something to say I love you but in a I am thinking about you a lot kind of way. I paid with Wayne's debit card as I only had cash and that was that, $150 worth of a gift for Christmas morning for Irene.

Chapter 21.

When Christmas passed, I did not go back on the boat to Alaska as I was in an argument over the checks and the insufficient funds and told them I quit. The owner tried to hold face and told me "good the new skipper doesn't want you anyway". I hooked up with the Irish guy who had the boat,

Paddy and he was in some kind of legal pickle, which meant he couldn't go out fishing so he had another guy doing captain, Timmy.

Timmy was a local to half moon bay California and his dad had actually built the boat that Paddy now owned. I was coming and going between Irene's apartment to the boat and back and some weekends or odd days going to Healdsburg to visit Wayne and Deni's. They had come down and we did a double date, me and my new girlfriend Irene and Wayne and his wife. A good friend of Irene's worked concierge at a nice restaurant on Haight street "cha cha cha", good old Hugh Irish descendant himself born to an Irish mother and father, but as American as they came. Irene being such good friends with him meant we never had to wait for a table, the line might be a 40 minute or sometimes over an hour wait, Hugh always hooked us up. So we double dated with them there. They got along but Deni was protective of me all the way and giving me the vibe she was not good enough for me, for that reason I liked Deni even more as she was for sure on the watch out for me.

The crab fishing continued and Irene had a Toyota pick-up truck so I used it sometimes to go back and forth to the harbour, I had picked up a second job now that the summer months were coming on a squid boat. Same type of fishing as the salmon boats do in Alaska in the summer, purse seining but this time the catch is calamari, that's the little pencil sized squid. The fishery was open from Sunday afternoon to Friday afternoon, so no fishing on the weekends and the best way to catch them was using lights at night to attract them, for some reason they think it is the moon or something and so are attracted to the lights, when they are all balled up to the lights, we shut the lights off and lay the net around them and start hauling back. These little critters squirt ink everywhere but when you are making $1,250 per boat load you love that ink squirting all over you. I had the fortunate luck of being on a boat with the sharpest captain of the whole entire fleet from Monterrey bay all the way up; none of the other boats could catch squid like him. Some nights we filled the boat with squid three times between 8pm and 4 am in the morning, that's go ashore offload and back out again, most other boats spent all night trying to fill once and rarely did they fill up at all. The checks were good again, I mean making $4000 in one night squid fishing was another part of the dream from when I was younger all coming true. I was fishing, making money and in the Pacific Ocean.

I had been living with Irene full time now and I had been professing my undying love to her, she always said, you are not in love with me, you are just overcome with emotion, I said no this is love alright, I am so in love I want to marry you. She without hesitation said yes and we went and got married by some minister in his office down off of Mission Street in San Francisco. Irene didn't mind that we just ran off and did it one Saturday, but she did want a ring. I said look let's do this I will save and get you whatever ring you want and we can save and do a full church wedding when the time is right. That girl was very happy about that, she was married to me and we were going to get married. We didn't say anything to anyone about us being legally married, we just were happy and in love and started to plan a wedding, well outline plan it at least. One Sunday morning on the way to squid fishing, I was T boned, that means someone ran into me on the side on sunset Blvd, while I was heading south bound to go fishing. Irene's truck was screwed, the back axle was destroyed, the other driver had five of his friends there before the cops came and they all said they were witness and I ran a red light, not the case but hey that's how they worked it. I felt bad and promised Irene I will replace it for her, one day. So now we had no vehicle. It didn't matter much to Irene as she took the bus to work downtown every day; we lived right along the 21 line in a beautiful neighbourhood just below Haight Ashbury in the pan handle area of San Francisco. Right on CENTRAL. Here I was again on "c block" it took me a few years even to register I live on "c block" but last time I lived there it was in the comfort of a cell on the north circular road in Dublin. Hadn't I come a long way since then? The night myself and Irene got married I drank 7 creamy pints of Guinness and Irene was all nervous because she was not used to me ever drinking at all. I had always promised myself the day I get married I will have a few pints and so I did, I enjoyed them to the fullest and got a nice little buzz going and the day was wonderful. The only "c block" I was going to was our new home together, well Irene's apartment but we called it ours by this time.

Back when I met Irene the very first night back at thanks giving in 2000 I had told her all about Darra and she was cool with that as she had no desire to have any children yet and I was cool with that too because I said my love for my child was unbreakable and I cannot even think how I could split myself with how I felt about Darra and having another baby with someone else, I even in a moment of madness thought maybe I should ask Clare if she wants to make a full brother or sister to Darra, no strings just a full sibling. The madness never left me did it?

Myself and Irene enjoyed weekends away to Las Vegas, to Monterrey bay to Texas, oh yeah major piece there, Irene is originally from El Paso Texas.

We drove all night while we had the truck back then, as in before the crash. About 17 hours' drive the route, San Fran, to LA and on out to Phoenix and then across the desert through New Mexico and into El Paso Texas. El Paso or EP as the locals call it, is a city that joins directly with Juarez Mexico on the tip of Texas, there is a big long border between the states and Mexico and three bridges from El Paso into Juarez. We went to visit Irene's family and did not say we were married but that at least they could know we were serious because Irene never brought a boyfriend home ever in her life. Her brothers were cool and welcomed me and her father was studying me but he loved his daughter so he saw her happy I guess and he was cool with me. Irene's parents spoke Spanish and were not good with the English so it was always me asking her to repeat it to me in English and me speaking back and her repeating to her in dad in Spanish. Irene's mom was getting old too and had dementia or Alzheimer's one of the two or both, she loved stealing shinny things and when nobody was looking she would be in our suitcase and taking things from Irene's make up bag and hiding them. Irene would freak out calling her dad, "she is taking my stuff again" I found this quite funny. I would sit on the couch and watch TV and Irene's mom would sit beside me and speak to me about all kinds of things and I would keep replying I don't understand a word but I really wish I did, that didn't stop her mom from chatting away, from what I could make out she was telling me when she was younger she loved to go dancing and then she met him, and she would make faces nodding her head towards the kitchen where Irene and her dad might be. One of the days I remember it so cute, I had a hankering for a McDonalds and so I headed out to go get a big mac meal and came back to the house.

Out in the desert in El Paso it gets so hot by 11am. In the mornings if you have something to do, get it done and get back home or the heat will melt you. I couldn't get back to the house quick enough, what a great idea Mc Donald's was the heat worth it? Yes! Reminded me of when I had been in phoenix the year or so before and I had seen a sign saying cigarettes cheaper, so I decided to walk from the apartment building as it was only two blocks away. Well two blocks in phoenix is a long way and I nearly melted that day too. Desert heat is no joke folks, nothing to be messed with I had a full understanding then of why they were always reports of people dying from the heat.

Anyway this day I came back to the house with the big mac meal and nobody else had wanted anything and so I munched away, Irene's mom took a few French fries from me as she would eat all day, but it was important for her father to keep her on a diet of, in and around set times of meals, because with her condition she would forget if she had eaten or not. Irene came in to the sitting room laughing, she said her mom had gone out the back and asked her, what is wrong with the white kid, and he must have problems at his house because he always comes over here. He even brings his lunch with him. "That poor white kid". I was whitey to her as she was Mexican mixed with a little bit of Native American too. She was one of those old women who you could tell was a really nice lady in her good times. The front door was always locked so as to stop her mom from opening it and going wandering through the neighbourhood so when someone would come by or Irene's brothers would come home they had to knock as the security lock was always on. Her mom would come whizzing through the house with probably the only English I ever heard her speak, "coming through" everybody smiled or laughed when she did this. She seemed very happy and content in her state. But when Irene would come after her to try and get back the makeup items, her mom would even try and bite her hand off, it was funny in an endearingly sad kind of way. How fickle is the human mind and what really goes on in someone's head when they are in that condition?

It started to rain one day when we were visiting El Paso and it was an ironic occurrence, when the rain comes slightly in the desert people come outside as it is a cooler breeze usually with the rain, I was laughing explaining to her brothers, dam if you like rain you should go to Ireland everybody runs indoors when it rains over there and here in the desert you all hide from the sun and come out when it rains, how much of a reverse is that. I loved the heat and the sun but this desert heat is too much even for an Irish person who thinks sunning themselves is the best past time anyone could ever have.

We headed back the long road to San Francisco, stopping off halfway along the road around Palm Springs, I went into the casino and played some black jack and Irene said she was going to take a nap in the truck and don't be too long, well the black jack kept flowing and in the casino it is impossible to know what time of day or night it is, Irene came in all "grumpy head" saying she was thirsty and she nearly died out there. "Thanks for checking on me, it is 7am and the heat is ridiculous". We went across the street and took a motel room to let the day pass and drove the rest of the trip through the night again, as it was cooler to drive through the night across the desert. We were still about 10 hours from San Francisco.

It was coming on for winter again and time to get crabs pots ready for the crab season again in half moon bay, I met up with big Paddy and he explained if I would rig all his gear for him and get all the pots ready he would buy me a pick-up truck, I said deal. I got the truck and started working on the gear. Timmy was going to run the boat again this year. The squid boat I had worked on wanted crew too but I had already made the deal to get the pickup truck and so I was committed. A couple of Irish lads had come around and said they knew Paddy and were looking to crab fish for the season, I explained to them I needed one crew man and so the brother said he would come with me, the other Tommy ten wheeler he was known as in the city as he had dump trucks he ran for construction sites. Tommy I knew from my days fishing in Howth I had seen him there a few times in Howth, Ireland, and remembered him, but himself and his brother were from the same town in Galway as Big paddy, it really is a small world in the fishing industry when you think, we mended nets together in Howth harbour and now here we were rigging crab pots on the pacific coast. The season was fast approaching and that meant it was going to be Darra's birthday again, man I was missing him, I spoke to him on the phone as often as possible and I had many nights where I wanted to just go home and be with him but it could not be, he was with his mammy and I needed to stay in touch and wait. That was my main thing when it came to Darra, it was my private thing as it was not Irene's baby he was mine, but with us discussing applying for a green card and the lawyer had advised us that if I get the green card, well Darra would pretty much automatically get it too, so I figured this is a good way to provide for his future too. Lay the ground work for when he is older. I am sure he really didn't understand how I could be doing so much fishing, the thing with my status was that I was illegal, but all the fishermen took that I was married so my green card must be in order. I renewed my fishing licenses with the same fake social security number each year now and this year's crab season was going to be no different. I sent Darra toys in the mail and cards with dollars in them to have the novelty at least having dollars to show off to his friends. But here we were again heading into November, all eyes were on making it a good crab season, I had a wife now who wanted an engagement ring so the pressure was on. Also lawyers who we needed to start the immigration process, as I had over stayed my tourist visa by a long shot and if I leave now I will not be allowed back in as the lawyer says, it is important to submit and do the whole green card process from within the country, if you leave they will keep you out and make you do the process through their embassy and this could take forever.

Crab season was a go and the price fell through the floor, even Timmy the captain didn't want any more of it, so I took over as captain. I was able to squeeze $800 to $1000 a week so I was living and enjoying it. One crew man and myself go out every other day, in my in between days I had met a guy a year ago from Midleton county Cork, we actually worked together around San Francisco for a moving company, we would head out in a truck and move people and their furniture and belongings from one apartment to the other or one city to the next, we got paid by the hour and usually got some tips, when we had met, I said where are you from he said a little town in east Cork called Midleton, I said I know it well and he took the attitude oh yeah the dubs always know everything, I said yeah! Well I played rugby there for a few years, he stood back in shock, he said I was the only Midleton man to wear the Irish jersey, u18 or u21 rugby from Midleton.

Adrian was blown away that maybe even the year he left Midleton to head out to the states, was right around the year I had joined them, but hey, there we were and met finally in the U S of A. myself and Adrian stayed in touch all the way through and for example, my friend Wayne, his brother and Adrian were best friends all their lives through schooling and on up rugby together etc. So the circle was complete there. Anyway in my off days Adrian and

I would work together on whatever construction project he had going on, he was into laying the fake grass for people and putting in putting greens in people's back yards. On occasion he used to hook up with this other guy who would lay paving stones, cobble stone driveways so I would pick up some labour from them in between going fishing.

Actually that year even Wayne's brother came out on the boat with me for a trip hauling the crab pots, the poor fella Ryan is his name, Adrian's good friend, he was sick as a dog on the back deck I did most of the work myself.

Chapter 22.

Back to me and Adrian, we would get together and cruise around San Francisco when there was nothing to do of a day. I was not fishing and his work was off due to the weather or something, many evenings we would go and play a 9 hole round of golf, we had taken this up as a hobby and on a few occasions braved an 18 hole. Irene liked Adrian and so it was good times.

I fished squid that summer again and was able to buy Irene the ring she wanted, she designed it herself with the help of a jeweller and I was dreading the price, to make matters worse I knew I had my check for 9 thousand dollars coming from the squid so I hoped that would cover it. When in the squid fishing, we got paid like three weeks behind which was great because when things slowed down and there was no work you still were getting checks for the following three weeks, I knew at that time I had 9 grand coming and I did not know the next couple of checks but I knew they were in the same ball park maybe one for 7 or 8 and another for 9. So the ring was for sure to be bought, Irene was happy she was picking what she wanted and I was going to pay for it. I drove to half moon bay and picked up my check 9 thousand 600 and change and straight to mission street san Francisco to cash it. That day I had hooked up with one of the old timers who was a horse racing fanatic, I had met him at the race track a few times Bay meadows in the peninsula of the bay area, Neilus was his name, divorced out of work construction worker, who many talked about having such a gambling problem it had cost him his life, somehow I ended up with him that day. There were many a Sunday or Saturday myself and Irene headed out to the race track and done some betting and the Irish crowd there were a good laugh, Irene knew some of the older crew from the Irish bar on Haight street, yes the same bar we had met at, Martin Macs. As it would go, that day I was with Neilus driving me around and I was going to throw him a couple of hundred for doing the driving, I got the check cashed and Neilus said, let's go to cache creek the casino up north, we could double that money and you could give me a loan then and buy the ring. I was keeping my money tight as he wanted a loan and I kept saying the ring the ring the ring, I cannot do it. It was about 10.30 in the morning and I gave in to it, Irene was at work until six anyway so why not. I called Irene and told her I was heading out to haul some crab pots and away we went up the freeway towards Sacramento to hit up the casino.

I really could not believe it, it is Vegas style casino and they have restaurants and food and slot machines everywhere, the only two things they didn't have were roulette and craps, I had never knew how to play craps anyway so it didn't make a difference. All the way up the road I had been telling Neilus how I was a wizard at roulette and could win a fortune and he was loving the story, Years before, the year Darra was born actually, I used to load my car up with fish from the harbour in union hall and drive it around all the Chinese restaurants, I would make 5 or 6 hundred extra money then from the Chinese. The fish delivery run to them was not for them to serve in the restaurant it was for them to eat themselves so it needed to be fresh, still kicking and be delivered around 11 pm at night; they would cook up a feed for themselves when they shut the restaurant down for the night. Many times wherever the last stop I had I would eat with them too, I remember one Chinese new year there were about 30 Chinese and me all at a long end to end table, all seafood provided by me and a 1000 pounds in my pocket, my cost for the fish might have been about 200 direct from the boat. After we were finished eating we would head to a private club on the south mall in Cork city. It had a Caribbean stud table, two black jack tables, three roulette tables and an eating area upstairs. I was telling Neilus all the stories of roulette in cork and Neilus being originally from cork was loving the stories and Neilus knew, Clare's dad, so that would be Darra's grand dad, him being a bookmaker and having a betting shop in Clonakilty and Bandon, Neilus being a gambler all his life knew Christy Clare's dad pretty well. Funny isn't it, My buddy was from the rugby club in Midleton, Wayne grew up in Midleton all his life, lives there today, Irene's friend Bridget had a brother married to a girl from Midleton, as my buddy Wayne always said, Midleton, "the centre of the universe"

We arrived at cache creek casino owned by a Native American tribe and so the laws allowed the casino to operate in California. By 7pm that night to make a long story short I had 1000 dollars left, I could not believe it, Neilus was in to me for about 800 and what was I going to do, I am supposed to be buying a ring this Saturday, to the best of my knowledge the ring was 4 grand and the diamond was three. So I had it all covered in the check, but no the good old gambling rush took over and I was feeling kind of miserable. Me and Neilus went and had something to eat and I said to him, typical, they don't have roulette and I am down 8 grand in just as many hours, what now? I said to him while we snacked on some food, please don't ask me for any more money just hang with me and I will win it back, I know how to play black jack and even though I hate it as it so boring I know the game, he being ever the optimist, not! Says, you were the wizard of roulette on the way up in the car, there is no roulette now 8 grand down you surprise me with, you know how to play black jack, he laughed. I said yes, my dad thought us when we were kids, we used to sit around the kitchen table at home and my dad had a bag of old time pennies, Old Irish pennies, they are really big old copper looking coins, we used to use them as chips, Neilus laughed, old pennies and copper coins, and here we are almost broke, that was his witty side, a deep laugh out of him, them too and an "ah sure" in a heavy west cork accent.

I sat up at the black jack table and I had said to Neilus, this is my lucky shirt we will be alright, He pulled on his underwear waist band and said, sure I wore my lucky jocks today and that didn't help, I could see the holes all along the waist band, he must have had them years. I started playing $25 chips not going so good and then I got a bit off a run and then down again, and another $100 bill flew across the table. I sat at seat 7 on the table so no one could sit behind me and I had one hand in my left pocket and it never left there, that hand had a fist clinched around my last hundred dollar bill, it was getting sweaty in that pocket that is what I can remember for sure. I played on, I had some chips starting to build, sometimes playing two boxes some playing one, some a big stack of chips some just one chip. In this casino you can double any number so when I would double on 13, the dealer would announce to the pitt boss," doubling 13" Neilus had not been by for a while and I was getting a good run, I was changing black chips for pink chips, pink chips were 500 and black were 100. I was putting pink chips in the breast pocket of my lucky shirt. Neilus showed up all disorientated and saying the security were about to chase him out of the place as he was trying to take a nap and the security kept waking him up and saying "no sleeping sir! Not allowed sleep in the casino sir". He said can he get a whiskey or something, Neilus usually didn't drink and so it was funny to see him all warn out and desperate, his eyes opened wide when he saw I had chips in front of me, a quick glance he said sure that's a couple of grand come on let's call it a day. I turned and said here's the last hundred a black chip go cash it in and play a penny slot or something and get lucky would ya, or go play "Indian bingo" with all your crowd the pensioners. I continued grinding away win some and lose some, the "pitt boss" came over and said, would you and your father like some breakfast, the restaurant has started serving breakfast now, I said is it full Irish, they had not got a clue what I was talking about. I had been cashing pink chips in for white chips now and the white chips were worth $1000. Neilus said he would take a breakfast and I kept playing, soon after I was getting really tired and I said screw it, I took the sweaty hand out of my pocket, the poor old hundred dollar bill was crumpled to bits and I went to the breast pocket and started cashing all black chips to pinks and pinks to white, I had $18,500 and I was ready to go home. Neilus was bouncing around like a jennet as they say in Ireland, he was delighted he said I have never seen a professional black jack player at work in all my years, but you are a professional, of course I was smiling ear to ear with the dough and off to the cage to cash the money. At the cage they said may we have your ID please sir, I said why ID I am not paying taxes on this, this was hard earned, he explained no, no this is just in case for example if you are stopped by the police on the way home, then you can say you won the money here, they call us and we verify, I thought that is cool handed my ID and got the cash. We were walking to go and get the car back from the valet parking and Neilus, said to me; hey you have the ticket for the car right? I said oh yeah I think so, I reached in my pocket, and said to him hold on I will be right back; I had another 11,000 in white chips in my denims pocket. I ran back to the cage and cashed them and we hit the road home. That's right 29,500 and one wrinkled sweaty hundred dollar bill. I broke off 3,000 to Neilus as he only thought I won 18,500 and minus my 9 and half starting he thought it was very fair I keep six grand and give him three. Fair it was dam right generous of me, but that's how the gamblers mind works. That Saturday I treated Irene to the visit to the jewellers who had worked with her on the design, we done some upgrades of white gold and platinum and got a bigger more expensive, diamond, well more expensive because of its clarity not really the size. Everything was hunky dory.

Irene and myself didn't fight much through those years in the early days, but we did have arguments and one of the key arguments was my son, I wanted to go to Ireland every possible chance and Irene would say wait until the lawyer and the papers and then why is it that my husband wants to spend my vacation time running to Ireland to play with his kid. I resented her for that when she took that attitude as I always felt that, I was wasting my time trying to explain to her, that my son Darra is a child and he should not have to make a sacrifice, I would tell my wife, "you are my wife, you knew I had a son from the beginning and it is the adults who have to sacrifice for the children, that's the world I believe in" she would reply with, I grew up around so many Mexican girls who were getting pregnant in high school and dropping out of school and I went to college and made sure to live my life not to get pregnant and now I am old enough to enjoy life without kids I am stuck in a situation because you were not responsible some years ago. Well reading back over it now in words, yeah they were fights. I told her many times Darra will not come second to anyone, and she told me many times, she deserved to be number one to her man and that was that. With the extra money in hand and the rings taken care of I said to my wife, I am going to go to Ireland and renew my passport and that way we can get the green card process going as it will be better if I try to get the green card while I have a passport in good standing not an out dated expired tourist visa. In Ireland you can have your passport in either Irish or English it is your choice as we have both languages.

My passport in my English version name was in the system in the united states with an expired tourist visa on it, I said I will go to Ireland and exchange my passport for the Irish version and return and

why not. It will mean a one way ticket back to
Dublin and then a new tourist return ticket, Dublin
to San Francisco and back to Dublin and I will get
my passport stamped for 90 day visa again. I will be
able to visit with Darra and then with my new
passport I will be able to get the green card process
started. We told the immigration lawyer the plan
and she said go ahead and if it works it will be
great.

Chapter 23.

I booked the trip to Ireland and as the days before
travel approached Irene started getting nervous, am
I ever going to see you again, I said of course, you
are my wife, this is a good thing to do and the right
step, the lawyer even said so. Don't worry. I will
call you and Skype you when I land. I landed in
Dublin and headed out to the family home and we
had some sausages and club orange and tons of
bread and butter, along with a major raid on the
chocolate section of the local shop, everything you
couldn't get in the states all available again, I had
missed that chocolate and the king crisps oh so bad.
A pound of kerns sausages and Brennan's bread and
Kerry gold, this was luxury. I spoke with Irene and
she had calmed down and told me how much she
loved me and missed me like crazy already, I told

her I had the same feeling but once I take care of this I will be back. I had no ticket out yet because I needed the passport first, I called to chat with Darra and he was his normal quiet self, I said guess what I am calling you from granny's house, he said oh yeah ok. Then after a pause he said what you are in Dublin all excited, I said yes and we are gonna see each other soon, he was so excited I almost cried on the end of the phone, I was so excited myself. His mom came on the phone, what is this you are home, I said yes Clare and I would love to see him, she said no problem I will drive him up for the weekend, she then said and I could tell she was a little embarrassed or something, " I am 7 months pregnant by the way" I said oh that's great news for you, congratulations, she said "so don't be surprised by how fat I am" I said not at all relax, that's great news. Clare had been married and this was their first baby, Clare's second but their first as a couple and I was happy for her, I mean we might not have ended on the best of a note but I thought and according to the psychologist at the time was try and allow her to live her life and get on with things and just try and maintain contact with Darra. So I was genuinely happy for her and I was an emotional wreck to think about seeing Darra this weekend. Darra would be 7 in a couple of months and I had not seen him in so long, I had guilt and all kinds of emotions, but the best one was the excitement that we were going to be hanging out together. I used to satisfy or justify my guilt to myself by thinking, well I am paving the way for him, he could come to the states and play sports or go to college or will not have to worry about a green card, the doors will be open so I always comforted myself that I was doing a good thing for him even though I missed him and I had many a down evening living the so called wonderful life in California. The Irish always think living anywhere else is just wonderful, and California sounds as glam and glitz and all the sunshine, so it is assumed, living the wonderful life. I was living yes, wonderful many times but it was all just life and normal to me.

I submitted my passport application got the photos and all the required stuff and applied for the Irish passport that was done first week.

Friday afternoon, Clare arrives with Darra, man is he getting big, and I had not seen him in almost three years. He was the image of me as a child, Clare was big a fat and looking well. My thoughts were well there goes the idea of a full brother or sister, lol. I offered to make her some tea, but she said she had other plans, now this is another weirdness about the whole thing. I come from a small village well actually I live about three quarters of a mile from the village so I grew up in farm land nowhere really but it is classed as Loughshinny. Our immediate neighbours are a good field and half away to the east, you can make out their roof top from our front door, these are the Matthews, so yes they are our neighbour but if you walk the road, there is a cottage right at the top of their lane so technically old Mr and Mrs Ferguson are our neighbours and then Matthews lane, the Matthews are four, Andy the eldest, Caroline a year or so older than me and a little bit younger than my older brother, Patricia who is my age and was in my class growing up from 4 years of age to 11 or so and their baby brother Brian who is the same age as one of my younger brothers. We would have mixed through the years, I mean when it came time to experimenting with kissing and the likes I can remember me and Patricia, who we called Tricia, well we had our moments behind the school after school, we were probably 8 or 9 at the time, Now that I think of it, was Tricia the first girl I ever kissed?, maybe so. Their mam was a nurse from down the country somewhere, Limerick I believe and I remember them talking about their country cousins over the years. The eldest brother Andy Andrew of course, he was a few years older than me but when I was a tyke at three and hanging out or trying to hang out with Garret my older brother and his school friends Andy would have been there then, so when I started school for the first day at 4 I was crying my eyes out and the older classes came over to comfort us and be with us if any of them knew us and Andy came and sat with me all that first day of school. So this would give you an idea of the long integration of us and our neighbours over the years. Well what do you know Clare was married to the Matthews first cousins from Limerick, yes there mom the house she grew up in as a child was where Clare married in to. So the guy who sat with me on my first day of school, and probably the first girl I ever kissed, my first kiss were now indirectly related to my first born child in a way through marriage.

Clare was not stopping for tea or anything as she was heading up to the Matthews for a visit, after all they are her in-laws.

Me and Darra were outside playing football. He wanted to show me his skills and he was good with the ball and handled it well and had the same kind of walk as his uncle Noel, Clare's older brother, I remember thinking this is what happens when you are not around he didn't pick up your habits, his role model of a man has been his uncle. Oh well, he is a fine young man and I love him and I love to be with him right now, thank you Jesus for this moment. Imagine all that while playing kick ball in the front lawn.

I was in goals up against the shed door and Darra took a good few cracks at me I saved one or two and some he scored, Darra was letting rip showing me he was a strong boot of a young fella and letting me know he knew how to strike a ball, he went in goals then and I tried a few sneaky soft shots he saved them, he was enjoying the fun too and all smiles and then he started being a bit cheeky saying, "is that all you have" so I let rip to show him I had a good boot of my own, he put his hands up to stop it and it rattled him. I could see he hurt his wrists, to be honest I knew when it left my foot it was a touch too hard, the ball hopped off his hands and hit the shed doors and out into the field a bit, I walked towards him are you ok, I AM SORRY, he shrugged away from me got the ball and tried to kick it as hard as he could at me, a drop kick. And he started walking out into the field. I said, "hey I am sorry, you made a great save" he turned around and with a big red face full of tears, "yeah well you just fucked off and left me you are a prick, I hate you" and he turned to walk further into the field, wow! I thought unbelievable, how do you answer a 7 year old child to that one, he had every right and great grounds for his point. I didn't just fuck off and leave you man, it was the way it had to be; I will tell you the whole story if you want. He said I don't want to hear it. I said ok I am going in to make dinner I will call you when it is ready or if you want to help me cook I will be in the kitchen.

I always enjoyed a bit of cooking as it was part of working on any boat, one had to be able to prepare a meal that 7 hungry men might need so they can keep going another 36 or so hours. I had promised my mam I would cook up a feed that evening as I thought Clare might be staying and her being pregnant might need a big dinner, so I went into the kitchen and started cooking. Darra had come in for a drink of water, he was outside playing football with his uncle, my younger brother who himself was a hot shot on the soccer pitch. We sat and ate and watched some TV and eventually it was bed time, my mam had set me up in what we called the middle room as it was the middle bedroom of the three in the house, the bottom room had the five bunk beds and the middle room had two single beds for visitors should we have any, so me and Darra had a bed each in the middle room.

Darra had some questions for me about what kind of cars do they have in California and do you see Porsches and Ferraris, yes I was able to tell him how up in Marin county across the golden gate bridge there is a dealership for both, but the coolest thing is the Ferrari dealership because all of those cars are custom made in the factory and delivered out of the truck brand new and I had seen them being delivered a few times, reason being Adrian's boss had a warehouse of tools really close to the Ferrari dealership and on days working with him I had seen this. I had said to Darra if he wanted a hug? and he without even saying yes he jumped into the bed beside me, I put him in front of my chest and wrapped my arms around him, I could feel his happiness, this was exactly how we would cuddle when he was a baby and when I used to visit him on weekends when he was 3 and we would be staying in a local hotel, I said now that I have you and you can't move, what's this shit about I fucked off and left you, he said I am sorry for the language I said I don't care about the language I am proud of you to say that to me, that took some guts. I know you are strong and have guts and that's what makes you wonderful to me. I love you and had two options try and fight with mammy all the time or leave and not break your heart every other weekend or break mine having to leave you over and over again. It just worked out that way and we are here now and I love you very much and am proud of you how you let your emotions out to me today after we haven't seen each other in so long. He said with all his heart, I love you dad and I know you love me I wish we could be together always but I understand it is just not the way it is, I said Darra we are together now for the next few days so let's make the most of them, he agreed and we fell asleep.

We had a great weekend together and it was like our bond had never been broken, he was a mini me the way he looked, his way about him I mean he had a mad Limerick accent which I kept slagging him about and he didn't like that too much so he would slag me about the American accent so we were even on that front. We visited my friend Donna and Keith who were married now and had their own bundle of joy Katie who Darra got upset with because she was too young for him, him being almost 7. But it was a good weekend, well a great weekend really. I made a plan with Clare that I would like to come down and visit next weekend too before I head back and she was cool with that, so that was the plan.

I rented a car that next weekend and drove down to Limerick to see him again, his mom brought him into the local town to meet with me and we headed off for the weekend, we drove out to a beach and walked along it we ate at a Chinese restaurant that he liked. One of the days driving Saturday, he wanted me to pull handbrake turns in the car and so I drove down by the river Shannon there was a parking lot of gravel and I spun the car a few times for him, he thought this was "class lads class", I said to him there is a ferry at the end of the river that goes to America, do you want to come with me he said yes, all smiles and I said ok don't worry about clothes I will buy you all new stuff when we get to America. There is a ferry out in Listowel which is in Kerry and we were in limerick almost in Kerry, Darra rolled down his window in the back, laughing yelling out the window, help I am been kidnapped and taken to America, we got a good laugh out of that. We drove over to west Cork that afternoon and showed up at his Nana and granddad's house, Clare's mam and dad's and the front door was open so as I parked Darra jumped out and went in the door, his dog Rigby was still there and happy to see him and Rigby recognized me too, I was chuffed really the dog I bought Darra when he was two was kicking away strong, good and fat now too living with Na-Na, Rigby was probably the only dog in west cork that got a steak cooked medium rare for himself, or Ireland for that matter, I had never seen it before, but Na-Na took care of Rigby well. Darra made it to the kitchen door of Na Na's as I was walking in the front hall door and they were sitting having their evening tea, Darra with the chest out was pointing behind him, who is with you Darra said his Na-Na with a shock and concern in her voice, oh my god its Daddy, well how are you Aidan and big hugs from Na-Na. We had tea and chatted and were booked into the local hotel but the plan I made with Darra is when Na-Na asks just tell her we are staying in a ditch out the road a bit. Darra loved telling it and his granddad copped on to this so every so often he would say, "and sure, it is getting kind of late, where are ye staying" and Darra would come right back "ah in a ditch out the road". To keep it going Na-Na would say "ah sure that's ridiculous, I will make up a couple of beds" Darra would come right back having a great laugh, "nah its fine, we are staying in the ditch we will be grand". Of course I had told them we are staying at the hotel in Roscarberry and hopefully we will go swimming in the morning. The room in the hotel had two single beds and Darra spent most of the night changing channels on the TV and jumping from one bed to the next and acting the maggot, but who was I to stop him he was over the moon it appeared and was enjoying himself to the fullest, as any child would when on cloud nine.

The next morning we missed breakfast and it was check out time, so the swimming was a no go, I decided I would take advantage and we could visit with Sister Angela up in the convent, so up we went. The hotel and the convent are about a stone's throw away from each other at the edge of the town square of Roscarberry. Darra used to always call the nuns the Marys when he was smaller I guess because to him they all represented Holy Mary, I used to bring him to visit the convent and the nuns when he was smaller and when Darra was a baby he loved giving the cute eyes to the women and the attention, so the Marys were no different, they loved playing with him and talking to him, one time I thought about this and I always viewed nuns as strict and religious and different, when you see the nuns around a child you realize they are just like any other woman who have taken some vows and have the same loving motherly qualities as any other woman. It was good to see Angela, well sister Angela and we walked the convent and visited the church inside of the convent or chapel I forget what they called it. Darra used to go in there in the terrible two's and scream his head off because of the great echo, there might be a nun deep in prayer in the chapel and I would be embarrassed trying to stop Darra from yelling but sister Angela always laughed and smiled and said let him, that's what children do, it is a wonderful sound in the convent a child's voice. We mounted up the car after our visit and headed for Limerick.

Of course the drive back was not as nice as the conversation was about me heading back to America and I would be going next week and I would be in touch and he said it sucks, that he had a great two weekends but he held it back well, he didn't cry it was me who was about to burst out, so we had almost like an unmentioned competition going who would hold it back the longest. I gave him a big hug and he gave me and even bigger squeeze and I told Clare thanks so much I would be in touch and away I drove the road home to Dublin.

That week I booked my ticket with my new Irish version passport and it was a ticket from London to Minnesota and then Minnesota to San Francisco. I said my good byes to my friends, Kenneth and James and Donna and Donal and away I went. They were the close friends I had really around the home place as anyone else I grew up with was either in jail or strung out on drugs and still living the same old life, so I had a small group of friends at the time, of course I had been away for years too. I boarded my planes and was heading back to my life and my wife; I could not wait to see her. I had missed her so much now too as I had been on an emotional couple of weeks and I felt I needed her to comfort me and be with me, maybe next time I thought.

Chapter 24.

I flew to England first and was nervous about my new passport and will I be stopped going into the states, however the English flight and ground crew were not doing anything to the tickets just check 'em and fly you out there, the immigration piece would take part in Minnesota. When at the British airways check in desk in London, the lady stalled as she entered my passport and said, hmmm and uhhh and hmmm I thought, already I am not gonna make it past her even, why my passport is new and good for 10 years, she looked up at me and said, you are tall and I have given you the exit row seat, so you can have a comfortable trip. Handed me the ticket and circled the gate number and time for boarding, ok cool. It was a big British airways plane, I do not know what model exactly but it was big and the exit door I was sitting at had two luxurious seats right behind the first class area, myself and another Irish guy were sharing the trip. I was able to stretch out and catch just a few hours' sleep but it was a hook up none the less. Me and my travel companion for the trip discussed everything, soccer, economies, penny stocks, stock market, fishing, building laws in Ireland, it was really an enjoyable and relaxing flight. It is hard to find one of those most of the time going trans-Atlantic but it was and I was on my way back home. Home obviously to my wife, to my life, sunny San Francisco was now my home at least that's how I felt about it and I had just spent some wonderful time with my son, maybe that's where the relaxed came into it and it had nothing to do with British airways.

We landed in Minneapolis Saint Paul, they are twin cities I guess two cities adjoin each other and so it is Minneapolis and Saint Paul in Minnesota, state of. I joined the lines and remember thinking they are watching like hawks for nervousness and anything suspicious, just relax your passport is fresh and clean and they will in no way snag you. I had a forwarding ticket to California so I was feeling good relaxed and confident. I tell you once before when I said about coincidences and the truth being hard to believe, well here we go.

I step forward when beckoned from behind the yellow line, anyone who has ever done this travel know it, it says in bold letters, stand behind the yellow line, if you do not, some strong American accent officer will be quick to tell you, behind the yellow line please sir. I try and throw the Irish accent a bit at the immigration officer as passing my ticket and visa form and passport. "How's it going, jaysus there is a lot of snow outside, how cold is it here" she reads it checks it with a pen and swipes my passport in this electronic barcode scanner thing. She answers me with "Oh it is cold but it is mild for this time of year, you won't have to worry about it I see you are heading to California, I am jealous of all the sunshine there" she swipes the passport again and she puts a funny kind of confused look on her face and she calls across to the officer in the next booth, he replies, one moment as she picks up her telephone. She repeats "ah ha, uh huh. Ah ah, ok thank you" she hangs up the phone. Then I had to try and keep the innocence going and lean over a little to try and see her screen on her computer, "is there some kind of problem I asked" she says one moment and walks out of her booth and to the one next to us behind me, now at this stage all the people in line are looking like there must be something wrong with me and I am beginning to think it myself, she comes back to the booth and picks up the phone again, I am standing not knowing which way to look, poor old tom hanks in that movie where is he is stuck in the airport is starting to creep into my thoughts, while she has the phone to her ear, the officer from the booth behind is asking for the passport, I am like what is going on, she hangs up the phone and says. "for some reason sir, this new system has shut down and will not swipe your passport, I am going to have to do it the old way, I just needed to check with my supervisor" the officer from behind me was trying to take my passport and swipe it through his machine as his was working fine, she told him nah it is ok supervisor said go ahead the old way. So she pulled out the big old stamp, stamped my passport and I was in. Could they have swiped it and it came up knowing me probably, but it meant no finger prints and no photo taken and I was in again, it was a sweat for a minute or two, of course it felt like 30 minutes but I held it together and got back into the states.

My immigration lawyer and my wife had me all on edge that maybe I get turned back and between me and my wife, we agreed if that happened we would figure out another application through the embassies and she would look for a visa for Ireland or whatever was needed, we were ready but all averted due to the immigration officers system shut down for absolutely no reason except God wanted to give me a break and let me through. Coincidence again popping its head into my life at the crucial moment in time, who cares I was in and off to my wifey, Irene.

This was time now for crab fishing again and the squid season was over, I spent my days around the harbour rigging pots and getting gear ready. The big tall Scottish guy I had fished in Alaska with, he had bought this tiny little boat and he wanted to make money and wanted me to help him, so we made a few fish pots where each boat could catch a certain amount of kilos per week of a particular fish, black cod or as some people call them butter fish, they are just like a regular cod fish except there skin is black and they live deep in the canyons of the ocean. The pots we made to catch them are simple like any type of fish pot except the catching them trick was to go out to the edge of the canyon and try and rest the pots along the wall of the canyon if you miss the spot, the pots will keep sinking and bye bye to all the hard work as the pots sink into the abyss. These pots because they were for fish they had rope type netting which was soft and made it easy to stack the fish pots one inside each other, whereas crab pots are all metal and steel and have to be stacked high one on top of each other and are heavy, these things were light enough and easy to stack. Luckily because the boat this guy, laddie was his nickname around the harbour, big guy six four or six, six maybe and me six 2 we looked a funny sight on this little boat. There is another kind of crab that had a good market with the Chinese was a rock crab found in along the shore and had no season or permit needed so we rigged some of them pots too. I said we should rig the boat for tuna too because that is all light and will be easy if the boat can go fast enough, I mean this boat was maybe 35 feet and a tiny 35 feet a little bath tub and when we were both on the boat, it looked much smaller. We headed out for the night to catch black cod, steamed out a few hours to the edge of one of the canyons, just to explain, Ireland for example has this great continental shelf that extends out to the west for a few hundred miles and so it doesn't really get too deep off the coast of Ireland, that is said to be why it has always been a great breeding grounds for fish. Not too deep would be maybe 1000 feet deep maybe and out where the porcupine bank is maybe a little deeper but that is 120 to 150 miles off the west coast of Ireland. In the Bering sea the depth does not change too dramatically and again another great breeding ground for fish as it stays about 600 feet deep at the maximum approx. now no need to quote me on these figures.

The pacific ocean along the California and Oregon coast line, well for example Monterrey bay in California, this has a floor along and around the bay and as soon as you turn the corner on the southern tip of Monterrey bay down by the village of Monterrey itself, the ocean floor disappears. Literally it is the abyss. Monterrey is where they had a famous writer who took refuge there and wrote some books, one being cannery row. That is a real place in Monterrey; it is along the California coast. So off of San Francisco and surrounding bay area the ocean holds its depth for a while and then in parts there are big canyons that the bottom is unknown where it is and then there are what they call mountains as the ground comes back up to a peak and disappears again. We headed out to an area of ocean just outside the Farollon islands; these are a group of small islands outside of the golden gate bridge west of San Francisco and ocean beach. The islands are one of the few spots in the world where it is a natural breeding ground for the great white shark one of three popular spots for them, so no skinny dipping there. In and around this part of the Pacific Ocean are the inbound and outbound shipping lanes for pan pacific shipping, meaning goods between the United States and Japan or China. A lot of ships would come and go in and out through the Golden Gate Bridge to the port of Oakland California.

So we set the pots, now in fishing it is always good to use enough rope to allow for a couple of times or three times the depth of the water, so the most expensive piece of fishing for these black cod is the rope, we are trying to set these pots on the edge of a cliff on the ocean floor, the depth is about 800 meters down and so we needed about 2000 meters of rope, then we need floats to know where the fishing gear is so we can retrieve it when it is time to haul. The reason for all the rope is the float will be taken by the tide and so the rope can swing and switch with the tide, if the tide is too strong we need that the floats will not be strong enough to lift the fishing pots and so it is all a science really. We threw the last pot over and watched the rope spin wildly into the sea, and then at the end throw the floats in, buoy we call those, BU WEE. Then watch and see and wait, is the buoy going to go down with the gear because we missed the canyon edge and just throw our pots into the canyon or will it go with the tide a bit and settle. Guess what? Yup success the buoy stayed there, now the stress of that was off we needed to sit by there and sleep and wait for the pots to do their fishing while we waited. We figured 16 hours would be good enough. In the oceans of the world there are things people refer to as sand flees or skinners, what they are, are little bugs in the ocean down deep and if they find fish that is trapped they prey on them and they eat the fish from the inside out and when we haul up the catch we get nothing but skin, a complete perfect looking, no meat inside fish, just skin, hence the name skinners so in order not to lose all your catch to skinners, it is best to not leave the pots for 24 hours or more or you will end up with pots full of skins and nothing to sell. This fish sold for approx. $2.40 to $3.60 per kilo with a cap or restriction on us of 800kilos per week that is what was allowed per anyone who wanted to try and go catch them. So we were looking to make about $800 each for the night after expenses. The options to us at that time were go back ashore another three hour boat ride home to the harbour and three hours back out in the morning, which costs as we would be burning fuel all the time or sit and wait, so we went to a shallower part of the area and tried to drop these long lines with fish hooks and see could we catch any of the more expensive fish, these red snapper looking things, I don't remember the exact names as the fish in the pacific have many weird names, Cabazon's and things like that.

We started to haul the pots the following evening after we had toyed around a bit and had gotten some sleep drifting around the back of the Farollon islands, a ton of rope and a slow hauler on Laddie's new boat, well new to him at least. And up came the pot and before we could see it break the water it looked like nothing in it. Because the fish are black remember and in the water a few feet under it looks all black, then up comes the pot and bunch of fish all swimming and kicking. We open the pot and put the fish into boxes and keep hauling for the next one, we had 5 pots in total and figured, 160 kilos per pot would do us, the second pot came up and the real weight only comes on when you try to haul it out of the water. This pot had more fish in it, this pot alone had 800 kilos in it, this was too much, but when fishing and the killer instinct the hunter in you comes out, and you just want to see each pot full full full. We had to let the rest go as each pot came up full and that was us for black cod for the week, we tried to get the fish buyer to buy a little extra from us but he said no way, the authorities will know if we deliver exactly 800 kilos, so he would take 760 kilos the rest we threw back into the ocean and the sea lions had a good feast courtesy of me and laddie.

We made our money and the plan was I would continue rigging crab pots and he would start rigging the boat for tuna, albacore tuna there was no limit on how much of those you could catch.

The process with the lawyer had been funded and she was beginning working to get me legal status within the US and more importantly was the wedding. We had looked at some venues in San Francisco and as soon as you mention wedding to any venues the prices take a few jumps on the scale, 12k for the hall and catering for a dinner, "oh yes we were thinking for our wedding" well in that case our basic wedding plan starts at $20k. Needless to say it was a long road of ideas and every new place we viewed we had instant dreams and then the price became the ultimate in dream killers. I figured a good squid season will cover it and squid ends usually into September, the crab season kicks off in November and in between that there is always tuna, so options for making money, lets aim for November. The date or preliminary date was set and of course we would change if we could get the right venue. I had the few odd days here and there with Adrian my buddy in the hardscaping business too so I was not worried and Irene always worked a steady job, so when you are young and making money, what's not to do, go find a wedding to plan and spend the money. As it turned out the crab season this particular year was crap and I just barely was scrapping by and really there were times we were totally dependent on Irene's income to help cover everything. We used to always split the rent cost, and then she would pay the phone and the light, I would put up cash for the groceries or anything after that. I would pay usually with cash, a night out or she would pay with her card. So I was just back through the Minnesota trip and a few dollars left over, the lawyer paid to start the process of immigration and not much other spare money and the internal pressure of, what am I doing? I am taking on a wedding I could never afford. I decided I have a plan maybe I should go to the casino again and in my mind I will win another twenty thousand dollars. I had about eight hundred dollars and I went and gave it a shot and negative, nothing doing there plus a whole day wasted. I had gotten a day's work from Adrian so I was able to have some pocket money and I just didn't want to tell Irene I was broke. I had been rigging pots all year long it seemed and I had been out fishing as many good weather days as god sends but it was not adding up. Irene did not understand that sometimes in fishing you do all the same work or sometimes even harder and the resulting pay is less. I was fishing the boat for Big Paddy and Timmy wanted no part of it because there was no money in it, so after losing the money in the cache creek casino I went and visited

Timmy, I borrowed from him 2,000 dollars just to tie me over the hump.

Chapter 25.

Timmy was a real investor type of guy and he saw better loan me 2000 and take back 400 a week for 6 weeks than have no extra income himself.

I headed to the race track that Saturday with 1000 dollars and had spent my week studying the horses all geared for Saturday. Now with the horses the study of the recent races and using the information to try and predict the outcome of the new race between the competitors is called "handicapping" so I had handicapped the race card for this upcoming Saturday and to the track I went. Good old Neilus was almost part of the furniture at the race track. I made my bets sat back and watched the races unfold, they have a type of bet there called the pick six, what this means is you have to select the winners of 6 races in a row at the same track, but it is like combinations and permutations, you could select all the horses in every race and be certain you would win but with 8 and ten horses in each race, that would be a very expensive ticket to play as it would be a $2 stake times 8 horses in the first leg… 10 in the second …8 in the third…..10 in the fourth…10 in the fifth… and 8 in the last, many times the last would have 12 or 14 runners so very difficult and if you want to cover all possible combinations, well that would be the bet, $2 x 8x10x8x10x10x12 let's say that ticket would cost 1.5 million dollars just to place the bet, but you would be certain to win and sometimes the pool for the races might touch 2 million or 3 million but of course you would have to share the pool with any other lucky winner, so the idea is to handicap, study the races and try and narrow the fields down to the ones that have a chance. How do you do that, I do not really know but I will try and explain. Ok 8 horses racing in a particular class of an event, so look for the horse that performed well the last time they ran, look for the horse who is dropping down in class of event, look for the horse who is stepping up in class, look for the horse who is trying to run a new longer distance, look for the horse who is shortening in distance so their last event was a mile & today's event is six furlongs which is only three quarters of a mile. These are some basic pointers I would study what they call the "fractions" the fractions are the time it took for the portions of the race, example the race is one mile long, that would be eight furlongs. Ok now my view point is how quickly did they run the first 2 furlongs, how quickly the second two furlongs and how quickly the third two furlongs and how quickly did they finish the last two furlongs. To give you a layman's view of this it is a given that an average time for a horse in race speed to cover one furlong is approximately 12 seconds. So two furlongs would calculate to 24 seconds. An eight furlong race follows the same calculations 8x12 seconds, 1 minute and 36 seconds. So handicapping means you are looking for a horse in the field that can run a 1 mile race in 1 minute and 25 seconds, which means he can cover one furlong in an average speed of 10 and half seconds, that's pretty fast. Does he run on sand or prefer grass, grass in horse racing they would call the turf. The racing newspaper for Saturday used to be available on Friday around noon time in the shop one of the local stores near my house and I bought it and started studying. Irene came home from work and we ate dinner and I continued to study the racing paper and look around the internet for any video replays of recent horse races where I could watch any particular horse how it ran, did it run from the front and get tired at the end, did it go a steady slow pace at the beginning and then finish like a bullet, all factors of handicapping horse racing. I went to the race track and made a few bets on races I thought I could win on and was doing well, I was up about 4000 dollars, I played my study of the pick six at Belmont park which is a New York track and I sat back and watched. I had played a pick six ticket worth 512 dollars, so this was a big investment for me the 512 comes about like this 4x4x1x2x4x2 so that was my combination of selections for amount of horses running for me in each race, of course by the $2 stake. The first race I had the winner, the second race I had the winner, the third race the hardest one because I only had one single selection running for me in that race, winner the fourth race winner, the fifth race winner the sixth race winner. I was ecstatic I hit the pick six in Belmont park, that day I had a bet of $200 to win on a horse running in California at a different track and the horse was 10/1 so I was looking to pick up 2 thousand dollars on that race also, the horse slipped as he angled out to make his run in the final furlong, just like my study said he would he was winding up to explode like a train and he put his foot wrong and slipped and finished third. I was so bitter over that. But the day finished well, I had come home with almost 14 thousand dollars, the pick six pool that day had 9 winning tickets and each paid 11 thousand dollars. So all in all it was a great day.

I came home and told Irene and she was so happy, I said maybe we could spend Christmas in Ireland and you can meet all my family and some of my friends. And meet Darra. I was still within my three months 90 days tourist visa so the lawyer could see no harm and they would let me back into the country. I thought using these winnings would be a great way to spend it, I planned a whole trip we would go to Ireland for Christmas and then we would spend new year's eve in Paris, I booked a lovely hotel so we would be right on the plaza by the Eifel tower for new year's eve, then we would return to Ireland a few days and off to San Fran again. Irene said let's do it, no sooner did she say yes I pressed confirm on the booking and we were off to Ireland again. Christmas came and we did the usual Christmas dinner, Darra came to visit so we got to hang out then off to Paris to show my loved one I was a romantic at heart and the city of love was the place to be. We popped champagne in the streets and watched the tower light up for New Year's. And back to cold, cold Ireland visited a few more friends and away back to the states. That's what winning on the horses meant to me.

Irene was convinced I was a genius at this and so did I so she would print the racing guide for me in her office and bring me home the charts for the horses and I would go when the racing was on. Sometimes for very little investment my handicapping was working and I would cash winning tickets for 3 and 4 thousand dollars so it was working well. There was no more crab season and the squid season was looking like it was going to be late or non-existent this particular year and I was getting married in November with friends and family coming to the wedding, I was starting to panic. I was working as much as I could I even hooked up with another Irish construction crew who did stucco, that is just plain old plastering really. The good thing was they were Bridget's brothers who had done the building and I would carry the hose that the concrete was being pumped up in along the scaffolding while the guy sprayed it on the wall. This job lasted three weeks and netted me 2 thousand dollars, I had a few two and three day stints with Adrian which would get me 3 and 4 hundred dollars and I had a few squid trips here and there that netted me about 15 grand so I was paying things off for the wedding. Irene had a place picked out which would provide the room and had 14 guest rooms which our guest could stay. I bought all the alcohol in a discount store through my friend on the local corner store, he used it as a purchase for his liquor store, George and his family ran the store, one of the nicest Palestinian people and families you will ever meet.

For the wedding we had settled at a location in Las Cruces, New Mexico for the wedding obviously it fit our budget and Irene had taken a trip home one weekend to visit her family and scout out venues for the wedding, it was about 30 minute drive from El Paso so we figured get married in the church around the corner from where she grew up and have the reception for about 40 people in this venue in Las Cruces New Mexico. Here we go 2002 November 2nd it is all coming together. I knew I was going to be broke after the wedding but who cared at least I was going to be able to make it happen and that was what was important at the time.

The wedding was on, the crab gear was getting ready again for another season and I went to the races must have been a Thursday in October. I had done my handicapping and around the 20th or 23rd of October. I played a pick six ticket with a cost of only $256 dollars this time and I hit the first four races and a race track hustler who obviously had be friended me because he saw I used to win, he came and said he could get someone to buy 25% of the ticket before the last two legs and I could walk out of there with $5grand in my pocket at least even if I lose the last two races. I thought that is a good deal I give up 25% for $5000 now why not I need the cash, the hustler, Tom was working his angle for a percentage on both ends, if it hits the other guy has to take care of Tom and if it doesn't hit I have to take care of Tom, that is how a race track hustler stays alive. I hit the fifth leg and it was all eyes on the last race I had two selections running for me. The screen put up the possible payoffs for the pick six ahead of the last race, my two horses the 3 and the 8 were both paying 148 thousand dollars. Every other horse in the race was only paying for five out of 6 which meant the pool would carryover if any other horse wins, if one of my horses wins, then I, my ticket is the only ticket in the whole United States that will be paid out and I win the whole pool for the day. People came around us, there are about 28 minutes between races, and people came around. What have you got? Oh they have no chance, some said, go to the window get in line you are an automatic winner others had said. A few others were just simply hating and some were genuinely rooting for me. Sixth race started, I had a little few butterflies and watched the race, my 3 horse had a good lead turning for home but the pack were coming to catch him, I thought I am screwed he is not going to hang on. The 4 horse moved out from the rail and started a run; the 8 horse came off the final bend covering the move by the 4. At this stage we are all in a corner in the club house of bay meadows race track gripping each other and screaming at the TV, the 3 horse the poor jockey is doing his best to try and keep the horses head in front while the four is battling away resiliently, the 8 is gaining with every stride and seems like the finishing wire might just come too soon, I thought, FUCK IT I AM GOING TO BE SPLIT, this would mean the four horse would get his nose up on the line and the 3 and 8 would finish second and third respectively. I have to admit the poor jockey did everything he could to try and win that race for me, I know the jockey didn't know I had a chance at 148 thousand dollars but for me at that time I felt he was putting all that effort in for me and it was gonna fall just a little short, with one final burst the 8 horse gets his head in front and the 3 finished second 4 horse was third, I just hit the only ticket in a pick six at Santa Anita park about 10 days before my wedding for a cool $148,000.

Not too shabby for a little kid from Loughshinny. I had someone else sign for the ticket as the IRS take percentages in taxes and I ended up with 95 thousand dollars cash, the guy who bought in got 30 thousand and the taxes got the rest. I went home that evening the guy Tom drove me he was ecstatic, I stopped at the bank and deposited nine thousand dollars as anything under ten thousand keeps the IRS away and Tom thought I was going to go party and spend all the money and go for steak dinners, I took him through the drive thru of taco bell and told him take me home. I remember a movie from new Zealand where the guy Jake won on the horse and they were supposed to visit their son in prison, the movie Once Were Warriors, with his winnings he threw the money on the table when he got home, I did the same. I said to Irene quoting Jake the Mus, short for muscle from the film. "Irene about this wedding we have a lot of expenses and as I slapped a brick of 100 dollar bills on the table and said, "rent a fucking limousine" she was over the moon, we were getting married and now could pay off all the little extras and go overboard a bit at the same time. We were in good shape as far as no more of the penny pinching for our wedding.

My youngest brother flew out to San Francisco the following week and the plan was Irene would fly down ahead, her and her bridesmaid were going to take delivery of the special flowers, she had these special orange coloured roses not bright orange but orange, ordered and needed to take delivery and hope the desert heat would not ruin them. She needed her dress fitted and the venue to have all the décor she wanted. I in the meantime would get fitted for my suit and my brothers best man suit and I would drive with all the Napa valley wine through the night to El Paso to get their the day before the wedding. Also that week my good friend Donal and his wife and daughter flew into San Francisco to take a few days in San Fran and then they would go visit a friend of theirs in LA and meet us back in El Paso for the wedding. Donal and I had fished together back in Skerries right around the year or two before I ended up in prison, we used to enjoy doing the cross word on the boat on the way out fishing in the mornings and shared many a laugh on a Friday evening when getting paid in the pub at the top of the harbour in Skerries. He had an eye for things and was an avid camera hobbyist or enthusiast and so as we had remained good friends over the years I asked him would he do me a favour and take the wedding photos for me. He agreed and as he now worked in the airport in Dublin and would love to take advantage of his staff travel. So I met him in San Fran that week also and he enjoyed his stay there and went on his travels with his family, we met again in El Paso for the wedding.

For the long drive down the country I had rented a big ford explorer for the wedding festivities and trip to EP. I had the trunk or the boot full with boxes of alcohol. A friend of mine who I sat my leaving cert with and who had gone through the house in Father Roch's named Keith, he had flown to San Francisco, so myself him and my younger brother Brian hit the trail for LA first stop so they could have a one day seeing the sites, universal studios and the Hollywood scene, Beverly hills etc. As I would be stopping in LA really for the first time since leaving Jimmy behind on the Venice beach Blvd. I shot him an email to see if we could meet up. We drove the night from San Francisco and hit LA early in the morning I had the new mobile phone number for Jimmy through email and we met and had breakfast together in a diner near Redondo beach, Jimmy now had amassed a small fortune selling Australian bird callers, he had a big motor home parked near the beach and explained me how he follows the weather now to county fairs and shows and does all the east coast in the summer and back along the west coast in the winter, telling me I was lucky to catch him actually. I told him things were going good and he said to hell with getting married, look at me, motor home and four by four car to tow around the country, let's go to Australia and live up and down the west coast we can take the money we have right now and buy all the gold from the small miners, gold is cheaper than weed right now it has never been so cheap we could get very rich, we buy all the gold up and deliver it to the Perth mint, they store it for us and when it hits a peak again we sell it to them at the mint and they will melt it and keep it in bars. I said sounds great man but I am about to get married man what is wrong with you. He had his joking smiley face on and was still the larger than life character. We finished up and I left him with his thoughts and hit the trail to go "touristing" around Hollywood for the Irish guys, Keith and Brian to see some sites. We promised not to leave it so long the next time. When we were in Beverly Hills pottering around looking for celebrities, we bumped into a real one but not an American celebrity, an Irish one. Rodeo drive, Ronan Tynan was shopping for something for his dad's birthday, we said hi and we chatted a bit, I joked saying you would be a great surprise as the wedding singer, how much do you want. He laughed and said he had a gig already lined up he was in LA to sing for the dodgers game tonight or the angels one of the baseball teams anyway and he was the guy going to sing the American national anthem at the game that night. It could have even been the Lakers game, I cannot remember for sure but it was one of those big games. Or he had to fly back to New York to sing at a game, hard to recall but it involved him being tied up singing a national anthem somewhere nonetheless and he declined my wedding. We headed east from LA that evening the guys had a good laugh and we stopped off on the way in Palm Springs for an evening meal and show the guys a full swing casino. They had gotten some sleep along the way and I was beat tired, so I let Keith drive for a while, we were trying to time everything so we could pick up another brother John, he was flying from Australia as he had been working and travelling down there for a year or so and was making a return trip home to Ireland via my wedding, so we had some time to kill along the way awaiting his arrival. He was flying into to LA from Australia but it made more sense for the timing of the drive for him to catch up with us in Phoenix and then four of us spend the night driving across the desert.

John got off the LA flight in phoenix with long curly hair and a pair of shorts a big back pack and a surf board under his arm, I thought ah here, driving through the desert with a surfboard strapped to the roof, now we really look like clowns, where will I tell the border patrol we are going, to surf sand dunes in the desert.

I had let Keith do the driving like I said and when I woke up I was in a panic he was over taking big semi-trucks and driving like he had no fear I woke up convinced I had fallen asleep at the wheel and I was about to drive under the truck, Keith was laughing away "it's alright hoss, I got the wheel" I took over again and finished out the ride. When we got to El Paso a bunch more people were there and we had a pre wedding night dinner at a ribs spots and all ate well, Irene had been running and tearing like crazy all week and she was happy her husband had arrived.

The next morning I awoke in the hotel and could not wait to get to the church and have the day roll by I was anxious, nervous, embarrassed by my mother of course, the heat was killing I was not getting into the suit until the last minute, I had always hated a tie or dickie bow tie or anything even the top button closed as I hated the feeling on my neck and I didn't want to sweat up the shirt too much. For those that do not know, El Paso has a huge Mexican population and the churches being catholic are usually full of Mexicans too which, they are like the Irish really but a different colour and a much warmer part of the world, but November 2nd is "the day of the dead" "dia de los muertos" like an all souls day for us in Ireland and the churches are decorated accordingly. The symbols are quite often candles with skull motifs or kind of ugly death symbols, it is a celebratory day in the church for letting the spirits go to heaven kind of thing, but for the Irish contingent who didn't understand this, some of the decorations in the church were a little creepy.

I got to the church in the rented car and walked in and the family and few friends who could make it were there and some of Irene's relatives who could make it were there too, the one good thing about the church was it was nice and cool, that helped calm me down a lot, with the collar of the shirt and the jitters of getting married and this is really happening. I mean I had been married with Irene for a while but doing all this in the church suits and dresses and the full issue was an emotional time, a good emotion though. Irene came in and she looked stunning, she had her hair up in a way I had never seen done before and her makeup was perfect and she was an absolutely stunningly beautiful bride. I mean obviously I had the hots for her anyway any time of day or night, but that day she did it alright, beautiful. She came to the alter delivered by her dad, her brothers had the suits on and looked like the feds, two big stropping dudes and her mom was there not really sure what was going on but her dad had her by the hand, my crew were there too. Mexican traditions would have a few little differences and the priest put this rope like a lasso and that's what they call it in Spanish too, a lasso or something spelled like that and it symbolized or was supposed to mean the tying us together, the unity. The priest rambled on a bit and we made our vows and put the rings and did the full ceremony and mass and then we kissed and the cheer went up the round of applause and the photographs started. I had my woman in a beautiful white dress and she was everything to me right then and there.

Off to the reception, the speeches, champagne, fondue fountain, the mariachis playing for us, the meal, the wine, cake the first dance the dj and the night of love making in the presidential suite, yup we had a no holds barred wedding. I don't care what anyone ever says and me and Irene were married already for a while now but that wedding night, hmmm yummy yummy she gave me some loving, the wedding night sex is the best....I can see why people renew the vows several times just to have that night all over again and then why some divorce and re marry and divorce and re marry.

Hell of a night. The breakfast the next morning and all were happy with the hotel and the service and the wedding party. I paid the hotel whatever they were due and me and Irene were simply in love.

My family hung around for a few days and we hung out too and enjoyed hanging with our families together, many of the other guests had flown home and that was it. We didn't have a honey moon and I had to drive the car back to San Fran and Irene took a flight, I drove back as fast as I could to be with her and my two brothers tagged along for the ride, they were leaving for Ireland out of San Fran as well.

I remember Irene's mom, funny, Irene had made these little gift sets for the tables for every bodies place setting and in them were these special chocolates and everyone had a little box of chocolates in them, Irene's mom had spent her few hours at the wedding dinner and when the dancing started she was going around filling her pockets with peoples little boxes, Irene was mad at her for that I thought it was great.

Another funny part from the whole wedding trip, gold was 300 an ounce approx. back then and Jimmy was right within the next few years it hit more than a thousand an ounce, missed opportunity. But I had my gold in my wife.

Chapter 26.

I had received an injury back in union hall when fishing on the boats and I now had the money to try and do something about it, so I pursued the route to fix my leg injury. What happened simply was, one night out fishing of the south coast of Ireland I well we caught a rather large boulder in the net, we struggled with it to get the catch aboard the boat on the winches and this rock was really large and it hit the deck with a thud. The night was a little rough in the terms of the weather and so it was upon us to secure the massive boulder immediately and work around it for sorting the catch that had not already been squeezed and squashed to pieces by the mass. For a couple of days we tried to work around the boulder, now when I say big, there is of course a limit to the winches and the equipment of what size or weight we can actually physically haul aboard the boat. So that particular night we caught this big rock about 4 and half feet high and about 5 to 6 feet wide, so it would have had a circumference of about say lay a tape all the way around the thing, maybe 15 feet maybe. A solid dead weight. The day before we headed for the shore to finish our fishing trip and offload the fish from down below in the freezer room, the captain said, let's dump this rock out over the side of the boat as we are on top of an old ship wreck and that way the boulder is off the fishing grounds. I disagreed with him and said, we have put up with it all week now let's do it at the safety of the harbour where the boat will not be moving so much, I remember taking the rock aboard the other night and it is heavy. He said, nah it won't be a problem I am sick of looking at it. I said ok.

In the deck of a boat there can quite often be areas for sorting the fish called pounds. A pound is made up of timber pound boards stacked on top of each other, more often than not lengths of timber of size of 12 inches from top to bottom and by 2 to 3 inches thick and maybe 6 to 8 feet long. The boards would be planed at one end and slot into what are known as stanchions, or stanchion posts. A stanchion post for this kind of use on a fishing boat gives a cornered off area and forms a box, the boards may be three high so three feet or even four high so four feet and then running long ways six feet so you get a box built on top of the deck where the fish can be securely set in one place, as you sort down you can take out one individual board at a time allowing ease of access and the fish are not rolling all over the deck when the boat sways "on the roll" of the ocean. When we would haul the fish in with the help of the winches, the pound boards would be all in place and then if it started to over flow it would only fill into the next pound. When we fished for herrings as we catch them by the tons, the pounds really have an important role to blockade and be used as an alleyway by removing middle pound boards and leaving the side boards so an alley can be created to direct the fish across to the other side of the boat to fill the fish room evenly, then for the next big lift of herring put the pound boards back in and the herring will flow a different direction. So on this particular boat we always landed the catch in the main pound and worked out of it from there, the second pound aft the deck, which means down the deck a little bit towards the stern, or the back of the boat. The second pound was longer and never took the real pressure of the catch as it was an area where we could sort the fish by removing pound boards from the main pound and let it flow, over into the second pound where we could sort through it.

So the decision had been made to remove the rock from the deck and dump it over the side into the ocean and allow it to sink down to the ship wreck at the bottom of the ocean floor. In order to perform this we must get new wires and ropes and secure the wires and ropes into a basket type formation or some form of cradle to be able to haul on the winch and all ropes and wires would take the weight of the boulder at the same time, increasing our chances to lift it evenly. The man on the winch is usually a seasoned fisherman and knows how and what to watch for, on this particular boat the winch man was maybe a little under qualified but he was the winch man, so the order was given up, he started to heave upwards and the boulder was starting to move a little slightly like a centimetre, but once you take the weight it now becomes a pendulum and it is deadly dangerous, so it is either up up and away fast and have to time the roll of the boat too at the precise time or this pendulum will start acting like a wrecking ball and make pieces of everything in its path. So the inexperience then of the winch man was he needed to having taken the strain of the boulder continue the motion while we would stand around the boulder with our weight and hands on it to prevent it from getting any momentum, he heaved a bit too fast and then stopped causing us to lose our grip, then because it was swinging dropped it to the deck immediately now the boulder was free and rolling around, the deck of the boat is slanted from the bow to the stern (front to back) so the boulder wanted to move aft (toward the back) my right leg was next to the railings and one of the more experienced crewman shouted your leg I pulled my right leg out of harm's way and the boulder kept moving it crashed off the side rail with a thud where my leg had just been and continued aft, I was retreating backwards and before I could get the second step in retreat the boulder had trapped my left ankle in the second pound where there was one base board, my ankle was trapped by the boulder with my foot pointing straight along the board not away from the board my body was knocked completely back and I was on the ground, well the deck really so, in a sense we can all roll our ankles inwards a little bit well mine was as if you rolled your ankle outwards at a complete 90degrees from the leg as my foot was flat on the deck but so was my body, I was yelping like a dog, rolling and screaming, I could see the water over the rail beside me and all I wanted to do was jump in I do not know why I thought the cold would make the pain go away, the base board of timber had a full crack/break in it exactly where my ankle was, if that board did not give way in that sense, well it did not break completely but had a full crack and was held together only by some fibres, if it did not give way or was a solid material like metal or steel my ankle bones would have been crushed to pieces. The pain was unbearable at that exact minute in time, the winch man was in shock or something because it seemed to take 5 minutes to heave again and take the weight of the rock off me and my trapped leg where I had been bent in a way the body is just not supposed to bend. The drama guy on the boat was trying to tend to me and the captain had come out from the side door of the wheelhouse and watch looking down on me as if to ask are you alright but stunned in shock of the pain I was expressing, they took my rubber boot off and did it quickly because I had said no and then my sock, my foot looked fine and had a slight grazing of a scrape across the skin after I removed my sock. They went below to the ice and filled a big bag and we got a towel and placed it on my ankle immediately. I said to the captain; get me a helicopter to take me ashore. He laughed and said, sure you will be alright we are going in the morning. There are a couple of reasons for that because a captain owner of a boat does not want to raise alarms bells and have to list an inquiry as to what happened and end up paying something of a higher insurance premium and or just ignorance, who knows.

I was in pain, big time it was not only throbbing under the ice but everything from my knee to my foot hurt and I told him I cannot feel my toes. You would have to imagine reaching down to your ankle and turning your foot outwards to make it like the wing of airplane 90 degree angle to your leg, it just doesn't go that way it is not meant to be. This was sore, I could not move and did not sleep with the pain and they fished away. We made it into the harbour, I guess they got the rock out I do not remember if it was that night or they waited until the next day, I really was hurt and so I could not take notice what was going on outside. When we got ashore, I was helped onto the harbour and one of the guys drove me home in my car and there I sat to figure out a doctor and the hospital and x-rays etc. etc., I remember Darra at the time he was just learning to talk, "daddy has a broka leg" I was on pain killers and something for anti-inflammatory and some other thing. It was a wreck of a situation.

This time round fishing had gone quiet out in California I had some money from my winnings and I wanted to try and straighten things out in my leg, I had suffered with it for a long time now and had tried Chinese medicines and different acupunctures and alternative options but nothing worked, I could not run I could not walk for long periods and it was always swelling up and causing me all kinds of problems, my toes always felt cold and I did not know what was going on. When I had the ankle problem I would have to stretch my calf and my upper thigh all the time or I would not last a few hours before I would just have to put it up and all the time fishing on the steel boats I would just nurse it along and thought it was the vibration of the boat that caused the extra pain not the damaged ankle. Nothing had actually broke in the ankle what had occurred that all the tendons in the leg down there had been stretched beyond capacity, they had now healed themselves through time and shrunk or healed themselves tighter causing the joint of the ankle to be non-existent really, what it was that the leg basically went straight to the foot and there was no cushion or joint between them so I was a bit of gimp really for want of better terms but I braved it well. I started this course of treatment with a foot specialist I found in down town San Francisco, he told me a funny story about his history with Ireland as he had always wanted to visit the rains and the cold and convinced his wife to honeymoon there. He waited to get married at the end of summer and headed off to Ireland and had talked up the cold and the rain of Ireland and the feeling of a warm fire and the idea of renting a cottage and having his new wife next to him and the rain beating off the windows, he went in September and said the Irish government declared a national holiday and gave the kids two weeks extra off school for the summer holidays as it was a heat wave that September in Ireland, he said, his new wife, was looking at him like he was crazy and that all the Irish kids were on the beaches frying themselves pink. I laughed so hard at him I remembered the exact September he was talking about.

This was my foot doctor an accredited surgeon and I visited with him twice for him to perform some tests and then he put me into what they call a walking boot, he said he will take an MRI in 6 weeks and gave me pain killers anti-inflammatory pills and a course of steroids. He explained we are going to retrain your ankle and fix you. I never experienced the head racing that I experienced that next ten days while taking the steroid pills, I did not sleep a regular pattern I was taking these heavy pain killers and Irene used to laugh and say I love you when you are high, you act so stupid. I didn't know I was high even with all my days of being high as a youth, I felt so weird and crazy. If they ever offer you steroids say no and ask for something else, although they do not have the same effect on everybody.

I sat there high and used to go to the corner store as the doctor said get out and walk every day, he said do not worry the walking boot will help you, and keep it on for the full six weeks. I followed his instructions and my routine was wake up shower very awkwardly, relax do some horse study watch the stock market on TV and then go to the corner store for a sandwich and lunch. I would sit and chat with my buddy George again one of the nicest people you could meet, funny guy all the way and a real good man. We would watch the stock market TV and hang out I would take a sandwich sitting behind the deli and he would go about his duties. George and I shared some laughs in his store, home service market on central and Hayes San Francisco.

That was my routine for the 6 weeks in the walking boot, Irene would come home from work and I might have cooked and most all the time the thing to do was, keep my foot elevated. The time had come to take the boot off, the doctor had given me an extra prescription for pain only if I needed them as he wanted me to get the MRI of the foot tomorrow when I take the boot off and then come to him the next day. He said really stay away from any pills if possible as he had wanted to have a clear natural MRI picture and then once the MRI had been taken I could take the inflammatory pills if I felt I needed them or the pain pills. I awoke and my buddy Adrian had said he would take me to the MRI. He dropped me off and I said no need to wait I will be fine, I went inside the clinic for the MRI test and they took the boot off, I lay there and the thing went whoosh, whoosh, whoosh, whoosh and then after ten minutes or maybe twenty the thing was done and they said thank you I paid and left. You have no idea the pain, absolutely no idea the mental crazy mess I was in, I could not tip my toes never mind my foot off the ground, it was impossible. I called Adrian saying please come back and pick me up I was standing outside an MRI clinic on California street maybe, it was near the presidio area of San Fran and I was about to keel over with pain, I was losing my mind, I called the doctor immediately and sincerely asked him if this was some kind of joke, he said eat the pills go home keep the foot up and he would see me tomorrow. Adrian came quickly; he said he had never heard me talk like that so he knew something was wrong. He helped me into my apartment and I swallowed down a couple of pills, I was high alright but the pain was only barely gone I could not believe I had just set myself back like five years since the accident and this is where I was at I could not walk. Irene came home to take care of me that evening and made me some soup, the pills had me sweating I hardly knew my name and she caressed me and looked after me, then again she got a good laugh out of me being stupid when I was high.

I attended the doctor the next day, Marino or Marinero was his name something of Italian decent, his clinic was down town near the financial district in SF he said he had looked at the MRI and the options of surgery were that he could go into the joint and scrape all the scar tissue out by key hole type surgery but where is the guarantee that new scar tissue will not form from the surgery and then be in a cycle of scrapping the joint every six to twelve months. His recommendation was I was young and not an elderly person and so I could probably get used to living and dealing with a 25% disability.

My take on this was a surgeon who I am paying cash too, is telling me keep my money and try all these therapies he has lined out for me and maybe I will be ok, well usually now, think about it I am in the states where doctors thrive off cash paying patients and he is advising me no. I like this doctor and my confidence in him shot through the roof, I liked him even more when he gave me a shot of cortisone that day directly into the joint and I could walk like normal like magic a big needle into the middle of the joint and I was walking with ease and no pain although he did tell me the cortisone will wear off and I will need to be in physio therapy the very next day. I attended the therapist, she was an ex-ballet dancer who specialized in ballet dancers ankles, and apparently they go through hell just to be able to stay on their toes, so to speak. They said there was some genius had some gateway to the mind theory and it was common therapy, first she pulled and tugged and stretched the ankle, left and right, up, down, in, out the whole issue and then had me practice some stretches lightly though she said we will get more intense as the weeks go by, I was two weeks of this therapy and then the plan we would go to every other day and so on until I was walking like brand new. So here we are first session keeping it light I can handle that and then they wrapped me in ice but first had stuck multiple little electronic pads and wires on my foot all over it, hooked it up all electrical and then wrapped it in ice and I lay there with a machine which had a dial on it and the electronic pulses I could feel zapping my ankle and then she turned it up a bit so they were faster, a little bit, as I had said no not really that sore, she turned them up until I said ok I can really feel them now, she explained the gateway was a trick to confuse the mind in a sense, the electronic pulses made the brain think I was exercising extensively and so the blood was rushing to the joint with all oxygen and the body's natural healing properties, then the ice was forcing the new blood to run away quickly back up the system so they were enhancing the body's natural way of healing but in a major multiplied by a million of the normal process way. Two weeks we did this and I was walking like a champ then the therapy every other day and then twice a week and then once a week, but the joint was pulling itself back down tight again and without the constant therapy it was just going back to the way it was, the doctor gave me another cortisone shot during this time and it was only after physio when the stretching and the ice was applied would I feel my best. I mean it was an improvement for sure just not what I had hoped for. I thought my ankle would be fixed and brand new, the doctor had explained to me already, just learn to cope and deal with it, here is an open prescription for pain killers and anti-inflammatory medications or we do surgery every year for life. That pretty much was the end of that idea, I will just never run too much or strain it too much and that will be that, I still to this day do the muscle stretches but I have given up the ice packs a long time ago, live with the pain is the answer.

By this time Christmas had come again and we were spending Christmas with Irene's family for the first time. Of course we were the married couple now and so to visit her family was a nice thing to do. So we visited and took her mom and dad out to a few restaurants and enjoyed the holiday time, When I was in El Paso I phoned home to Ireland to wish them all a happy Christmas, to phone home from the states in those times I always bought a phone card and scratched off the panel and revealed a number, then you call and 800 number, the recording tells you, "You have $10 credit, please enter your destination number now" Phone cards sometimes were a scam and then some worked fine, some gave you three minutes some gave you 40 it all just depended on the card, I called home and spoke to the gang and whoever was at home in the folks house and in that phone call that year, something weird happened. Dad asked me on the phone "and how are Clare's parents" I said Dad what the fuck I am married to Irene, you flew out here for the wedding don't you mean Irene's parents. My dad got a little flustered, oh yeah Irene and kept on speaking like nothing. If you knew my dad at all, well he would not make such a mistake in conversation he was a smart man who knew what he was saying all of the time, so this was really really weird, I finished up chatting with him and then I asked could I speak to mam again. My mother came back to the phone and I asked her straight out, is there something wrong with Dad? My mother said, no not really, I asked had he been drinking today she said no in the house he never drinks. I expressed the concern to my mother there is something wrong with him, I explained what he had said and then she laughed and said he just made a mistake, I disagreed and mentioned to my mother you better keep an eye on him because that was not his normal self, something weird, but maybe it is nothing, Ok happy Christmas and all the best for the new year.

I returned to my wife's family home and was quiet and she thought something was wrong and so later that evening I said to her the conversation I had and my feelings were something is not right. She advised me I was reading too much into it and of course what wife wants to hear her husband and his dad were talking about his ex. Now Clare was always going to be a part of things as she was my son Darra's mom so my wife did not need to be hearing her name and so we finished out our Christmas vacation and headed back to San Francisco. January was here the rains were coming because in the bay area January can be a really wet month with storms and all kinds of heavy weather, so not much by way of fishing, construction or any form of work. I would still play the horses on the weekends though.

I was pressing the issue for the green card with the lawyer before my money ran out. I wanted to get this wrapped up but what had happened was I had won a number of the pick 6 bets recently, one I had two horses ending the bet the 1 and the 6 and they finished first and second, if the one horse wins I win the whole pool 152 thousand dollars if the 6 wins I share the pool with one other ticket, 76 thousand dollars, a few days later I hit another bet which I told a buddy he could have half, the pay-out for the pick 6 was 41 thousand dollars, because of new York rules of racing there had been a horse entered and then taken out at the last minute and so we had the horse removed from the ticket also and so it paid 41 thousand twice, so that's was 41k each. I had bought myself a nice pick-up truck at auction, not new but new to me and my first nice vehicle, dodge ram pick-up truck, I was living this carefree lifestyle of going racing and betting on football, American football on the weekend and eat out most nights of the week life was good, marriage was great and there were no pressures, then the lawyer started to apply herself, with the flow of cash and get me to sign all the papers and it was in that month of January that I spoke with my brother John, he is the next below me in line of the five of us, this phone call was not a good one, not a good one at all.

Chapter 27.

John explains to me that he is in the hospital, the mater hospital in Dublin with mam and dad, dad has been going for some tests since Christmas and they have called him back in for further testing, he has cancer.

Panic bells and alarms are ringing around my head I do not know how to figure this one out, John is trying to relay to me what the doctors have just spent an hour explaining to him and mam in the hospital corridors I really didn't know how to take this news, I was a little mad about it and trying to stay calm and discuss with John who he didn't really know either. I tried to get some straight answers from him but all he could tell me is they are saying maybe a month or three weeks to live they don't know they are going to do more tests. I called him back in a little while and said ah fuck man I am coming home, what else did the doctor say, John had given me the number to the oncologist doctor in charge of the case of my father as the doctor had advised if any family members wanted to know anything she would be available to discuss. Irene came home that evening soon after and I told her the news and I was freaked out, I wanted to go home. My wife calmed me down and was upset that I was saying screw the immigration policies and process I have to go home it is my dad. The following morning, first thing, I called the lawyer for the immigration and explained what I had just found out and that I would be calling the doctor at the hospital and see where we go from there. The lawyer explained well maybe a few more months and the process should be finished but I have an appointment tomorrow with the immigration department, so I can apply for an emergency travel visa based upon this recent news and they might allow. It could slow the whole green card process but it is worth trying. Just sit tight find out what you can let's see if I can get this accomplished tomorrow.

I called and spoke to the doctor in the mater hospital explaining who I was and who my father was and I wanted to know something, the doctor explained to me about metastases and cancer growths and stages of cancer, I with the American attitude said, doctor give me the straight and short version how long does he have to live?, she replied three weeks maybe six but he could last a long time with successful treatment, chemo therapy has come a long way, I explained to her at that exact moment my own delicate situation immigrating into the states but if she could give me a simple answer to the case, "doctor I want to know should I come home immediately to see my father or should I wait for treatment?" the doctor had listened careful to everything I had mentioned to her and to this question her reply was "come now if you can" my father had stage three, Lung cancer. I needed to wait until the following day as my lawyer had an after lunch appointment in the immigration offices. I spent the night discussing with my wife, what will I do? How can we manage this? The tensions were high but spirits were low contradictory it sounds but it was that my wife wanted me to be with my dad and she wanted to be with me. How does one juggle this dilemma? I had looked at flights and prices and routes and make a preliminary plan that evening to travel. The following morning I awoke, Irene was getting ready for work; our routine at that time was I would drive her to work in the mornings most mornings that way she could delay a bit as not running for the bus. I drove her and then went to my safe deposit box where I kept my cash and deposited some money into my bank account as I will be booking a flight later is what was in my mind. I went back home and was driving myself crazy watching the clock tick by, it seemed an eternity just to get from 10 am to 11 am I needed to wait until after lunch this was killing me, I made a phone call to my brother John who was having to be the strong one making the hospital visits with mam and faced with the face to face dealing with this new horrible situation.

Because I was going stir crazy in the apartment I went by the store to my good friend George and explained to him about my dad's diagnosis and he was genuinely saddened but it was good to talk to him and rather break down and have all the tears I decided to walk the block and just try and think. I walked up by the panhandle and thought about a walk to the beach and headed that direction, with all my years fishing and at sea I often just went and looked at the ocean and felt some peace and so the idea was head for the beach, although that is quite a long walk, I found myself four or so blocks from my house and there was this big fancy church on Fulton street, myself and Irene had been before in this church looking to get married there as it would be considered our parish church within our neighbourhood. There I was thinking yes I will pray why not I will walk in here with all the anger I feel toward God right now and ask him to help make things easy for my dad. I sat about 45 mins in the church admiring it really as it is a rather large and well-built church with a ton to be admired. On returning home I checked the answering machine, no messages I went down to the store to my friend George and immediately he greets me with any news, any updates. I say no and order a deli sandwich to go, I am waiting for a big phone call so I have to get back to the house and wait for this phone call from my lawyer. I sat there eating my sandwich on the couch starring at the phone, I had about as much interest in "the closing bell" this particular day as the man on the moon, 1.45 pm the phone rings, the lawyer says Hi "book your ticket" I am confused, she says if I can make myself available today at the bureau of investigations and have my finger prints taken and then take the copy directly to the immigration office downtown that I am good to go. She said in 19 years a lawyer doing immigration this is the fastest green card she has ever gotten. She said the actual green card will take some time, but you are in the system full green card no restriction, travel permit I have gotten it all today within one hour, this is something that would usually take up to 6 months or even a year and usually then a green card comes with a two year probation restriction. This green card is free and clear no probation, full travel permit, work permit the whole nine yards, "book your flight and get down to the finger printing place immediately".

I rang Irene immediately and told her while on the phone with her I booked a ticket to Ireland I was leaving at 6pm with air France. I booked a one way ticket that day because who actually knew what the plan was going to be when I got there. Irene came home and we hugged a lot and it was sad day yet a joyous one for the green card but the circumstances really sucked. I boarded the plane and off I went again with a lot of deep thoughts that evening flying across the Atlantic.

I took a taxi that morning from Dublin airport to my parents' home in Loughshinny in and around 30 or 40 euro's, my mother came out of the kitchen as I entered the hall door a big hug and she brought me into the kitchen to explain, I had not got the focus or patience to listen but I let her speak as I knew she must be going through some rough time herself. When she was done explaining I said where is he in hospital, she said no over in his bed but there is a priest there as with his medications right now and awaiting a chemotherapy plan from the hospital I think he might be a bit depressed and he has not been out of the bed for the last couple of days. I was tired from the long flight and wanted to punch the wall as my emotions were getting the better of me I remember telling my mother, who the fuck wouldn't be depressed with a priest over there, what is he doing giving him his last rights or something? I walked over to the room and the priest happened to be just leaving he said, my mom introduced "Paddy, Paddy look who it is" my mom was getting a laugh out of he might not recognize you because they have him on some heavy drugs this past few days and yes dad was a bit out of it alright, he was a bit loopy. He peered at me as if he couldn't see me at the end of the bed, his words "I knew you wouldn't be long" I said what dad, "I knew it wouldn't take YOU long to get here". I just sighed and said yes and asked him to get up and come have a cup of tea with me in the kitchen as mam had kept saying to me to try and get him up out of bed when you visit him in the room, so I said exactly that, Dad are you getting up, he said did you bring the money? And laughed to himself. I was for the first time in my life in a state of shock to see my loved one high and know he was sick and thinking of the doctor saying three to six weeks. I asked again come on dad let's go to the kitchen and get out of that bed, let's go have some tea. He asked looking at me directly "do you have cigarettes?" of course I said and as I was replying my mother was raising her voice in disgust, no, no, there is to be no more smoking in this house, my dad was getting out of bed with his feet now on the floor. Ah give over Teresa he said, "The damage is already done" laughing to himself again. I said "yeah mam give up that crack will ya" I walked ahead and mam waited to make sure dad could walk ok and we headed for the kitchen. When we got there dad had stopped to take a leak along the way in the toilet and I said mam

"for fuck sake you are giving out he won't get up, if it is a cigarette he wants to get up and enjoy then so be it, which would you rather he is in the bed depressed, you told me try and get him up out of bed now we have gotten that far so why start with this no smoking crap" Dad was up and the tea was on and we started chatting and going back and forth with mam about the smoking I knew she was happy he was up and moving and she was just saying whatever for the hell of it at that point. John had gotten up from bed and came and joined us and we decided to grill a few sausages while we were at it, the good old kerns were under the grill again. You can say what you like about God and the church and religions around the world; I received that green card so easily and full status that day because God had listened to my words in that church.

I know that anyone could say well that is the way that makes you happy or if that fits for ya, but here I was again with a strange and in my favour coincidence that happened through a church visit. And that is the only coincidence.

The next few days at home were the same routine, mam giving out about the smoking and dad only getting up if I could tease him out of bed in the morning for a cup of tea and a smoke, the heavy medications seemed to be wearing off and the local nurses and doctors had seen to it that for his first chemo trip to the hospital he was entitled to a taxi to drive him to and from the hospital, he was beginning to look sick now whatever the pills he was taking and he said to me he probably will get worse as the doctors told him the first chemo can cause some really harsh side effects. And he had explained to me he was worried to be too sick, I just had told him basically don't worry we will deal with whatever we have to deal with and let's keep going and see what happens. I really didn't know what to feel as my conversations with my dad were all serious feeling now and the state of affairs in the McNally family had a cloud of bleak wrapped around them without the silver lining.

I had discussed with my brothers at night sitting around the house and the feeling seemed the same from them, the simplest way to describe the majority of conversation with them of that week "THIS JUST SUCKS"

Mam and Dad headed off the following Wednesday in the taxi away for the hospital for chemo number one, dad had to sign some extra forms when he got there about consent to start receiving chemo therapy and I stayed at home waiting for their return. I made a few bets on the horses that day in the local town and sat around the house watching horse racing on TV and waiting for the taxi to return to hear of how the day went. I didn't know of anyone at the time to just call up and talk about cancer, this was all new for us. When they returned that evening about 5.30pm dad came in and just went straight for his bed, mam and me and John had dinner and mam gave us the rundown of the day. Dad was up the next day without any bribing and enjoying himself, his face was flush red and he was having a good day, he said they gave him this cocktail along with chemo and it had him feeling great, he called it his "energy juice" as he said it gave him great energy but he was definitely more of himself and normal and so we watched the horses chatted and got caught up on things and this good energy lasted some few days. The following Wednesday he was flat to his bed exhausted and no chemo was scheduled for another week. I had been meeting my few select friends around the local town of Skerries and letting them know the news and that I was home for a while until we knew more. The chemo followed this pattern chemo then an energy cocktail, for the first week it had dad flying high and buzzing around to do everything he wanted to do, I drove him out for a beer or two and one of the cycles of chemo he was booked on a flight to Amsterdam with a rental car all ready when he got there to go to all the coastal ports looking to buy a yacht as he always wanted one, three days later he was still flying from the energy juice he returned and was full of life. He went for pints in Skerries that week and I asked if I could drive him, he laughed "why?" I said well now that all this shit is happening there is no need to get stopped for drunken driving, his reply " I will put the window down take the ticket and tell the cop, I don't think I will be around to make the court date , sorry" He laughed. I ended up having a few deeper conversations with my dad at that time and it involved the tougher things to speak about, I mean I was not prepared to be back home laying on the edge of my dad's bed while he lay there taking the brunt of chemo therapy and letting it kick his ass. And I could not understand his high tolerance not for the physical pain but the emotional minefield he was now in he replied to that issue "what can I do, it is here it's a life sentence, might as well enjoy it" we got to share a moment and I was able to apologize for being a little shit of a kid and I was only the man I am today because he never gave up on me. I am deeply grateful that he never turned his back on me and I got the chance to tell him that, he held out his hand and I held it which I probably didn't do since shopping on Christmas eve in Dublin city with my father when I was four years of age. He said "I blamed myself for pushing you too far, that the more I chased you the deeper into the messed up life you were living and thought if I had not chased you, you would never have ended up in jail and messed up" Holding his hand laying on the bedside with him that day I was able to tell him that if it was not for that chasing I never would have made it out alive. Drugs and the lifestyle I was living had me on the slipperiest roads I have ever known and his fight to win me back had paid off and I was deeply grateful. My dad squeezed my hand a little right then and said that's the best words he could ever hear, I tried not to cry but when I saw his tears too I wept and he let the tears just roll down his face without any further words or expression.

You see I had been in these alcoholics anonymous rooms and heard many people share their stories of how they got sober and what it meant to them and how one of their big regrets was standing by a graveside of their close friend or wife or husband or father or mother and there they had their moment of trying to speak to their loved one and they wished they had not been such a drunk and had the chance to do it face to face with the person while they were alive. I was given this special moment to share with my dad and it uplifted me to a level I had never known before. I always felt I was more of a spiritual person than a bible basher type but God worked to help us bury any misconceptions between us that very day.

Me and my brothers had shared the laughs with dad now together at the dinner table when he was hopped up on the energy juice and individually by his bedside when he was in the down cycle. The cycle was energy first week and real low lows the following week and off to therapy again, it was a two week cycle for his chemo therapies. Soon to be introduced they had talked of additional radiation also, but not to worry they had new medicine now where he would not lose his hair, I know he was glad for that. In taking our turns at hanging out with dad and sitting with him bedside him at night we, me and my brothers had fallen in to a pattern by default, there was no plan but I would go out and meet my friend Donal and maybe go play some darts in the local pub because my brother was sitting in with dad, it worked wonders to have a little distraction from my friends at the time.

My wife's birthday was coming up in February and even though we telephoned and skyped almost every day, we wanted to be together and of course for her birthday it was only right. So my good friend Donal who worked for the airlines, yup the same one the man I had fished with as crew men together many years ago and since had taken the job in the airport and yes had flew out to my wedding to Irene to take photographs for me, well the very same he was able to score me a staff travel airline ticket from Dublin to LA for something like pay taxes only $140 so I made a plan with Irene we would be together for her birthday and we would do a long peaceful weekend together somewhere around the LA area.

Catalina Island became the venue, we met in LAX she flying in from San Francisco and me from Dublin. Mid-February 2005 we spent Irene's birthday on Catalina, the weather sucked and it was raining so heavy shopping mall roofs were collapsing in LA and we were out off the coast getting a good hammering from the weather. It was great to see my wife amidst this personal mess that was going on and spend this time with her and try and make her feel special too as it is not easy to juggle the two. The new woman whom I love so very much on the weekend of her birthday and the man whom I had his blood flow through my veins, however through opportunity and friends this was able to happen and we had a very nice peaceful weekend together that worked for both of us. The weekend went off without a glitch and because at that time of year would be very much an offseason time for Catalina island it was like we had the whole place to ourselves to do nothing except be together and be in love. Tell her I love her very much for the opportunity to spend with my dad and her to tell me she loved me very much and she was there for me all the way. I flew back to Dublin and she to San Francisco and I had a renewed energy to be with my dad and watch him be sick.

Now that I was in Ireland for this time I had been to Limerick to visit with Darra, we had spent a cool night together eating Chinese in his favourite local place and I went to a hotel and then came and watched him play hurling the following morning and I headed back to Dublin, but I had to tell him grand dad was sick and let him know that something was going on. So on saint Patrick's day in march 17th to be precise, I arranged for Darra to come up to Dublin with me and we would meet up with his cousin my brothers daughter Kessia and planned with my brother to take the children to the St. Patrick's day parade in Dublin city, just like dad used to take us when we were their age. A trip to McDonalds for the kids and out to home and hang out with their granddad. Dad was fading by this time in his treatment and was becoming a smaller framed man, you can tell someone is going through the sickness when their own head just starts looking too big for their body, the body is losing weight and he was gaunt in the face, but he shuffled over to the kitchen that day in his slippers to play and have fun with the grandchildren. I took a photo of Darra and dad that day as dad sat at the kitchen table and Darra stood beside him, for the times I was fishing and not home in Ireland it was dad who drove to Limerick to pick up Darra and take him to Dublin for the weekend, it was dad who kept the connection strong in my absence with Darra's mom and so to have a picture of the two men I loved in my life was a real important thing for my personal emotions, my son and my dad. The following week March 23rd 2005 my dad took his last breath in his bed around 10.30 pm at night. I have never felt so sad in my entire life.

The following morning arrangements needed to be made and it was like I was seeing the world in Technicolor, I went to the town of Skerries for a haircut in the morning as the funeral services people had removed the body and I felt horrible, sick in my stomach but thirsty with dry mouth and then, well I just saw the town and the people with some other form of colouring, Technicolor was the simplest way to describe it then, as we know today I was on high definition for some reason. Because of the catholic church and the traditions and this was holy week that year there are no mass services on good Friday so the wake or the laying out of my father went for two days, holy Thursday and good Friday with mass service to be Easter Saturday and that is when we laid his body to rest in our local graveyard. There was a slight mist on the ground that morning and people said as we carried his coffin along the laneway to the grave yard from their view point they could not see our feet because of the mist and it looked like we floated along the lane to the grave yard gates, a friend of my brother played the pipes and the crowd was there and all his friends and family members as me and my four brothers and our first cousin the next McNally boy as we saw it, carried him and we lowered him down, I could hear my brother Patrick heave in his throat as the pipes were playing and I almost broke to complete tears myself on hearing how close he was himself, I guess seeing as I had travelled from the states and he from Australia the pipes made the hair stand on our necks that morning to be grave side with our dad. That Saturday was a fine sunny day afterwards and it was back to the house for sandwiches and beers and teas and coffees and a large crowd was there, the house was full and the garden too. Darra had travelled the trip and his Na-Na and granddad too I was so happy Darra was fine and delighted to see Christy and Vera too.

The strange thing about the night Dad died was it had been my brother Johns turn to take a little break from it all and go and visit with his girlfriend who lived in Sweden, I had taken a break to spend Irene's birthday with her and on that Wednesday night I called John to tell him dad had taken his last breath, John was freaked out on the other end of the phone as I said, " he is gone John, he has taken his last breath" John asked me are you sure I said well I think so yes, John freaked "ah what the fuck are you telling me is he breathing or is he not" I said no John he is gone, the irony if there could be any irony was John had been the one at home calling me in San Francisco when this diagnosis and Cancer came into our family and now I was the one at home having to tell him he was dead. I returned to San Francisco to my wife and my life soon after, my dad was dead.

When I was home that year with my dad a funny piece that must be told, I met an old friend from school, I had been out at a local bar and this kid I had not seen since we played soccer back at ten years of age, well actually he was a classmate from the local school. I walked out from the night club bar and he was "well on" with a few beers in him, Aidan McNally, you are a fucker he said, you ruined our lives. I thought not more, never his why would he say this, he repeated it a few times being under the influence. Aidan seriously though you made our lives hell I said what are you talking about man, he said him and all my class mates from the first year of secondary school were never allowed to forget my name. He went on, do you remember that math class where the teacher surprised us with the test, remember you showed up for it and had been saying you should not have come for this. I said yes you have a good memory, oh he said it was not easy to forget, you got of course 100% in that test, we did not do so well. That teacher made fools of us and reminded us regularly, saying "Aidan mc Nally does not come to one class from one end of a semester to the next and he aces the exam, why are all you here every day if you cannot do better than a guy that never comes" the guy told me how the teacher belittled them regularly over my achievement in a math test and they were not allowed to live it down for a long time. That was about the only funny piece of the battle with cancer and memory of fondness of the time, just wanted to share that laugh.

Chapter 28.

On my return to San Francisco I decided to work every day god sends at that time and the years of laying around and playing horses and sports was something not for me anymore, I still was involved in being a bookie and taking bets over the internet at the time but someone else was running that and handling it for me. I worked with my friend Adrian and we did more and more installations of astro turf and fake lawns and indoor football pitches and putting green installations at people's homes and with that came additional hard scraping jobs and laying cobble stone driveways. We decided to make a company Double A Paving. Naturally Aidan and Adrian for this we needed a license to operate and be an active recognized construction type company, so the study began. I was back studying engineering and construction plans and drawings and all the stuff that my dad had done all his life about figuring out and designing and plans and permission and construction industry stuff all in front of me now on a daily basis. I passed the California state license exam in about twenty minutes and I was away to operate. I got really big into the engineering and construction of retaining walls and laying cobble stone driveways and the company took off immediately. There was a boom time at that time that I remember and work was piling up people wanted Double A Paving for the job, the more work we did the more little fancy things like a built in barbecue or a fountain or pond or pillars at the end of the driveway with the mail box set into the stone. Drainage issue on people's property that was undermining their home or driveway. Things got technical and jobs kept on coming. I recall sitting in meetings with project managers and engineers and architects and advising them of why they were wrong and using the plans and the technical details to explain to them why. I felt so good hoping that dad could look down upon me and be proud that I was studying architects drawings and designing peoples back yard "outdoor living spaces" I thought this is in my genes it is so easy to listen to the clients wants and then turn them into reality for them and dad would be so proud how I can show up to any meeting and read the plans and know what to do.

Myself and Irene were going strong and still no interest to have babies and with some extra money rolling in we used our tax return to buy her a nice new car and took a couple of nice vacations, Cabo in Mexico was one five day mini vacation and another time I had wanted to visit Jamaica and so we did a luxurious stay there for seven days. Irene loved me and I loved her and life was rolling merrily along I was able to take a couple of extra trips to Ireland to visit with Darra and sent him gifts and clothes for Christmas and his birthdays now and he was getting older, too fast. He called me up one evening well what he would do is send me a text saying "can you talk" and I would get a phone card and call him back. George's son B and his cousin Omar worked at the local store now by the apartment and I would call them and have them scratch off the number and tell it or text it too me and I would call Darra, I remember one evening when we were speaking he was asking me about the cars and the movie stars and the dollars and the sports and all the basketball games I would go to and all interested in the NBA and I knew it was because he was out with a friend or his friends and wanted to be cool as they were all saying hello that evening. One evening when we spoke he started asking me what was San Francisco like, and how far is the city and where I live from the airport and how much would it costs in a taxi, that evening I was expecting him to show up at the door the next morning the way he was asking the questions.

Those phone calls were great and technology moving so fast I was able to speak with him about things of school and girls and sports and we had agreed on some rules, we agreed or he agreed with me, 5 rules well the first and had been a long running thing was always to show respect to his mother, I used to always tell him that and it was like he could repeat or speak it with me simultaneously when I would say it as it was the number one rule going way back, so in addition to that one we had 5 more.

1. Your family comes first and no one can come between him and his little brother and

sister, that's right he had a little sister now too.

2. Nobody could come between him and his school work
3. Nobody could come between him and his sports training
4. He had to be respectful first to everyone
5. He would never tell lies and we would never keep secrets.

To these rules he adhered strongly and he understood although he asked me one evening when we were not even talking about anything of rules to clarify for him what did I mean when I said nobody could come between him and these things, I explained as I knew he was having all the girls chase him now that if he had or must have a girlfriend that wants all off his time and attention and she request he doesn't spend his night with his family, then she is no good. That if he has a girlfriend that wants him to hang out with her instead of study, she has to go. That if he finds himself a girlfriend that wants Thursday night to be him spending time with her and not go to practice for the sports, she has to go. The important one was the lies we could not have secrets as there had been a time earlier where his mom had said to me he had gotten in some trouble earlier in school that day and it involved a kid getting hit in the face and Darra got in trouble for it. When Darra came to the phone that night I asked him what happened in school that day, he said nothing; I said come on man I want to know I heard you are in trouble. He said yeah but I am already grounded for it so what is the point. I explained, "Darra you will never do any wrong in my eyes and I will always take your side as long as you tell me the truth, you will never be in trouble with me and I will never be mad at you for anything. Providing you tell me the truth" he went ahead and told me what happened, a boy had taken his friends ball and he didn't like to see his friend sad for this and so he went to the big bully and took the ball back, through the other kid grabbing the ball as well the ball bounced between their heads while Darra was wrestling to take it back and it burst his nose, it was an accident but he said I hit him. We discussed as we had many times before how Darra was bigger than most kids his age and he had much stronger arms, muscles and body and so he would always have to take an easier approach to people as they might not be as strong as him and so in order not to do any damage to anyone, Darra understood this and he always knew that if any problem that occurred, we would discuss it and learn from it and learn to know the wrong piece of anything or situation and the right thing in any situation and for those reasons I would never be mad at him and never judge him as long as, he always told the truth.

I was able to take some trips home more often now as the money my company was earning was good and I used it to run and see and spend time with him. I would fly into Dublin spend a night with my mother and then try and get Darra for a week if I could or whatever worked into his mom's plans and have our time together. I had been worried about him when he had started to be an altar boy for the masses in church and all the media was full of news and stories about sex offenses within the church and what do you tell your son without breaking their innocence, how do you discuss the horrible sexual abuse that was all coming to light about priests. We discussed it like this, if anyone every touches you inappropriately, of course he wanted to know what is inappropriately, so I had to explain if anyone ever asks you to do anything that is not right or does not feel right or you find yourself in any situation where an adult is trying to touch your penis or your ass or tries to show you naked magazines or they want to be naked around you, you have my full permission to kick that person in the teeth as hard as you can and I mean break their teeth, smash their mouth wide open to be sure two or three teeth are missing, call me and I will be on the next plane and you will not be in trouble for this.

He laughed and said "yeah right I will never get away with busting someone in the face" I explained to him if any adult finds themselves with smashed in teeth because you did it I will know why and it will be the adult who will have to explain to everybody why you did it in the first place, remember that. It will not be you who has to explain anything Darra, it will be the adult who will have to explain to everyone what they were doing or trying to do at the time, but remember it is not about bust them in the head, you must draw back a kick so hard that at least three teeth come out and really make it hurt. You will never be in trouble with me and I will make sure you are in trouble with nobody else should this ever occur. Luckily Darra never bust any body's teeth out.

I remember Darra was a bit older maybe 13 now and I went to visit him and he had been talking about his girlfriend a lot lately and this particular trip when I picked him up it was like he wanted to come spend time with me in Dublin but he was going to be missing his girlfriend and he was texting her every five minutes and no way would he share his phone. So that night in the middle room at my mother's house in the two single beds I said to him as he turned out the light, now what do you know about sex? He said "oh no not the talk, I heard this a hundred times from everyone" I thought how funny is that; they call it "the talk" still. I said seriously what do you mean, he explained "I have had the talk, in school from the religion teacher, in school from the guidance counsellor, at home from mam, in church when we altar boys" I told him oh well I guess you definitely don't want it from me then, but I didn't say anything about "the talk" I asked what do you know about sex, but if you know it all I told him it is ok, I just wanted to offer my knowledge should you have anything you are unclear about or have been too afraid to ask anybody so you could use me to explain it to you. That night I thought immediately well that was easy gets me off the hook in the sexual education part of things. Then he said "well there is one thing" I was cringing in the dark of the room in the other bed and trying to bite the duvet cover and not laugh or blurt out, "holy shit" I answered go ahead. The question came and I was biting down on the duvet, the thing was stuffed completely in my mouth as I didn't want him to notice me breathing differently or about to laugh, and so he flowed and continued to ask his question. Now I did not think it would be an easy question nor did I think it would be too difficult only the fact we were about to start talking about this. "When a girl says she wants to do it and then she says she doesn't want to do it, what does she really want to do?" "Yes she wants or No she doesn't"? I could not get any more duvet into my mouth and there was a longer than normal pause so I could compose my voice to give an explanation. I went on to turn the conversation quickly and gave some generic answer and continued mostly on a talk about hygiene and why waiting for sex was probably just the best option to take, it worked out a good conversation actually and now Darra understood why I wash my hands before going to pee and after. He seemed satisfied with our conversation as we had discussed the cleanliness importance of fooling around and protection and I discussed with him how easy it is for girls to encounter such simple infections of the urinary tract and how embarrassing it would be or might be to be sitting in his girlfriend's house for Sunday lunch with the family and the girl has returned from a doctor's appointment with her mam on the Saturday before and how the parents may look to him as a filthy little chap who was fooling around with their daughter, we laughed as to that would not be a good situation to be in. I think he got the message, stay away for a while and wait a year or two more.

On the drive home to Limerick that Sunday, before I would return to the states that week, Darra was super anxious as the county board of the Limerick hurlers was going to meet and on this night they will decide who is going to make the team for the Limerick hurling team of underage players. Darra had been training hard and been to the trials for the team during the year. No word had come yet and as we drove the road from Dublin to Limerick that evening and as luck would have it when we pulled into the town of New Castle west, the call came. Darra's mom had just received the word; Darra had been selected to the county team. He was beaming "this is unbelievable" "this is absolutely amazing" he kept repeating things like this and he was texting his friends as his best friend had made the team too and so they would both be together through the journey and the experience. We got to Darra's home and he invited me in to stop and take a tea or something I said No and got out to give him a hug and he came around the car from the passenger seat of the car and threw his arms open and just hugged me so hard, he was becoming a man now with his big arms and the length of them he had no problem embracing me in a full wrap around, Darra's words at the time of that hug, "Dad this is the best night of my life" I hugged him back and agreed I was so happy for him to make the team and that all his hard work had paid off and now he just had to keep it up and take it all to the next level. When my son hugged me that night I felt his sincerity and his emotions were high on his recent news, this was the pinnacle of his life right now and cloud nine was where he was walking, I felt special to be able to share that moment with my baby. Though grown and growing very fast these days, this was still my baby and he was so happy and I had not been around him every year and missed so many things as I was his father at the end of a phone or a weeklong visit or a parcel in the post, but this night the hairs stood on the back of my neck. I drove back to Dublin that night and was so proud of him, for one making the team but for the most important reason he was a genuine man and he knew how to express himself and show his emotions and hug me so well, Darra was becoming a true man and a fine fit tall and strong man with goals and dedication that were beginning to pay off for him this early in life. He could recognize it and see life is good and even when you put in the hard work life is great.

I headed back for the states that week to take a driveway project from a client and landed a new retaining wall project so even in the downward economy I still was picking up some of the scraps of work available.

Myself and Irene had separated at this stage in our life and we had agreed we were not going to work any longer, she accused me of cheating on her and she could not be with me anymore, I said I cannot be with someone who is going to take such a strong stance of this idea of me cheating on them and I cannot be together any more either and we split. We had gone through the fights and the makeup sex and we had had nasty name calling fights and we were drifting apart. We carried on a sexual relationship for a while to see could we maybe make it work but we could not so by around august 2011 I was on a trip out of the country to Ireland and I would not be returning as I had taken a job offer for 6 months in Costa Rica. Irene actually dropped me to the airport that day but we were fully separated by that time and the little hope we had to resolve this was down to low percentages. The construction projects had become non-existent as the economies of the world were under the biggest recession pressure on a hundred years or so and the point to keep staff and an office and things related to my little empire I had built was shot to pieces. Off I went to Ireland that day again to visit with Darra and from Ireland I would fly straight to costa Rica to take this new job, it was to come with $600 a week with my accommodations paid for. I was ready for a new challenge now working on the other side of the phone lines as to those I had bet on before.

When I got to Ireland, Darra was spending two weeks of his summer holidays from school in a Gaeltacht summer school; I thought this was amazing as I had done the same thing when I was about his age. I wanted to spend time with him before heading to Central America and let him know that I would not be visiting until sometime in march or April of the next year as the job I was taking would run that time of an unwritten or informal contract type to run at least six months. Of course I wanted to continue seeing him more and more and this was just the path of employment I had entered in to that would be the first time in a long time and actually the first time in my life I would be in a position where it meant being in an office every day to work on a computer and behind a desk. The job keeping up with all the latest and greatest in the sports betting industry and the back end of the online gaming industry to provide customers who make wagers online over the internet with support and a voice at the end of a phone that knew the game of betting and knew how to speak to the people who used such methods to bet on sports.

Of course I did not explain all the details to Darra when I saw him just that I was on my way to make work and I wouldn't be home to hang out with him until next year.

Darra got to call me from the Gaeltacht and we arranged a meet. He and the Limerick panel / team were going to play a match on the outskirts of Dublin/ Kildare area in a clubhouse grounds known as commercials. The match was set for the team to travel up by bus from Limerick, go play the game against Dublin under age team then they had activities planned for that afternoon in the Wicklow Mountains and they would return to their hotel and stay the night. The team, the Limerick team and Darra was one of them. So I showed up at the commercials grounds and they were togging off in the dressing rooms, Darra came out to me and as this was like a test match or just a friendly preparation match the coaches were giving everyone a chance to show their stuff and get a run. The coaches could now test strategies in this friendly game and see the players play in prep for the season to come, as this is how I understood it. Darra asked the coach could he wait a bit and go in in a while as he was visiting with his dad, and we walked the side-line and chatted. These guys were fourteen now and the kids on the side lines and those in the field were big strong men already, thick hairy legs and muscles. My baby was definitely not a baby any more he had found a place for himself and I could see how his friends on the team respected him too and the coaches, they had high admiration for him.

Darra's best friend was on the team also and he was in the game playing that day and Darra called me down the side-line a bit and explained to me the weirdest thing. His friend Kieran's sister had died a little while ago and nobody knew why, he said she just collapsed walking out the door to school one morning or something, She was 19 only I believe and Darra said to me he found it hard to be there for his friend because the whole situation was weird, one minute she was there and next she was gone, something about no heart attack or anything just a sudden death they were calling it. I said back to him was she poisoned or something, no he said, just no explanation. One minute walking out the door the next minute dead. Darra said how the whole parish by his house was in shock and it was a terrible time and that his friend Kieran was a tough nut to battling on through it. Kieran and Darra were best friends and so it was weird like Darra had said.

The Dublin team put in a big half forward and so, the coach said Darra come on its your time, get in there and mark that fella, this other kid on the field was bigger than me and I could see Darra putting the moves on him shuffling the feet and working the elbows and keeping the player tightly marked and just making his game uncomfortable. They went up for the ball and Darra did not shy away but he needed a little more meat on his bones to tackle a kid of that size, now Darra at 14 was touching close to 6 feet and was broadening out in the chest and arms but this other kid was, well he looked to be 25 to be honest and when they went up for that ball, Darra came away the worst with a thud to the ground, he came up holding his arm and the ref gave a free out against the mammoth guy from the dub team. I was ready to go in and beat the shit out of the other guy but kept a lid on it, this was my instinct on the first time I ever saw someone push my baby to the ground. It was a great day watching Darra play that day. After the game the teams changed and came out to their bus in the parking lot and Darra was ok with spending the day with me and I encouraged him to go with the team as the activities planned for them that afternoon would be great team building when you not only play and train together but you have fun together too. Darra came out from the dressing room and toward the team bus where I was waiting in the parking lot. I gave him some money into his hand as he approached and most of the team were already on the bus and waiting for the last few stragglers, and without hesitation Darra spread the big wing span and gave me a big hug and I hugged him back. We said we would be in touch, I was surprised but delighted that Darra had no fears of all the lads watching from the bus and he was able to give me my place as his daddy in front of all and had no awkwardness in him at all, what a fine man he was that day.

I returned home to my mam's house and got ready for the travel to the new job in costa Rica, myself and Darra shared a few calls before I left and he had told me how great that day had been with the team and he was so glad I made it to his game. I had now seen him over the years, play hurling as an 8 year old, soccer as they won the cup in the schools probably when they were twelve and now here in his fine hour with the county team. I was so proud of him as his efforts really were paying off.

Chapter 29.

I boarded the plane for Madrid Spain out of Dublin and this route requires a night stay in Madrid and then connects to the airline Iberia in Madrid the following morning to fly 10 or so hours to Central America, San Jose Costa Rica. August 2011 and I was on my travels again.

When I arrived I was met at the airport by the owner of the company who I had had a dinner meeting with in California some months previously and his administrative office manager who was doing the driving. The assistant had found me an apartment to live in and had located me in a safe neighbourhood near to a hotel with a casino in the lobby restaurant to the front and bar. She didn't know who I was or what might be my taste so she tried to fit me in to a nice accommodation as they had all been prepared that a new replacement boss was coming and they wanted to treat me right.

Flying in to Costa Rica I could see a lot of red tin roofs as we approached the runway and this, was very new and strange to see so many houses from corrugated sheets of roofing, in Ireland this is a cow shed I thought oh, shit, this place is poor. Being the new guy around many people had their advice about do this, don't do that, go here don't go there. I really was only pretending to listen and making peoples acquaintances for the first time a smile and a few words were polite enough from me I thought. The office was pretty cool, a call centre for taking customers calls and there were the tech side of things, the administrative side of things and my job was going to be holding on to customers really, keeping them happy when they called as many customers didn't like to speak to someone who spoke English but with a Spanish accent. So for all purposes this was going to be my job in the end, take calls from the difficult customers and the higher echelon of customers to let them know they were in good hands. Some of the staff there in the call centre had this idea I was to be their new boss but I had no real interest in being any body's boss but the owner and I shared a few nights out that week as he was there for a week to greet me and show me the ropes and explain what he was looking for. I had told him I have no interest in firing people if that is what you want me to do and he said no but employees had to be handled strictly here in Costa

Rica or they will just take advantage of you. He left the country and I went to work. There was nothing new for me to learn about the betting industry I had been around this since I was 11 or 12 years of age and with Darra's granddad and all the horse racing stuff I knew how to make a book as they call it. Then with all my own success in gambling on sports within the United States, this kind of operation I could handle with my eyes closed. I was still in communications with my wife and she looked at the possibility of transferring her job as she was now working for the united states government and the possibility of her moving to Costa Rica by taking a US government job here with the embassy or something gave light to an idea of us trying again. However I think we both knew it was an idea that we both wanted but both were reluctant at the same time. I would go to work and return home in the evenings and then reflect a lot on my time in the relationship with my wife and the years of fun we had spent together.

We had lived an ideal life, with always having enough money and taking weekend breaks and road trips, looking back I could count up where we had been and the countries visited, Spain, Ireland, England, Holland, France, Jamaica, Mexico some more than once but that was just the international trips we had done New York, Washington dc, that trip was because Irene had run the marine corps marathon one year, I was proud of her at the finish line that afternoon. We had done a nice trip to New Orleans a train ride to Oregon, Portland to visit some friends and some road trips to Texas. On a couple of occasion we took a flight from San Francisco to LA and spent the night at Hollywood park Friday night horse racing and this was luxurious too although we didn't win it was a weekend break and a hotel and all the feelings of vacation and so as I sat reflecting. I explained to her many times we have had a very spoiled time together where we have eaten wherever we wanted and gone where ever we wanted and we were quite spoiled in our life. The time came where we just had no real focus on the relationship and we drifted though we had a good 11 years together through all these trips and fancy living and going to sporting events and sitting court side at the basketball games and doing the VIP status of anything or anywhere we went, NFL games, MLB games, NBA games, concerts in Vegas. That reminded me that the weekend we went to Vegas to see Gwen Stefani was a great concert and Irene was such a fan of hers just another great night, a part of our life style of living in those times. The highlights were not the trip to New Orleans and following our favourite team from the bay area to watch and be front and centre of the game in our VIP seating, but more the fact that I was having fun and enjoying myself and my wife was right there with me doing the same. That is what did it for me I had a good partner who loved to have fun and be alive and feel alive. Many times I would be somewhere or doing something for example, myself and Irene flew into LA to go and watch our team the Warriors play the clippers one Friday evening, the rental car was a service that meets you at the airport curb side with your car as soon as you walk out of the terminal and we had this nice escalade monstrosity of a car and off to the game, we always bought seats close to the bench of the team and shouted them on. Then for the rest of the weekend cruising around LA checking out the sites in our luxury car and staying in nice hotels and being together finding nice restaurants, eating and enjoying our time. When doing such weekend trips to follow the team and attending NBA games is a special highlight as it is an awesome experience to be at the game. I always remember the feeling to myself that someday soon I will show all this to Darra and do it all over again because I was on a high with the glam and the glitz of everything and can you imagine a young guy growing up in Limerick attending an NBA game courtside and slapping hands with the players and talking to the players after the game. Riding around Hollywood in an escalade and cruising the areas and surrounding hills of Beverly Hills. Or even back in San

Francisco my neighbours from the block on central hanging out and going to VIP parties of rappers and actors, I always felt Darra is going to be impressed and blown away at this and so I got an extra kick from it like a child when I would think of when he comes to visit how he will be really blown away.

Me and my friend Russ from central had even thought to make an outfit and call ourselves the road warriors, to plan trips and be the home fans on the away game as our team was the warriors and we liked travelling out of state and supporting the team in their away games. Arenas we have been too are many Cleveland to see them play LeBron, Boston, new Orleans, phoenix, Washington, LA new York, the list goes on but we, well me, I had a great time and many times it was me and Russ and many times me, Russ and Irene and many other times me and Irene.

I always thought on my dad in those time too, not just about when Darra comes to visit in the future what it will be like but what my dad would think if he saw me standing next to Cindy Crawford in blue lounge in LA, my dad would like that or having the back stage wrist band and access all areas at a snoop dog rap concert or being on the guest list on NBA all-star weekend break at Bun B's private party. These are things that would blow Darra away. The lifestyle was fun and this was how I was going to show Darra around California.

I didn't have Darra with me then obviously and so I had a surrogate son, my friend Russ was a single dad and raising his son lil Russ as he was Russell too. So lil Russ got the benefit of being the kid I brought many places to the games to sit court side and chit chat with the players or get their autographs after the game, lil Russ used to call me uncle Aidan, now the funny part was Russ went to a catholic school in the Richmond district of San Francisco and used to tell all his school mates he was half Irish because his uncle is Irish. Lil Russ is a coloured kid, an African American to give the proper title and so one day at their gym when he was playing in a basketball game himself, he must have been 9 or 10 at the time, he called me from the seating area to follow him, then outside the door to where his class mates were and he stood there, saying, "see this is my uncle and he is Irish" and all the kids ran away. Russell knew it in his heart I treated him like any uncle would and for many times he represented Darra to me and so I never missed a birthday or graduation or his basketball games or an opportunity to take him somewhere and do something fun. Irene was very fond of lil Russ too and so he used to call her his aunty also. Me and his Dad Russ spent many trips together here there and everywhere and he would help me with office work for the construction company and we would check on his grandma and our lives became intertwined as good good friends really. Russ was someone I could count on and I was someone he could count on too.

All these people were gone now and I was in Costa Rica, I had lonely evenings reflecting on all those people George from the store had become a great friend over the years too and his entire family welcomed me, I was a regular arrival to the family events, church, the crab feeds they would have or his son Spiro (B) or his nephew Omar all had become good friends, my mechanic was George's nephew Sam and there were many cousins but the family of Palestinian Arabs welcomed me and made me feel very at home on any event we spent together. Sometimes you just meet good people, I had the greatest luck of meeting these people along my journey and it was great to know and befriend and be part of their lives. Russell had me at so many "African American" parties it was not even funny even in the ghettos Russ might have a cousin there and some form of something or other was going on and every one welcomed me, even though I was white it didn't matter. Aidan was one of the families.

Funny story about my friend Kenneth from Loughshinny, one time he had come to visit me in San Francisco as he liked to get some of the good California weed to smoke so he came to visit a couple of times but he had come to visit and it happened to be the week of lil Russ's birthday and so that Saturday evening we went and had a meal and brought a gift and it was lil Russ and his mom and her sister and husband. His grandmother was there and his great grandmother myself and Kenneth from Loughshinny, all laughing and having a nice meal and a fun evening all for lil Russ birthday. When we were travelling in the car back to the city of San Francisco across the bay bridge I said to Kenneth now that wasn't too bad was it, as he had spent the day saying he would just stay at home and get stoned and I could come and get him later, but I dragged him along anyway. Kenneth had his joint going and he turned to me driving and said "that was fucking great" I said what, he told me he never imagined in his life to be sitting down at a night out to dinner with a whole black family, that this is not the everyday thing in Ireland and he felt like he was in the movie "Big Mommas house" because of how lil Russ grandma's were, I laughed at him and he just kept getting high. I never noticed colour and thought it funny in a strange way that yes for someone from Ireland this could be a little strange but for me it was just normal life.

In Costa Rica there are a lot of beautiful women and girls and the nice thing is they look naturally beautiful not needing make up and all the trimmings to look good, they just have the thing that I find attractive I do not know what that is but it is something, skin tone, eye colour hair colour I really do not know but in my office there were many girls and the one that took my eye well to be honest two of the girls were good looking to me but one of them was a little out there with a slight hippy expression to her life and it was the turn off point and another was just simply beautiful to me, trouble with this was me as the acting boss at the time and the person the owners wanted me to replace and take over from or demote rather was the older brother of the girl who I like to spend time daydreaming about. How do I combat this as I have to work side by side with this guy and I want to get to know this girl. Not an easy task as I do not put everything out there on Front Street and I do not make known my feelings to everyone around me and so I thought this will be a hard task. I have to try and befriend her without anyone noticing, how do I do that, we exchanged a few glances and we spoke a few words in the kitchen area at work and I would ask her to run an errand or two for me from time to time, I had already been warned by her older brother. Well in not so many words exactly but he had said in a casual way, oh boy my sister, she is trouble and she makes bad decisions many times and so he has had his hands full with her all her life. I took it to be his protective older brother way of giving the subtle hint, stay away.

Well I continued working away with this sports book stuff and really didn't have much of a life, I got to go visit the beach with one of the workers in another office one day, it was my day off and he said he would drive to the beach and so that was fun, Costa Rica is like a tropical paradise, it stays sunny and nice most of the year and then it has a rainy season where it rains a lot and the thunder is unbelievable but the temperature does not change much throughout the year, always somewhere between 19 and 25 degrees maybe a really exceptional hot day of 31 or 32 but never dropping to cold temperatures. My favourite fruit of all time pineapple and this country has tons of the stuff and the smoothie drinks they make from fresh pineapples, for me they are to die for. I replaced my addiction to coca cola to these fruit drinks. If you want a sure fire way to lose weight, my schedule was this, swim in the morning in the pool, take a midmorning breakfast whatever I felt like eating, walk about 2 miles and quench the thirst with a pineapple smoothie and eat whatever was needed, excess fat drops off really quickly.

So at work I had braved the idea to search for Carmen on face book, now I knew her full name and I could search for her, but she was not using a simple face book name and so I just asked her for it, we had started taking smoke breaks together and chatting a little bit and so it was good, I was happy to go in pursuit of this woman, I got to know a little about her but I did not want to be obvious to her older brother as I did not feel right and did not know a straight forward way to tell him, hey I am digging your sister right now is that cool? So I asked her if she would like to meet on my day off and make a date and we did, we went to a chicken restaurant, "rostipollos" they call it and I went all excited to go and hang out with this girl, we took the lunch and chatted and walked through the park and sat on the benches and I got the real feeling she wanted to sit close to me and the potential was there to maybe kiss and I was just a touch, well not shy more like slow and wanted to see does this girl want what I want ? A partner or is she just into having a fling or what is the deal.

The park was nice that day and in our conversation and flirting that was going on she made it clear that she was not looking for a daddy to her son, as she had a 3 year old son and she was very happy being an independent mom who loved her son very much but she had not been in any relationship for a while now and was interested in dating, so with that being said I knew yes I could hang out with this girl and see where it goes. I had an attraction to her looks and her style and her laugh and I was "into" her. The weird thing was she was into me too and so there were some sparks there from the very beginning. For some reason we both agreed that, well more her than me, that we should wait to tell her brother as in my mind maybe nothing ever happens and there is no need to make him upset with her or anything and through time he would learn I am a good guy and responsible and a good guy to actually take care of his sister. So we started hanging out on lunch breaks and I invited her and her son out for dinner and we went to a ribs place that have a real life size pig and it is hairy as part of their décor and her son was loving petting it and he was climbing everywhere like a monkey and I made jokes this is a monkey and she was upset but she was enjoying the evening. They went home in a taxi and so I headed back to my apartment, a nice date had been had. November was here now and I called Darra for his birthday and he asked me why the funny number and I told him I am in Costa Rica, remember I told you I was taking a new job well I am in Costa Rica, he said oh that's weird I didn't know it was there. I could tell he was a little not upset but his tone was that I was hiding something from him or something, I was not hiding anything I just did not go into the big full details, the conversation was the usual and I had told him how it would be maybe February when I would get to see him and he told me how the hurling and all the schooling was going great and his girlfriend was good and the family were good. I had asked him was he still respecting mammy as now he was 15 and of course at 15 it can be tough, he said for sure, he told me how he was late for practice or to go to his practice and because he gave some back talk he said how mammy had no problem giving him a good slap across the ear that other evening, I laughed and said good, you are not too big yet, he laughed too. My baby was now 15 amazing. I was starting to fall in love and pineapple drinks were delicious. Here we are again with new life, new country, new love blooming; job is good and why not enjoy the place and make this home.

December came and one of our co-workers was leaving to get married in the United States and so for his last night he invited everybody to his house for drinks and a little party. I had said I would not be going as I had become used to my little life in my apartment and I would go home and visit the casino and eat the little tapas that came around and play a few games and go home and sleep, pretty simple were the evenings then I had a nice apartment now I had moved from the first place that had been arranged for me, it was a condo type place with the pool and a nice two bedroom condominium.

I had been to one party already that week as another co-worker was getting ready for Christmas and they had a little get together, and that evening Carmen masterminded herself to be in my taxi to share the ride home, we got to my place and I paid the cab for her to go home too, I think she may have thought I was going to invite her into my house but I was not ready to go there and she had a few drinks, I was into her but did not want to be having drunken sex and have a relationship that started there. So this second party they were all putting the pressure on me to go and I said no. I finished work about ten pm and headed home by 10.30 I was bored and called Marco and said, alright man give me the directions to your house and I will come. He was happy and I went to his house, nice layout larger open style patio area or garage area with TV on the wall a bar for drinks and a pool table.

When there I was playing pool and Carmen wanted to play, she wanted to play with me, but we stuck with the pool for now and the night ended, on the way home one of the guys I worked side by side with was driving and so five of us were in the car. Two got dropped off and that left me and Carmen, the driver had said to me earlier, she had said she wanted to be dropped off with me at my place, I thought hmmm I don't know about that too much.

We got to my apartment and out she came and we went in and then it was a long conversation night, she told me some stuff about her sons dad and what she thought and I gave the other side of the fence story as how I related things about Darra and how it is important to have the involvement and she said his dad just doesn't care. We talked about some of the staff and she brought me up to speed on any of the gossip, I told her we could sleep together but sex was not a good idea and I could see she was disappointed but she tried not to show it and we slept. The very next day at 3pm when her brother was leaving for the day I walked out the front down the stairs from the office with him and explained, hey before you hear any rumours or anything your sister stayed at my place last night and I wanted to tell you that nothing happened and she and I talked quite a bit, I said look I just want you to know before people start making stories, I have been hanging out with her a little bit and I don't want you to think I am not being respectful of you in this. Let's see if anything develops but just to not allow rumours to grow legs. Her brother was looking like he was embarrassed a bit but took it well and headed off.

On my day off the following week, Carmen ducked out of work and came over to my apartment, she showed up and we were ready and we tore into each other like animals, hot steamy fiery sex with tons of passion, it was good well worth the wait and we really enjoyed each other. She returned back to work and I spent my day off feeling great relaxing in the pool thinking about her and how I really really liked this girl.

That weekend I finished up work and went and spent the night at her place and we continued with more of the same, it was officially on and we were loving each other, something good was happening and we were two people getting involved and things felt right. I wanted to find a way and a time to let her brother know and then she wanted to keep things kind of quiet at work for now. It was fun I was liking this girl and she was liking me so what's to lose, go for it I thought, she is younger than me but she has some great looks and qualities and I could make something of this.

Chapter 30.

On Sundays I used to work from 11pm through 7 am due to some accounting for the week and that was my shift, so tired as all hell on Monday morning the guy leaving for the states, it was going to be his last night working with me and he drove me home close to my apartment and I walked up the hill from where he had dropped me off. On my way my cell phone was ringing from one of the guys who worked in the sales department of the office and said to me, hey I think your brother is looking for you, some guy John came on the customer service chat and is asking for you, he wants to get a hold of you, he told me that he had left a number. The guy from the office was Chris I had met him the first day I flew in and we had gone out a night or two over the short time four months I had been in Costa Rica, we would take smoke breaks together and discuss the job and have a laugh as to who we were and so in the office as far as circle of friends he was my friend. Now he was calling me to say some guy John is looking for me. So I took the number and got home to my apartment pretty tired but I better find out what is up with John.

I called the office and had them transfer my call to call Sweden as this was the cheapest way to make international calls by going through the office line,

I speak with John and he just is in bits, and telling me to call home, the conversation went something like this,

"Hey man what's up?" "Hey can you call home please and speak to mam"

John tell me what's wrong,

I can't Aidan just call home and talk to mam please.

John I am on a phone line that could cut off any minute just tell me, is it nana has nana passed away?

Please oh Aidan I can't as he wept please just call home please.

John, pull your-self together and tell me, what is going on is nana dead?

Aidan I don't have the words and he sobbed and he sobbed and said please call mam straight away, please just call mam.

I was getting angry with him I did not know what to think, I figured Na-Na is gone and they are a mess at home in Dublin, John is a weeping mess, ok I thought let's not get mad at him for it, whatever it is, it is definitely hard for him to tell me.

Ok John, just relax calm down and tell me what's up, is it Brian? Patrick in Australia, what's up? Just tell me please.

Aidan it's your son, Darra is dead, Aidan I am sorry please call home and speak to mam.

John don't you fuck with me right now, I am on a stupid phone that can cut off, make sure you are not trying to be some way sickly funny here.

Aidan I am sorry, I don't know he passed away please phone to mam at home please.

I hung up the phone with John right then and walked up and down the hallway of my apartment, I wanted to punch the walls, my fists were clenched, it was 12th of December 2011 and I had just had the sharpest dagger in my heart ever. I paced and picked up the phone, I called to the office and had them make a transfer to a number in Dublin Ireland. I called my mother, the tears flowed out of me trying to listen between her crying of what happened, that Clare had called my mother and told her and the next door neighbours who had been well like Darra's step cousins for want of a better word, had come to sit with my mam, They do not know, they are doing an autopsy and they are waiting to find out, he did not wake up to go school today. They do not know, Clare had said she wants this funeral quick quick quick she is distraught, she found him dead in his bed Monday morning when he didn't respond or she couldn't hear him in the shower getting ready for school. I cried hard, I cried and said I will be there soon, I called to a friend in California to book me a flight, he couldn't answer his phone that morning but responded with a text to say he had five grand waiting for me at the office just go and get it and do what I need to do. I telephoned the office again and the guy who was answering the local calls phone line I said to him as calmly as possible, I need you to come and pick me up and take me to the office right now, he said all casual as he was in his nature, sure I will come and get you after I do a lunch run for the gang, I said calmly, My son has died I need to get on a plane come and get me NOW!

He then replied. Pack a bag and I will be right there. Joe came and got me and I had tried to make another call to Clare through the office phone and Frank who was the mornings guy was trying to patch all my calls through, he stopped for a moment and said, everything ok, I was crying hard and told him, my son has passed away and I don't know why and I need to get to the airport immediately. Can you try the number again? I got to the office where, Frank and Kim and Joe were in the office and Chris who had told me my brother was looking for me, was looking at me as I walked in and saw me and wondered what was up, he knew something was wrong. I was in the office while they looked for flights and counted out 5 grand, there was nothing but flights for thousands of dollars thru online search engines. So Frank decided lets go to the airline Iberia offices in the city as they will be able to do a better price but looks like the most direct is Iberia leaving at 6pm today and then connect from Spain to Ireland. Everything else has 30 hour lay overs.

We stopped at American airlines office as it was close to the office and they wanted 7 grand to fly through New York and Paris and all kinds of messing. I said to the guy behind the counter, I thought there are emergency fares for flights in bereavement status. Why can you not get me to New York right now and a flight to Dublin, he said the bereavement specials only are for flights that originate from within the United States. I said this is American airlines right? I said to him if I ever meet you in civilian clothes on the street run, because right now I want to punch your face in for not trying to help and left. Frank drove to where we believed Iberia airlines was but they had moved to beside the airport apparently and we were stuck in the Christmas season traffic that was already under way and a whole bunch of down pours of rain, when it rains here in Costa Rica it is a deluge and then stops usually but this one was coming down hard and when that happens traffic gets worse. We made it to the airport, and the Iberia desk explained No there is no way to purchase a ticket at the airport, we would have to go to their main office which is just around the airport back along the freeway we had come in on and it is at the offices by the end of the runways. Not within the airport property but beside it.

We got there a little traffic again and walked into the office, they said they had 3 seats left and could get me on the plane although I will have to run as it is now four o clock.

From the office earlier, I had managed to speak with Clare on her cell phone and she said briefly, he is gone and I am here picking out a coffin, she was in an awful way and I told her I will be there but if you can't wait I understand. As I was leaving the office, I was able to tell Chris, who had a genuine look of concern that, my son has died. On leaving the office I left through a side door to avoid the crowd of staff and Carmen just happened to be returning from the rest room, she looked and saw me crying and did not understand what's up, but everybody knew something was going on.

The booking was ready with Iberia and the lady called the gate and explained she had a late arriving passenger with one bag to check in and please hold the gate he will run if he has to. Then Frank pulled out the money to pay we had all dollars and the lady explained it is only colones that are accepted which is local currency. I sat with the lady to make sure I am confirmed on that plane and Frank left to go find a bank to change the dollars to colones. He changed the exact amount and we paid the ticket and off to the terminal again. Traffic was worse now and we were literally 2 mins from the set down area of the airport but traffic was backed up and the rain still falling hard, I was smoking cigarettes back to back to back. My stomach was in the fast spin cycle of the washing and I kept having these waves come over me, where the tears just burst out, I could not think of anything I did not know why the tears would come for two minutes stop and then come again with serious upheaval from the pit of my stomach. I walked through the security line crying and stopping and crying and stopping and I saw computers with internet inside the terminal and I emailed my wife and told her Darra has just died and I am going to Ireland, she responded she will get the next available flight, I had been phoning my mother as she was arranging my brother Brian was to be picked up from the airport in Dublin by my friend Kenneth and James and driven to Darra's house, he was flying in from Egypt or somewhere he was on some travels, Patrick in Australia had not been told yet and John was trying to reach him.

John and his girl Ida were flying in from Sweden, my brother Garrett will be waiting for me at the airport when I arrive in Dublin. I made contact with my friend Donna in Skerries who had just heard the news and arranged that she be in touch with Irene and collect her from the airport. I was crying every couple of minutes uncontrollably, at one point I thought people must think I am completely crazy, I sat waiting for the plane in the waiting area to board. I managed a quick text message and call to Carmen and she was so so sad for me too. From there I waited for my group to be called and boarded the plane. My seat was centre aisle and beside me sat two priests who were speaking Italian and heading to Rome, I said to myself and the man upstairs, I am gonna open this emergency door and screw everybody on this plane, you piece of shit have taken my baby. And now you put these priests, your representatives next to me on the flight. FUCK YOU GOD!!!!!

I have never been afraid to fly nor worried about the length or journey of any flight, this flight I really did not care if we ended up in the bottom of the Atlantic, I could not sleep obviously and the waves of the crying continued and so I sobbed my way across the Atlantic that night with tears flowing into my little airline pillow. Spain was not a joyful sight although getting off and going to find my next flight from Madrid to Dublin just couldn't happen quickly enough. Then Dublin airport cold as usual and my older brother was waiting there with a car he had borrowed from his girlfriend who was supposed to join us later or tomorrow for the funeral. This borrowed status was the reason or the excuse I was not driving, the long road to Limerick from the airport terminal in Dublin, My older brother Garrett did not know what to make of it and the last thing I really wanted to hear was his opinion on life and death and how what must Clare feel and all the generic things people say in these situations, I think amidst the waves of crying which still continued I may have had a few words of , "shut the fuck up and drive the car a little faster".

It was a cold dark evening when we arrived into Newcastle West and as we drove out the road towards Darra's home, there was a big traffic road sign with flashing orange words, Funeral traffic this way. With an arrow as there is a split in the road ahead, I said fuck they must all be dying around here, I wonder who that is for. As we got closer there were cars parked and cars parking and guys in high visibility over coats directing traffic and this one guy was signalling Garrett to drive up the road and I said "stop here", Garrett replied, I can't stop here there is too much traffic and this cop is telling me keep driving, I said "you fucking park here and don't move I have to get some socks and shoes out of my bags in the back, this shit is freezing"

While I went to the back Garrett's starts to ease off as the person directing traffic is approaching him at the front waving his hand, and I was rummaging for a pair of socks and shoes in the boot of the car, Only because me and Darra are the image of each other I heard the other cop from down behind me calling to the traffic director hassling Garrett, the guy looked and the cop from behind me was now shoulder to shoulder with the other high vis jacket person and I could hear the whisper, "that's the father leave him park where ever he wants"

I closed the boot and headed for the laneway towards the house, there was a line of people in the laneway and along the driveway of their house and in the front door, I cut the line walked across the grass and made no apologies or excuses for cutting in the front door. In the room to the left the front room of the house, I saw the box and Darra's face as he was laid out, I met Clare with a hug I don't think in her own shock she knew it was me just another neighbour or friend who came to pay their respects and Darra's Na-Na was standing by the coffin with a handkerchief in one hand and red swollen eyes full of tears, I turned to hold his hand to touch it, and say oh my god, and lifted my head up and Darra's nana then realized it was me, "oh

Aidan" she said and we hugged and continued to cry together I could feel her body being weak and lifeless in my hug and was not sure will she collapse if I let her go. And there we were in a little room just outside of Newcastle west with my baby in a wooden box, he filled the length of it and was a real man lying there. I took a seat amongst the grieving family Clare's Dad and brothers and Tom Darra's step dad and family were there and people were coming in and shaking hands, I didn't want to shake any hands but just sit there and look at Darra's face, so peaceful and a nice expression of the Darra we all knew, fun loving and always up for a laugh. His step dad's sister Deidre came in and offered me tea and coffee and held me for a minute and then she told me, a joke, Deidre was always high spirits and funny but on this one was more of a quick story than a joke, she said all the family and locals were muttering and whispering in the kitchen about, how will we know the father and we want to make sure we don't do anything wrong but how will we know him when we see him, Deidre said she was sick of telling them, "don't worry if you know Darra you will know his daddy when you see him, sure they are the image of each other" she told me someone had come into the kitchen to tell her I was there and that she was right what she said, they are the image of each other. Darra's girlfriend was there at one end of the coffin and Clare his mammy and Tom his step dad and people kept filling into the room with their condolences. And the young people came all the school friends and their parents and the local team came through and what was a beautiful thing to see was the team from the county, the managers had gotten the news and they arranged a bus and meeting places to collect all the team from around the county and they showed up with their jerseys on and they owned him, It is a very powerful sight to see young 15 year old men, stand in the middle of a wake and stand with chests out that their lies their team mate. It was hard to see the young people own him so much that night but it was a beautiful thing. I didn't know that day and the waves of tears I felt would stay with me forever and that my tears would flow for many years, what I did know was I was none too happy to see my baby all grown up and in a coffin. I sat there in that room into the early hours of the morning and just had all the thoughts and dreams I had for him and me and it was going to be my time soon and he could visit me and I could spoil him and take him to NBA games and show him the fun side of life. It was all gone, the dreams had been shattered. A friend of their families offered us their house to sleep for me and my brothers and that we could shower there. My friends had gotten a hotel room in the town so I had options, I didn't care and went to the friend's house to sleep with a plan to get up early and find a shop that I could rent a suit and a place to get my hair cut. I said to my friends who had travelled down, James and Kenneth and James older brother Francey and another friend from Loughshinny done the driving, Damien, they were all in James family car a minivan type thing, Renault something or other, I said to them and my brothers of course, we have a big day tomorrow and let's get this done.

Francey came and picked me up in the morning bright and early it was freezing kind of day, that night while I sat with Darra I went out the back of the house for a cigarette and there were people that night that I had fished with from Clonakilty who were neighbours of Clare's growing up and people I had attended school in Roscarberry where I had met Clare, they had been Clare's friends from very young age. It was hard to take it all in. And when outside smoking the hailstones and almost snow was hard to bare.

Myself and Francey headed for the town and one barber shop was open and an old man was there cutting hair and I noticed a bunch of trophies and awards from the years 1992 and 1994 and things on the walls, this was an original old time barber shop alright, I explained what I wanted and he started cutting and would not cut down the hair at the front or on top and kept brushing it up to give it an old time quiff I guess you call it, I paid him and walked out and told Francey "we need to find a barber shop" he laughed and said it's not too bad the store with the suits wasn't open yet and we pulled into a parking lot to wait where up inside was a another barber shop, this was the modern kind young guy inside the door sweeping the floor and I said hair cut please, he started to cut and when I explained about the old man, he told me he himself had trained under him and the old man enters a bunch of hair cutting competitions and the competition style hair cut meant you always had to leave the top piece so it could be styled, we laughed about it. The conversation came to the topic of the young lad who died out the road and in the town it was a very sad day, I told him he is my son, and he said back to me, I used to cut his hair and do the lines in it for him, he said I was going to say something but I knew because he looks just like you, I tried to hold back the tears and I liked I had a haircut where Darra gets his hair cut. Got the suit and headed for the house.

There was Darra my baby in a box and the last kiss and they closed the coffin, Darra's step dad Tom had asked me that they were making plans on who would carry the coffin and there was so many team mates that wanted to carry the coffin that day and school friends and friends of the families and relatives, I said thank you for asking we will lower him into the ground, let them all carry him and we will lay him to rest.

Irene and Donna had made it to Darra's house and my mam and John and Ida and had made their way too and the funeral was about to take place, my baby Darra going to the church for a funeral, Life is not fair and that day was the toughest. I had said to a guy in a bar one night when we were just talking over crap, he asked can you remember the best day of your life and I said that is simple I can give you the best and the worst. The day my son was born was the best day of my life and the worst day the day I buried my father, he replied to me that maybe there is worse and maybe there is better in your future. Well he was right about one thing, I now had a new worst day of my life.

The hearse pulled up to the church and all along the driveway entrance to the church stood all the school mates and team mates of Darra, both sides of the little driveway up to the church. I lifted my head to see as Darra's uncles got their shoulder under the coffin and at the back of my leg, my knee went weak, I felt myself going down, I didn't know what was happening but my wife Irene was right there beside me and held my hand tight. Something to see all those young people and I knew Darra was not one of them. The mass was nice and his uncle Noel who Darra idolized gave a nice speech in the church and on to the graveyard, I walked holding my nieces hand and she carried some bouquet of flowers. The team mates of Darra were taking turns to get their shoulder under the coffin and me and my brothers walked along to the grave side. The priest had his words and then me and my three brothers as Patrick had not made it home from Australia yet. We took the ropes and we lowered Darra down to rest, I said careful now lads this is Darra we are talking about. In the corner of my eye I could see Clare go weak and almost collapse I felt horrible, this was a sad moment in the wonderful life of Aidan Mc Nally, a very sad moment. We prayed some more. I raised my head and I looked around the sky and the hills and the fields surrounding. Bye bye baba that's all, bye bye.

We took a meal close by and as Clare put it, there will not be a wedding for him, so eat up and enjoy. I drank four pints of Guinness and said fuck this place I need to get out of here. My mother and couple of brothers stayed in Newcastle west that night and I and the rest headed for home. Dublin. My uncle was supposed to be there in the house minding our granny but it was late when we arrived so I did not see him. For the next three weeks I sat on the couch and never stirred outside the room, my brothers brought me cigarettes and lucozade when I wanted it and Christmas was not Christmas any more now.

I returned to Dublin that night with my wife and I was upset beyond words, I told her it is not fair and, I know I have lost her and I have lost my son and what else is there to lose now. She was comforting and tried to be helpful but not to any fault of hers it was just "shit!" my mother and brothers returned the following evening. They went and visited Darra's room they told me, my mother said in his pants were a receipt for a snickers bar and a red bull.

The autopsy found nothing, they said it is now known as Sudden Adult Death Syndrome; SADS for short and it may be hereditary or just have formed. There is no way to detect it early and no way to know for sure and all the immediate family should get checked to see if the condition exists in either myself or his mom. I sat on the couch for three weeks, watching movies and I cannot recall if it was 3 am or 3pm I just had the curtains closed and smoking up a storm, my wife had flown back to the states already and I was in depression/shock/ I do not really know what to call it. Some friends of the area called up to shake my hand and offer their condolences and my mother kept sending my brothers in it seemed like every five minutes to tell me come and eat in the kitchen. I do not recall going to the bathroom but I believe I must have, but my memory says I did not use the bathroom once since December 12th 2011 until the day of January 7th 2012.

My birthday, I turned 36 that day and I got up and went and took a shower and a badly needed a shave, I looked at myself in the mirror on my wonderful birthday and tried with all my inner strength to shake this depression, this is not going to bring him back I thought, and what a cliché but the truest. I made contact with the clinic that tests for the SADS and scheduled an appointment with the clinic. I went and visited some local friends and most importantly I went and sat at the kitchen table for dinner. Christmas was now officially over and it was time for my mini hibernation to come to an end.

Many including my immediate family just did not know what to say to me, many greeted me on the street in Skerries with a warm Hiya and within minutes for some reason people who I had not seen for a year or two were trying to have a regular, normal chit chat with me had tears in their eyes. Was it me or was it them, could they see the pain in my heart or could they feel it in my words. I for the first time in my life had some idea of what completely empty felt like, the courts, the prison, the fights in prison the time in the treatment centre, the losing jobs and being in survival mode on the streets and marinas in Seattle, the movie stars and the rappers, the parties, the ball games and the jet setting, the kicking it in the ghettos with the thugs, the oceans of the world and my several wonderful touches with nature at its finest, the friends who had remained true friends, the loves that had come and gone all of it for what. For what died the sons of Ireland?? I posted a photo album of my baby on my face book page in and around that time and then I made my face book page only visible to me; I posted a couple of songs too. There is a good version of a song and it holds great words, REM, MAD WORLD. That helped me cry buckets and gallons.

Chapter 31.

I had a return ticket to Costa Rica for January 29th and so when the 29th came I jumped on the plane and for the first time with all my trips back and forth, I looked out the window over the clouds, the first time, I was bringing Darra with me on my travels. I looked across the sunny sky out of that airplane that day and wished so hard to see him high above the clouds, but in my being, my heart, my mind, my soul Darra was coming with me.

I returned to my job in Costa Rica and Chris from the office yup the one that put me in touch with my brother John that day, was there to say anytime you want to go and get drunk, I am right here it must be hard, as he too is a father of three beautiful daughters. Everybody had kind words and treated me with cotton gloves at the time of my return, but when I was at home after my shift what would I do sit and look at the walls the same walls I wanted to punch holes in only a month or so ago. I was in a bad place.

Carmen insisted to hang out with me and some days I had good days and I said yes come over and let's go for something to eat and other days I just didn't want to see anybody I wanted to be all alone and just cry. There were days where I knew people at work were talking about me because people were saying I was getting skinny and encouraging me to go meet up with them for dinner after work and let me buy you lunch. I was now a misfit in the world I felt displaced by my feelings and the whole process of trying deep inside to come to terms with my baby is not in this world anymore, this is not and anyone who has ever experienced this will know, it is not like the dye in a t shirt or the ink in a pen, it does not wear out finally, it is just is the way it is and that is how it goes. For a couple of nights I did go out and try the drinking the sorrows away but what seemed to happen was I convinced myself I was just going mad, I was talking to myself in my head thinking Darra was with me and could see what I see and I was talking to him in a drunken stupor. I was rejecting Carmen's advances through this time and sometimes she showed up at my door anyway, maybe with a combo meal from burger king or a pound of minced beef and encourage me to cook, she knew I liked to cook because I had tried to teach her how to make spaghetti before and she had showed up at my door, saying please teach me again. When I would chat with her on text in the evenings as my loneliness alone was killing me, she would call when my negativity showed even through the text messages and insist in the cutest accent, "come over here". One night I left work with Carmen and it was Friday, we had just been paid. We walked to the main street and hailed a taxi and when she was getting into the cab she said "oh sorry I have things to do, we can talk later", I really thought we were going to hang out as we had spoken of this earlier and she had waited for me at work, but she took off in the cab and left me standing there. I had never felt so alone in a foreign country and all my sorrows came over me strongly but as they say the devil makes work for idle hands, well along came another two work colleagues with an immediate invite to the pub for drinks. I was almost at a breakdown point of sadness right there on the side of the street and nothing sounded more inviting than the thought of getting completely wasted.

For all the years that I never drank alcohol I somewhat did not even like the taste of a beer, I still don't but that night I wanted and knew full well to escape my feelings like never before. I went to the casino and got completely drunk, wasted and lost all my wages playing some stupid table game or other and I was walking drunk up the street to go home when my phone rings, Carmen, "What are you doing where are you?" I thought I could lie, I could say I am at home and everything is wonderful but not in me, lies and me do not mix well, so I told her, I am walking the streets of San Jose trying to find my way home and she straight away started the drama and the panic, No it is dangerous where are you exactly, I said I don't know on my way home. She insisted I take a taxi I told her I do not have any money and it is ok I will walk. So she talked me into taking a taxi to her apartment and she would pay because the streets are too dangerous. I went and sat downstairs in her house for a while drinking water and looking at her ceiling and she said come to bed. I said no and drunken tears just flowed and flowed and flowed, Carmen came to my seat and held me and there was only the noise of me and my crying. The next day I was working and Carmen was off and so that evening she came over to spend the night with me at my apartment and we had gone to bed and were watching a movie and there was some fooling around going on, kissing and hugging and she noticed something wrong with me and I was not into it as much, when she braved the question, I told her I did not want to have sex with her at the moment as the only way I can be sure I will never have to go through this again will be no sex means no making babies. She said it is ok take my time and that is fine, she is happy to be with me and spend time with me as she had fallen in love with me, I said yes me too before I was falling all the way in love, but now I am just a sour angry person and this is not easy, so do not pressure me. She didn't understand but was trying.

The next few weeks we were hot and cold and some my fault as I didn't want to see anybody on some evenings just go home open my laptop look at Darra and his beautiful face in the pictures and play sad songs, smoke 40 or 60 cigarettes and go to sleep. Carmen would take a few moods and I would simply say, it is ok don't come over I have no interest to hear bullshit, quoting what I used to make fun of when I first met her, "the rules" to be with me. Sit down, look pretty, shut the fuck up and do what you're told. Yup they were the jokes I had before in 2011 now 2012, just was not so funny anymore. Everybody at work seemed to know we were hanging out now and there were some suspicions and I did not mind because who was I now, just a guy that lost his baby and seemed sad all the time. The fun loving idea of being a boss was gone, I really have no idea where it had gone, but it was lost.

Back when I was in San Francisco I had led a life of a construction company owner which was great and a lot of hard work but I also dabbled always in the gangster world too. The bookie business kept me in readily available cash and I middle manned a few deals here and there selling the great California weed products, from growers to clubs, which are dispensaries that distribute medical marijuana legally. I had a few connections there so I could make a thousand or two for twenty minutes work just pickup drop off and cash money. There were other times I may have come across some guns and did a little buying and selling and cocaine too sometimes, anything that could be got for x price and then sold on for a profit I was dabbling in which kept me in cash and I saw no harm in it, for this reason there were many gangster criminals who gave me the respect of the streets and it was all going along fun and games until a good friend and neighbour was shot to pieces from head to toe. I felt so bad for him and his family, I had just spoke to the guy the evening he was killed he had called me about finding some weed, I told him tomorrow. The signs of the streets were there, stay in this game and things might turn south quickly, this was part of making the decision to go to Costa Rica in the first place as I could see myself slipping as a person into this under world, where as in anything I would ever do I would be the best at it. I took a road trip to Texas at that time with ten pounds of marijuana, the guy who was going to buy said well it would be better if you hang out a few days and sell yourself you can keep all the profits, I thought I was making a quick stop and pick up cash and return home. While I was hanging out that week in Texas Houston actually, I was not affiliated to any turf or neighbourhood so I roamed around Houston Texas selling pounds of weed from California the good stuff to those out in Texas, for double the money but from south side of Houston to the west side to the wards, every time you step out of the car in those areas the possibility exists to get shot up, usually a white guy in the neighbourhoods is looking to buy some drugs so you are considered to have money, then when they find out you have the quality weed with you word spreads fast because everybody wants to chip in and piece their money together to buy the stuff, you might not be doing any business at all with someone but they heard why you are in the neighbourhood and that increases the risk even more.

I was hanging out with one of the big shots out there who sold more dope than I ever seen in my life, this guy was bringing it in and re selling it to all over the country, I sat in his house, "trap spot" and saw him weighing cash and handed over kilo after kilo of the stuff, there was no time for counting money, money got weighed just like the dope. We were sharing a beer or two and talking fun times and war stories and I heard some rattling outside the house, like as if the security gate was being opened but nobody came in. He said "you think you hear something" and laughed; I am not worried he said. There is nobody coming for me. I am protected and safe from the robbers in these parts, they do not mess with me. I asked him what about the police his response was "in that room behind me are all my weapons and not one single weapon is NOT military issue as he came from the door of the room with a bazooka. If they come for me the whole street is going to explode". I shook my head laughing and knew I was in the thick of this shit now for real. I was even paranoid of how much of the dope dust was getting on my clothes. This stuff was being sold five for New York, three for Florida, two for Utah. Three for Ohio. It was walking out the door and then cash and more cash.

Unbelievable operation but I did witness it all with my very own eyes. So it was in these times I had adopted the boss status and mentality of I am the boss and these women need to bow down to me because I am something. Well that will give you an idea of why I had the quote of, "Sit there, Look pretty, shut the fuck up and do what you are told" I had picked it up in ghetto Ville U.S of A.

I didn't really mean it with Carmen but it helped regulate a situation or two so I threw it out every once in a while. I began to give in to the advances of Carmen again and sometimes just wondered what did she see in me, I would not want to date me with what existed as the sour taste in my mouth. So this particular night I remember it so well we were in the throes of passion as they say and I let it go, no pull out here, I knew what I was doing too I said to myself at the exact moment, if it happens it happens she is my love right now and why not.

Over the next week or so I found myself in a deeper depression than ever and I stopped going to work, I stopped texting Carmen much and just drove myself stir crazy in my apartment, no drugs no alcohol just me and my thoughts and my loneliness. Looking back I can safely say I had no idea what was happening to me but I refer to it as a panic attack. I had to get out and get out fast. I had quit my job basically and left, my brother John jumped to the rescue with his credit card and booked me a flight to leave Costa Rica and return to Ireland. I was freaking out I took a taxi to the airport and headed for New York. When I got home to Dublin Ireland my good friend from years ago who I had coordinated through face book was there to pick me up at the airport, good old Bo he was now clean and sober after years of self-abuse with heroine and all drugs known to man. He had been my good buddy for many years back in the fishing days and when we chatted on face book that weak, through his own sobriety he knew I was not in a good place. He picked me up that morning and I was so appreciative to him for that and then I walked in to my mother's house of course I had travelled without any fore warning and my mother was a little shocked. I visited a few friends and they had ideas on me fishing, James was fishing his own boat and said come on, hop aboard the job is yours, let's put some money in your pocket and try and rebuild you to the man you once were.

So I went fishing with him for a week and we were back in Skerries tailing prawns on the deck of a Skerries fishing boat all over again. We were working as hard as we could and one morning when we had stayed out for the night, around 4 am my friend James wanted to get some sleep while everybody was sleeping before the next haul, I said sure I will take the wheel, I sat there as the sun started to come up that day in the Irish sea and I kept looking at the water, I had wanted to and was trying to convince myself to jump in and just end this torturous life. I knew it was my head and my sadness and everything working together, I mean I could not explain the panic attack that came over me to leave Costa Rica and I could not explain my thoughts that morning but they were as real as banging your head of a concrete wall, things were hurting. I said to myself things like, "just do it before they wake up", "it is still dark, they won't be able to find you", "it will be over before anyone has time to raise the alarm" well they awoke and we finished out the day and went ashore. The weekend was here and time to be paid for our efforts and I took the money and went home and just had the worst feeling.

Chapter 32.

I logged into my Facebook and emails and I had a couple of emails and messages from Carmen, "where the fuck are you?" "Where did you go?" Just call me please. Make contact so I know you are alright.

"I cannot believe you just left without saying good bye"

"Can you call and talk to me please" so I messaged her back and she happened to be online and she was upset to the nth degree that I was in Ireland and never told her anything, then she said we should Skype and chat she missed me and was so worried about me and where was I.

I had left costa Rica about three weeks now and she was still looking for me, I spoke with her on Skype and I told her I was sorry I got a panic attack and I was sorry it did not mean I didn't feel anything for her but some things just are difficult right now. Then the jaw dropper came, "I am pregnant" that were the words. I did not have the ideal reaction, I asked was she sure and how could it be and all the usual and she was crying as to I did not seem like I was happy. I tried to explain that I was in a very weird position or place in my life and a new baby was like I could not handle it but allow me some time. She was unhappy. We finished the call.

My friend James and his brother Francey came up to my house to chat and I had said sorry I quit. I cannot handle it right now I explained how James would be mad at me if I had of jumped that morning and why I could not in a mental state be safe on the boat right now, I just was not feeling it. I told them I was going to have another baby and they, both of them had been there that day we buried Darra it was Francey who drove me around for the hair cut that morning. Their eyes filled up and got all glassy looking and they said no pressure, James was really understanding and said it is there for you when you want it. I told my youngest brother Brian that I had my girlfriend pregnant and needed to tell the family the news, Brian being the comedian always. Said yeah the other brother John is trying to have a baby for the last couple of years and for you, you make them without hassle, "I don't know" his words of wisdom.

Funny thing was John and Ida were on a visit from Sweden that week in the summer months and I sat at the kitchen table with them and said to them all at the same time, I am going to have a new baby. I just found out and so let's not get over the moon just yet, I do not know how I feel about this yet and so I just needed to tell you all. John looked at me amazed and shook his head, my mother asked are you sure it is yours? My brother Garrett thought this was great news, ever the optimist of course and that was that Ida was happy but I could see what Brian had told me, all she wanted at these times was a baby. It was off my chest at least.

In the kitchen in my mother's house was a picture I had taken St. Patrick's day with Darra and dad back in 2005 it was on the side board so to speak with an album of photographs of Darra and a candle like a little vigil, I would look at it and think show me the way Darra, Show me the way, daddy is so torn and confused right now.

The Skype sessions continued with Carmen and she was a bit of handful for the pressure and when she went and got the scan and I asked her specifically that I didn't want to know the sex of the baby and she blurted out it is a boy, I was so over the moon and excited I got another panic attack. Something weird was happening to me ever since Darra had passed last Christmas I could not deal or feel stuff properly anymore. I didn't know if it was all still stemming from the shock that occurred that December or something just gone inside me. I got upset and told Carmen on email, her and the baby are dead to me and don't look for me anymore, I am out and want nothing to do with her. I don't want any more emails and leave me alone; her attitude and her pressure just were not working for me now. "I am nobody to her", these were her words and so "leave me alone". Of course Carmen, being who she is she followed up with an apology as did I and we smoothed it out that time.

My brother Garrett, he had been spending the week with his daughter and he said in the kitchen while we sat eating dinner that his daughter, my niece Kessia, he told her, Uncle Aidan is going to have another baby. The mother is out in Costa Rica, Kessia replied to her father, but daddy how is that possible Aidan has been home for a month or so, how could that even be possible? That's when old mother goose piped up, she is right; it is not possible I think you are being made a fool of. That's ridiculous. I ended my meal pretty quickly and made for the sitting room to watch some TV and get away from the discussion.

I signed on to the welfare program and was receiving money every week and one day I found myself standing in the kitchen in front of my mother, just breaking down crying again, mam I just am not able I cannot face people in the streets as many are seeing me for the first time since Darra died and it is just too hard to carry with me, I am not able. She answered me with I know and it will be ok, but you are able because you are my son and I reared you and you will be ok. We were coming up on Darra's birthday again and he should be turning sixteen with all his friends and having a wild party and it was these kinds of thoughts that just threw me into a spin.

I needed to work and start sending Carmen some money and get on track, fight back the demons and work through this pain, this is the only way I know how, even if I cannot defeat the pain, battle through it and fight that's the way forward. James and Kenneth said, they didn't understand exactly but they would help with whatever I needed to rebuild myself. I would help James to mend his nets for him for the boat and pick up some extra money there but I was looking or half planning to try and spend Christmas with Carmen if I could put the money together. I painted the whole house for my mother that summer for something to keep me occupied and so she made a deal with me if I did a few more odd jobs and painting around the house she would buy me a ticket to go visit Costa Rica. So that was the plan, I will spend Christmas with Carmen in her pregnancy state and her son. This was going to be my new family and so why not. I had now something to look forward to. I was getting my head around this idea of it is not a replacement for Darra this is a new life and so I must be a good father again and welcome this new baby and the blessing and now Darra can see the way of fatherhood through my eyes.

Carmen had been listening to the pressures from all her co-workers of how this guy won't be back and she was delusional to think anyone was coming back for her and a baby, I made her a promise in one of those Skype and email exchanges, that I would be back to take care of her and she will not be alone, she replied with "I will have to trust in you" and she hopes so. I made it for Christmas and had plenty of toys for Carmen's son Luciano and he was over the moon with a great Christmas, Carmen had to work some of the time and myself and Luciano hung out and played so that was a good time. Luciano was like a replacement Darra a new son, someone I could play with and help to grow but the love was flowing that Christmas and this bump in Carmen's belly was growing. We were planning, I will return to Ireland and fish and earn money and she can quit her job soon and when the baby comes we can discuss whether she should come to Ireland or I would come back to Costa Rica but at least we can make plans and have dreams.

Something had happened to me, I was scheduled to fly back to Ireland around January 8th which meant I would spend my birthday with Carmen, but she turned on me or she was being kind of cold and mean, for some reason I started this frantic panic and I got in a taxi and spent my last money to change my flight and flew back to the sanctuary of the homestead. Panic attacks maybe, I have no idea but it lasts for like 24 or 48 hours and it is just an intense feeling of, I HAVE TO GET OUT OF THIS SITUATION. Weird but it is the realest thing you will ever feel should you ever have the misfortune of having your emotions all jolted in your life. I cannot describe it in depth as it makes no sense to me even though, it is very real and it is extremely intense.

Good old technology helped me smooth things over, a Skype here and there and a few emails of loving words and we were back on track.

Carmen and I were planning the baby which was figured out to have a due date of March 10th 2013 and so I had a ticket booked for March 8th. I had taken a position on a small boat that would fish for razor fish and then as soon as I had the ins and outs of that I took the position of captain of a razor fishing boat, they are small boats with dredges and pumps to help clear the sand and move along the bottom catching this member of the clam family known as razor fish. Now these things are hard to come by and it takes a consistent grind to muster up a week's wages. I was working away and had sent money to Carmen via good old western union and she had what she needed for the baby. I was set to be out there for the birth and she was anxious and all was becoming a reality. I had prayed to god hard, "god I have not been happy with you for some time now, do not punish my new son, allow him the fullest of everything for his new life, we can pick up my argument again at another time"

The baby, Patrick, named after my dad was born on February 27th 2013 and he was a hungry lil fella and cute as a button. I missed the birth as he came early. I was rushing home from the boat when I was off to see him on Skype and to watch his hands grabbing for a bottle or food or something. Carmen was so happy on Skype and saying things, like say hi to daddy and I liked the idea my son is born and me and Darra are going to do this all the way. When I flew out in March which was the date of my pre booked ticket, I was so delighted taking pictures and videos and had two big bags of gifts from my mother and my friend Donna, baby clothes and tons of clothes for Carmen and gifts this baby was a real cool dude right from the beginning. Carmen had finished work and so I left my bank card with her as I would return to Ireland and continue fishing and send her money for now and I will see if I can indeed earn enough money to make it all happen. While I was in Costa Rica that time, I met up with my friend Chris and he had started a company in the betting world and he said he could not afford me right now but soon. As we had stayed in touch through Skype and emails we had shared again another Saint Patrick's Day in Costa Rica so it was almost a tradition for us to down a few pints on that special day and now I had a son Patrick I celebrated the birth and the day with Chris.

Work was very serious now back in Ireland I needed to earn money and make this family work, Carmen is out there relaxing and enjoying our new baby and it is on me to make the money and make a life for us. Well Chris came through for me he put a proposal together and said, look this company is new you come out here work it and I will give you equal partners in it. Chris valued my head for this kind of business and so I said deal. I packed in the fishing and was Costa Rica bound again. I would now begin again in the office life except this time a new light a new reason to live a new beginning in every sense of the words imaginable.

My depression days of sitting around my mother's house were a memory and through that time a good friend Donal who I had always been in touch with over the years, although to this day I don't think he knew it but he would on his day off from work call up to me and roust me out of bed and take me swimming to the airport, being that he was on the staff, the pool was relatively cheap and not too crowded as it was a gym for the staff. I would get a few laps in until I couldn't breathe anymore and take a sauna. I was like a Labrador when it came to the swimming I couldn't get enough of it going back to my days of swimming as a child I had always loved it. We would finish the afternoon with maybe a trip to Howth and walk the pier take a sandwich and a soup or do a set menu lunch in one of the bars close to the airport, although I believe he did not know it maybe he did, those days and those small tokens is what carried me through.

Now that I was all set with my new family and new job and energy for the first time in a year, I did reflect.

Sometimes in life you don't realize what doing anything is for or why or what anything is about and then little things like those swimming days, helped me work through a major depression and sadness, even though the sadness was still very real and strong at times, I enjoyed the heck out of holding Patrick and singing to him and feeding him and bathing him and all the baby things in life were looking good.

I packed in the fishing and flew to Costa Rica to set up life on July 19th 2013 to be with Carmen and surprise her as her birthday is the 20th Patrick was four months old now and had become a real ball he would cry all the time, I said feed him look at the size of him, he was born a normal weight and size but was for sure growing fast, the poor baby was starving. Carmen had been feeding him according to all the schedules and systems as to what a 4 month old child should be eating, this baby wanted more. He went from four ounces per feeding time to eight ounces overnight. My new baby was hungry and needed to grow some more and that is exactly what he did. Within a month or two of him eating happily he was becoming a huge baby not fat a little extra baby padding but a big boy, he was. All the heads would turn in the supermarket and everyone wanted to hold him and hug him and kiss him, he had that cute look about him that was simply irresistible.

The work was good and we were making money and Patrick had developed some kind of breathing problem and the doctor said nebulizers and asthma and I disagreed. It is the shitty apartment we are living in is too damp, so I looked for a house something bigger something newer and dryer. Within the first two weeks of this house no more breathing problem. The new house was three blocks from the office so it was great to take it easy in the mornings and shower myself and bath Patrick and then head to the office, sometimes Carmen would take the kids for a walk to the park which was right in front of my office basically well on the same block and I could go and kick football for a while or take an ice cream with them together.

Chapter 33.

Carmen had some issues it seemed with trust in the relationship as she doubted sometimes if I was at the office at all and would try and catch me and tell me I was somewhere I was not and that her friend had called her and said they seen me with another girl on the whole other side of town. I thought this is so weird and sometimes just put it down to she loves me so much she gets insecure and doesn't know how to deal with it.

Patrick's first birthday came along and we did a big birthday for him, my mother flew in from Ireland and we did a rented place with tables and chairs and a menu of different stuff for the kids and the adults. My mother spent a week with us as she still had to run back to Ireland to take care of my Na-Na who was slowly going downhill with Alzheimer's. But she came for Patrick's birthday and made a video of him playing peek a boo early in the morning while he was checking her out, like you could see in his face, who is this woman in my house, she must be here to play with me. Patrick was so happy with his balloon that I got for him and his big angry birds teddy, the red guy. The balloon was like a big cake full of helium and I tied it off to his buggy the whole day and he pulled it and tugged it and pushed it and hit it, what a great laugh he had with that teddy and the big balloon and his new playmate in the house too my mom.

I did my usual saint Patrick's day that year with my buddy and business partner Chris and we had become good friends and good work partners it was like when we touch something it turned to gold, this particular saint Patrick's day Carmen was not too impressed as I stayed drinking all night long and when I returned she was not happy, not happy at all.

She was livid accusing me of being with prostitutes and taking cocaine and a horrible person I was and came into the room where I wanted to sleep it off whipping me with her key chain. I could understand being upset for going out but I had just spent the best part of a whole year playing happy families and the father role I did not see the big deal in it, I showered and went to work. That evening when I returned all my clothes had been dumped in the garden and the house was locked. I picked up my clothes and headed to a hotel and thought to hell with her. She is crazy. Of course the texts and the insults kept flying until I turned off my phone, she finally the next day had calmed down and was apologizing and she did not want to be so mean but she didn't trust me and I needed to take a drug test to show her I was telling the truth. I went right up the street and took the drug test and said there ya go, she said this is not the cocaine test this is only a marijuana test, you have to give blood not just urine. I pleaded with her that I asked them in my best Spanish for the drug test the same as if I wanted to get a job, they told me to pee and come back in a few hours, so that is what I had done. Carmen had calmed down considerably and I was back at my house the next day and I was picking apart her emails to me and the discussion from me was, why she was so insecure and have I not shown her that I have been there all the way just like I promised before Patrick was born, what is all this nonsense about I don't care and all I want is Patrick and I do not care about her or Luciano. These things were so bizarre to me but I thought maybe something else to it, the monthly cycles had been weird ever since Patrick was born and it seemed like there was a little pattern to this and so we went to see a psychologist to see what recommendation they might have. The psychologist said that there was a possibility to make a research to see why Carmen explodes like this and if the hormones are unbalanced at any point through a 28 day cycle. So the plan was take blood tests through a six week time frame and let's monitor and see what's going on. Carmen was all for it and attended the first session and did not return for anymore so that idea was gone out the window and she said I am not nuts I just get like that sometimes, I thought ok if you promise no more of them, then fine. But it was at that outburst at that time that not only was she locking me out of the house she was calling her dad and telling him how I was a horrible person and I had been sitting in my house having my dinner when her dad arrived and the atmosphere was tense as she had just had her shouting and screaming the day before. Her dad walked into the kitchen with a serious tone of voice, telling me in Spanish which is hard to understand sometimes but if I listen closely I can figure it out. He said If I ever treat his daughter bad or lay a finger on her he will kill me, I interrupted him immediately in my best Spanish and explained to him, ask your daughter the truth, ask her why she threw all my clothes in the garden and locked me out of my house. If she wants to lock me out and I must waste good money to go and stay in a hotel then she cannot use it as an excuse to say I am sleeping with other women it is her who is the reason I did not sleep here, not me. Go and ask her before you make a fool out of yourself anymore in front of me in my house in my kitchen.

He went and asked her and some truth came out and a discussion was had and that is why she was in agreement to go to the psychologist to have another session, me and her both and we discussed what seemed to be going on. March finished out without another glitch and so did April & May so things were okay it seemed. Luciano was attending school and Patrick was growing at a rapid rate, his doctor had said, he is not fat he is normal, there is a chart that shows normal baby growth and within the guide lines are, the low line a small baby and the top line a big baby, the doctor explained , Yes Patrick is above the big baby line by quite some amount but he is following the exact same growth curve as is normal, he is just above the curve out there on his own but everything is following the correct course, this boy was a big 1 year old and his daddy was so proud. It was one of those mornings sitting by the front door and Patrick would wave at the people walking by the house out on the footpath that I sat there looking at the grass and felt that Darra was also proud and I had a feeling that Darra was enjoying this new baby grow up. I felt now at ease and comfortable for the first time really that Darra was not mad at me with this baby and he was all for it. As I used to feel some weird kind of guilt loving Patrick when Darra was gone.

Life was good and things were moving well , Patrick was walking now and the routine was simple and easy as with the office up the road and the house close by I could pop home for lunch or we could take a late breakfast maybe when there was no pressure to be in the office. I used to take one day off a week and most other days' work 10 am to 10pm or sometime before it but like I said I could pop into the house throughout the day if I wanted. Along came the summer and the world cup, it was on June 2014. I would shower with Patrick and watch the first half of the early game as it tied in to get me going to work about 10.45 then I would watch the second half in the office, the baby was washed and most days I would prepare the dinner for later so all Carmen had to do was turn on the oven and wait. I would eat when I came home but I knew they would have been all fed. Carmen might be sleeping but she would get up and tell me about the day and sit with me while I ate and maybe Patrick would wake for a bottle or a cry and I would tend to him.

Costa Rica were doing really well in the world cup and I walked for miles one morning to get the team shirts one for Patrick and one for Luciano and then we watched the match, I did my usual routine and Carmen wanted to go and celebrate with the people in the streets as Costa Rica had world cup fever at that time. Carmen was upset that I could not stay and have fun with them in the street and how come if I am a boss of the company I cannot just spend time with them this morning, but for me the job came first and without earning money our life would be a mess. I headed to the office and dropped them off to wave flags and have their fun. Then in the office that day, Carmen called me around lunch time and said, if you want your baby he will be in the park I am leaving him there cause that is all you care about. Now the trouble with that exact statement, that Carmen had in fact left Luciano when he was a baby in a laundry place and arrived home with no baby. Her dad as the story goes went frantically looking for him and some lady had thought she recognized the baby and was minding him until the father, Carmen's father eventually showed up and the lady beckoned him and said I think you are looking for this baby, so when that phone call came to me that day I freaked, I stood up at my desk and let out a sigh, my partner who had the desk behind me said what's up. He knew something had just happened, I turned to him with tears in my eyes and told him, she just said she was going to leave Patrick in the park and basically hung up. Chris said , "go quick go run to the park", I got outside the office and could see the crowd at a corner of the park with all the team jerseys on and so I hustled along the street to get there, I saw Carmen amongst the crowd with Luciano enjoying himself with the blow horns and Patrick in his buggy looking at the fun and activities, I put my hand to take the buggy and she would not let it go, with a smirk and a sick smile she said, "what do you think ?.. I am going to leave my baby", I said to her these words, "you are sick in the head and who knows what you will do". I would not leave their side the rest of the day which did not go on for much longer and I went home and she went and laid down and I cooked the dinner, the next morning I was full certain there is no way this is going to continue I did the usual routine and when it came time for me to go to work Carmen was preparing the buggy and was going to go to a different park nearer the house, I put my foot to the buggy wheels and told her she was not taking the baby outside the house today, she was going to have to get help from doctors and I am not allowing her to leave the house with the baby. She picked her phone from the carry tray by the handle of the buggy and called her dad. I spoke so as to make sure I was heard, she was screaming I was holding her hostage and wouldn't let her leave. I said call whoever you want you are not leaving this house with the baby. Never again until doctors are attended.

Carmen's father came rather quickly maybe an hour, Carmen of course was stomping around the house screaming all kinds of insults at me and I was just sitting watching the football in the front room where I could block the front door if needs be. Carmen came and slammed the door back and forth and actually damaged the handle of the door off the wall behind from banging it. She caught the remote of the TV and smashed it off the floor, I thought oh boy this is a mess, what the heck is really wrong with her. When her dad came I explained to him and she kept going with the high octane attitude and I explained to him there is no way she has to see a doctor there is something wrong. He reassured me nothing would happen now that he was there and I should just go to work so off I went feeling that there is no way she will do anything stupid with her dad there. That night when I returned from work there were two new chains around the gates of the house and her father blocking me standing in the porch behind the gates saying, she doesn't want you and to go or they will call the police. I said give me my computer bag and some clothes so I can go and stay in a hotel and he stood refusing and Carmen stood behind the door trying to make a few screams and shouts. I kept insisting I wanted my clothes, some at least and my computer bag so I could work but "no" was the answer and so I left.

I called her brother who I used to work with a couple of years ago and I explained him there is something wrong. I had called my partner Chris and went and stayed on his couch for the night, it is embarrassing to deal with when your business partner and your friend's family and his wife and kids are all looking at you bedding down on the couch for the night. The next morning I got the sorry and I am sorry to do this I do not want to lose you, can we talk on text. I insisted for doctors and Carmen said to me in our house, I will go to hospital I will do anything please I do not want to lose you I love you. I said I will look for something maybe not in treatment but a retreat perhaps in the mountains and she could go for a week and when she returns if she feels like she does not want to be together then I will find an apartment for her wherever she wants to live and we will just be once upon time in love and now apart but very much raise Patrick together still. I could not find a specific type of retreat on the internet and Carmen had said a hospital, but I had been discussing about visiting a colleague through work that had bought a new house somewhere by the beach, this was four hours' drive away and would be a first for me so I decided and Carmen agreed we will take a long weekend and go visit them and be their first guests so to speak in the new house.

That July weekend which would tie into the states seeing as it was fourth of July weekend we hit the road around lunch time to drive to a part of Costa Rica called Guanacaste, it is dotted with a bunch of beach towns and resorts in that part of Costa Rica. We took our time and I had just had the car reinforced as the chassis were not great but I did not want to make the trip without it being supported. As we drove we stopped along the way for a late lunch or early dinner in a restaurant and continued up the highway, night had come in on us and we were a little lost and it is much hotter in that part of the country. I had read the map to take a long straight road towards the beach town we were heading and was cruising along, we could see lightning out over the ocean as we drove and the show was great as the whole wind shield would light up. Patrick had gotten restless in the car seat and was hot and so we stopped and Carmen jumped in the back to hold him and let him out of the seat. I drove really carefully and even slower then as he stood right at my elbow resting himself on the little centre arm rest of mine, the driver's side. He was watching the lightning on the windshield and wasn't restless anymore, content. We were all a little tired by the time we reached my colleagues house and we set things up in the guest room, they had prepared four blow-up beds for us so we had a little feel of camping. We took a snack put the kids to bed and chatted for a while with our hosts and headed off to bed.

Chapter 34.

Tigran and his wife Marianella had one Daughter about ten or so years of age and the story they had told us of the great deal on their house and why so far away made perfect sense as this home was a very nicely built new and luxurious home. In the morning when we woke we saw the beautiful view of the ocean and the surrounding hills and this home was built, perched on one of the hills surrounding Playa de coco, coco beach. The kitchen and dining room were open plan and had sliding doors to a sand stone patio with a plunge pool in the patio area and a railing all along the patio as the house was high up on the hill with a couple of homes below.

We could see the Pacific Ocean and with a light breakfast and no signs of anyone waking up we decided lets head for the beach and off we went. Myself and Luciano played in the ocean and Patrick and mammy watched us from the deck chairs on the sand. It was a beautiful hot sunny day and the sunscreen was aplenty on Patrick and Luciano both. Patrick had a little inflatable dinghy and he wanted to go on it so I made the nose of a motor boat and would drag him across the little waves by the water's edge, Patrick walked or stepped funny when the tiny little waves would come towards his toes as this was all new to him. Luciano dug some sand castles and Patrick wanted to stomp them down and soon the waves came and made soupy sandy mess out of them and so Luciano started to try and bury Patrick's feet but he kept moving as Patrick was not tuned in to the game Luciano was trying to play.

I sat with Carmen and Patrick while Luciano was at the water's edge building his sand castles and Patrick was sitting alert watching him as he wanted to join in, I reached over and took Carmen's hand and asked her, isn't this beautiful?

She said yes for sure, I said honey this is our family and being in love she got up to kiss me as she agreed all this was wonderful and beautiful. I said see how easy to be relaxed and together having simple fun.

I saw a guy walking towards Luciano so I went down it was a guy renting another inflatable, a crocodile thing and I rented it for Luciano and he had it for an hour and enjoyed every minute of it. For me this was paradise and all the people I love were right here with me. Clear ocean sunny beach all the way from Loughshinny it does not get better than this. We went back to the house and the sun was really very hot still but we were beat and Marianella was preparing a beautiful meal for us for a late lunch, Tigran fired up the grill and barbecued some meat and we sat and watched, what turned out to be, Costa Rica's Last world cup game. That evening as the sun started to set and we chatted and ate and all were feeling beat from the sunny day at the beach. We made a plan to go to another beach tomorrow and everyone would get up early, Luciano had already headed for bed and Patrick was sitting in his buggy passed out with big puffy red checks as it was hot even still in the night. Marianella offered me some coolers or fans and I explained I prefer not as I don't like the fan blowing on me in the night and she said well if you need it, it is there and she turned in for the night. I was enjoying the warm evening on the patio chatting with Tigran and smoking a few cigarettes, Carmen had gone off to bed a little tired and so we finished up around midnight and decided to turn in. I asked Tigran do we leave the doors open and he said no as there are cats and some wild animals that live in the mountain here that will come in looking for food and so he locked things up and we said good night. When I got to bed in the blow up mattresses people seemed to be everywhere Luciano down one way and Carmen toward the bathroom and Patrick between us and I reached for Carmen and she was with an attitude of how I didn't include her in the conversation and I made her look stupid and so I thought here we go again never good enough. I turned my face to the other way and off to sleep.

I awoke to a howling noise, my dream kind of intertwined, the way when you wake to some noise or environment that was already in your dream, I could hear a deep bellowing and howling noise, I recognized it was Carmen, my mind half asleep was thinking there must be an animal like what Tigran had mentioned last night, this howling was from Carmen I could hear her saying NO and howling frantically, it was seconds between waking and the vision of an animal in my mind and I pulled my shorts on rapidly and came down the stairs, Carmen was at the side of the pool with Patrick laying there lifeless, I clambered over furniture perhaps covering twenty feet distance in four strides I didn't speak I just began CPR on Patrick He was lifeless by the pool Marianella was doing the compressions and I was blowing air, I could hear Tigran from the balcony above speaking to 911 for an ambulance. I was frantic now myself, I was blowing and compressions and I leaned back to look to the heavens, No I cried, No not my baby, Carmen was laying poolside crying and Marianella and Tigran were hollering in Spanish, I continued the CPR and Tigran said we need to drive to the bottom of the hill it will be faster to meet the ambulance, it is on its way. I gave two quick breaths to Patrick and picked him up in my arms, I was ever so careful to support his head and I cleared the 20 stairs in the stairway again with about four strides. I got into the back of the car and continued CPR while Tigran jumped in with Carmen, We drove to the bottom of the hill and the ambulance was there, we got Patrick strapped in and myself and Marianella were in the back with the Red Cross ambulance guy and Carmen went in the front. The Red Cross guy was fumbling with an oxygen mask and I ripped it from his hand, give me the fucking thing you clown, I tore it open and handed it back I was shouting at the driver, to drive, drive. I continued compressions on his chest and the oxygen mask was on. I saw then the oxygen hose had a kink in it behind the ambulance guys back and so I grabbed like a mad man to straighten it, I was standing across the bed/trolley Patrick was on, we stopped to pick up a doctor who was driving from the hospital towards us and she really screamed at the driver in Spanish, drive faggot drive the doctor screamed at the driver, my feet were wedged to the side of the base of the back of the ambulance as on every bend we took would throw me but I had wedged myself one hand to the roof of the far side and my feet set solid. The doctor continued the compression to give me assistance and Carmen was screaming at the traffic to get out of the way, it was about 6.30 am on the road that morning to the hospital and who on earth is out then around the sleepy beach towns of course, slow driving farmers. The doctor screamed at the driver to drive on the wrong side of the road and every entrance road feeding into this road we were on was blocked by local police as we whizzed through the villages on our way to the main city and emergency room of the hospital. We eventually arrived I had no idea if we were ten minutes or one hour all I felt it was tooooo fucking long, everybody ran for the emergency room and the ambulance men stayed back I was standing there in the emergency room with no shoes a pair of shorts and my fists clenched, my chest was bare as I had not put a t shirt and everything was code red emergency status, I was willing my baby back to life, I watched the nurses and doctors keep the air going and the compressions they hooked up a machine for the pulse there was a whisper off to the back of my left shoulder. I looked at who was talking behind me, the red cross man with the hospital administrator at a desk, he gave me a thumbs up signal and then I understood the administrator saying to him, you cannot say anything keep your mouth shut as she ushered him back out of the room, my focus was back with Patrick this occurred in a millisecond My fists clenched so tight they were hurting my fingers, my arms were in a rocking back and forward motion and I seemed to be rocking to my toes and back I was wanting my heart and my lungs and my breathe in my baby, I was willing him to live saying in my mind or out loud I cannot really say which I had my lip bitten, FIGHT, FIGHT, FIGHT,FIGHT FIGHT, FIGHT. The doctors had drawn blood from his ankle I noticed and the resuscitation continued, I saw the doctor writing numbers on the sheet and checking his watch then again the numbers and the watch, the security were trying to keep people back behind me I turned to look and I gave a look of death to the security, in my mind flashed the words, don't you dare tell me to move back I was in a position of ready to go to war. I could get in the ring with Tyson right now at this exact second in time, I saw the doctor calling it off and approaching me, Carmen then came into the room past the security that were keeping people out, all hearts were deflated none more so than mine, my anger and energy was still high, I could taste the taste of Patrick's lips and the little white bits he had spewed up at the pool. The doctor's explanation was brief, they drew blood he said and in order to continue with resuscitation efforts a minimum of 6% of oxygen would need to show up in the blood, Patrick had less than one, his blood had too much acid in it now which means the muscles had been without oxygen for too long. I understood exactly what he said to Carmen in Spanish I just did NOT want to hear it. I asked the nurse for some kind of blanket and I sat at his bed side, nurses shuffled around and the doctors and nurses who were involved in the rescue effort were all heads hanging low, I sat beside the bed with my head towards his and Carmen was laying on his bed crying, I was crying too.

The nurse came to wrap him and she caressed Carmen's hair I said I need a smoke, I walked outside while Carmen sat there, I lit a cigarette outside the hospital and the taste of that acid from Patrick's lungs was on my lips and in my mouth, I walked across the street to buy a coke and walked back into the hospital, on the way through the emergency entrance a doorman went to, as if to block me leaning my direction I pushed the door open and continued to the emergency room, about twenty paces. I was there again and offered Carmen some coca cola, we lay there with him and the nurse explained we would need a few minutes more while the doctor signs some papers and then we have to walk to the morgue. Carmen said she didn't want to speak to anyone and I had the task of calling the family. I walked outside again still shirtless and shoeless and as I exited the doorman leaned to me, and apologized to have thought to block me earlier he said he didn't know what had happened or who I was but he had been informed now and was sorry. I called my mother, I called Carmen's father, I received calls from Carmen's brother and his wife, they insisted to talk with her, I walked back in and she didn't want to speak with them. I now had the task to pick up my baby and walk the corridors to the morgue, three maybe four corridors with the sun beating in on us and I carried my baby wrapped in his hospital Blanket, his face pure and happy and soft, I laid him on a steel tray and I insisted to the doctor there in the morgue that is my baby and don't you dare touch him or cut him. I will kill somebody if they touch my baby and we were ushered outside the morgue. My Baby Patrick my new light in life had just been blown out. There was no sense of anything.

Upon exiting the morgue I was met with two detectives who came all heavy handed with their guns on their belts in full display, they introduced themselves as detectives and one judge had accompanied them, Carmen was deflated sitting on the ground with her back to a flower bed planting wall, one hand to her head and the detective started in on her, in Spanish of course, "was there any drugs and drink taken this night?". I said to him quite firmly while I stood up straight putting one leg to the front of Carmen to block her from him, "you better show some respect, I just laid my baby in the morgue and I am not going to take shit from you, you wanna ask questions then ask them with respect" He gave me the typical speech of don't make this difficult for yourself, I said to him again "you better show some respect, I am not afraid of your guns, I do not care who you think you are, are you a father" he was answering me to calm down and this is police business, I said again "are you a father,? Do you have children?" the judge was a female Judge and she called the two officers to the side, and they returned after a minute conference with the judge, I am a father he said and I do understand and apologize for not thinking of your situation, please answer us some questions. Carmen began speaking to the detective, I spoke directly to the judge I said if you are a judge I want an order not to cut my baby, he is pure and precious to me in this world and I want him perfect when he goes to heaven, she gave me the sympathy eyes and said "I understand" the detective wanted my passport for

ID and asked me what happened, I said to Carmen speak Spanish here I don't know whatever she said. "My baby is dead" and the tears were flowing again, all I know is I awoke to the screams and howling and from there it was CPR and this is the end result now what more do you want. I explained I came as quickly as I could from the bedroom and that's why I have no shoes or shirt, we went in the ambulance and this is the end result the morgue.

I was so upset and furious, I wanted to smoke but couldn't find a way out of the hospital grounds, because I had no sandals my feet were getting scalded by the asphalt as this place Liberia is a hot town in Guanacaste, it is about fifty miles from the Nicaragua boarder in the northwest of Costa Rica. My feet were roasting and my mouth tasted like Patrick's lips, we hid behind a building as all there seemed to be were fences and no exit and we smoked, myself, Carmen and Tigran's wife Marianella. I had to apologize to her for how I had been in the ambulance and in the hospital and the morgue; she definitely had no offense taken as she was right there in the thick of it with us.

The hospital would not release us, me and Carmen without us seeing the shrink of the hospital for the effects of shock and I had gone outside again to smoke and look for a shop that might sell a t shirt, Directly across from the emergency room entrance is a group of stalls or little shops and they had some pre used clothes for sale but everything was in large or smaller I needed 2x or 3x to fit me, I did get the worst looking polo shirt you could imagine big over grown paisley design blotted around it, I walked back into the waiting room where Marianella and Carmen were sitting, While we sat an aunt or grand aunt of Carmen's who lives somewhere close had shown up, she sat with us. The shrink called me first and explained to me about shock and what can happen and if I wanted anything of medication he would happily prescribe it for me right now as this is a horrible tragedy. I took my breath and wiped some tears and explained to him, as best I could in Spanish, You have no idea what this is as far as a tragedy, he interrupted me to explain how his brother committed suicide and it is his main reason for his job today, I said again my friend, you have no idea that this is my second son to die on me. I know now why some people show up to work and shoot everybody in the building, I never understood why someone would go to a church and kill twenty people, I have been in a heavy weight bout with god for quite some time now and the score is two- nil to god right now and I feel like taking all of his because he has taken two of mine. I am not going to do anything stupid and don't worry, I am worried about her outside though so let's get finished with me and see to her please, I don't need this waste of time. Carmen went in next and then I sat with her aunt, Marianella was off giving the clerks of the hospital some information. Her aunt and I exchanged what words we could and then the aunt went walking and came back out the same door of the shrink's office which I thought, that is strange, she called me and then said, Carmen has collapsed. I said, what, she was now in a hospital bed and high. They had her on a drip of some kind with something making her high. The shrink doctor said he saw her hands curling involuntarily towards herself, which indicates some form of high shock and he ordered a shot of a relaxant immediately. I stood by her side holding her hand and she said she was really thirsty. I went across the street to the stalls and bought some Gatorade and that was that, after a short time, they cleared us to go and Carmen's Aunt drove us back to the house. The whole rest of that evening people showed up and flew in and drove to Guanacaste, 6th of July 2014.

It did not get any easier the next day, operating on a numbness and 1 hour sleep I went with Carmen's brother to the hospital to try and put a stop to an autopsy, I had to go back to the court house, I found the same judge and we went to her office, she quoted law books and I insisted this is a baby, my baby the purest from god let him return pure, she said it was the law. I said I am Irish I don't recognize your laws, my baby is Irish too. The whole family of Carmen were afraid of me claiming that as that could delay the whole process of a funeral. I went to the morgue demanding to stop the doctor and he came out and said they were almost done, I wanted to kill. I wanted to kill something anything, I never felt the sickness inside me my baby was laying there and I could do nothing. Carmen's brother kept trying to be a voice of reason, it was not working. All that I achieved was a permission slip to transport the body back to our home in San Joaquin rather than in a van from the morgue where there were feelings that they may not handle him so well. I went to go buy a coffin and then Carmen had come with some clothes and I told her brother she is not to see him cut open, she has to wait outside until we dress him. The paper work was in order and I explained to Carmen's brother in law Alex, we will get him in the box and then straight to the freeway home no stopping for the friends and family outside the hospital gates. I went in with Carmen's brother Walter and I knew what I would see, I dressed him quickly and got some napkins to lay along the stitches so they would not show through his white polo shirt and we put him in the coffin, making sure to pad him well and headed straight the long road home, Once at road works we cut the whole line of traffic to many cars honking at us and when we got to the cop at the road works we showed him the paper and he waved us through.

At our house we laid the coffin on our bed and took some water to wash him and fill all his cuddly toys into his coffin and his blanket that he liked and many items, we were off to Carmen's sister's house to have a wake and a funeral and lay him out and say some prayers. The following day another church mass and a grave yard where I sat there and watched my second son be buried. The second time I had no mind to speak with or listen to anyone about anything, I wanted to be wreck less and fuck this life but I had to step up and protect and shelter my loved one the mother of my child and his little brother, we were now a family of three again and it wasn't fair. Patrick was lowered down and that was the end of another beautiful baby of mine, the tears will never end now I could feel the hardness spreading all over me when that coffin went in the ground.

At the sisters house when myself and Carmen's brother in law were approaching their home I explained him, let's just walk right in and lay him on your bed just the same as we had him on our bed in my house, lets walk by everybody, I do not care what they already have set up let's do it that way, he agreed and that is what we did, the long kitchen table had been set with a wreath and flowers ready to receive the coffin and we went right past and put him in the bedroom. We lay him there and I arranged the flowers so that no one could sit close to his head I didn't want a bunch of people touching his face, so I wanted to make so they could only stand at the end of the bed and view and say a prayer and keep it moving. As his position was set and I was confident he wouldn't have much or many people sit by his head because the flowers were blocking, somewhat at least. I stepped back to see my baby in his peaceful state and there above the bed was a painting drawn and painted by Alex's dad, a blue sea with two dolphins jumping out of the ocean, it is a night scene with the moon reflecting in the water.

Where my father lays, where we put him to rest in the graveyard near my home in Loughshinny, at his grave there is a head stone for which my mother took her time after his death to choose the head stone for him. She took her time as she said, she never saw anything she liked, the final design she chose was a black marble, shined & finished with one dolphin jumping up on one side and one returning from a jump on the other. The most striking thing above the bed where my baby lay was there were two dolphins painted above his head.

I felt one moment of appreciation to God and all the mysteries that exist, In Loughshinny lies my Dad with two dolphins above Patrick Mc Nally and here now in Costa Rica lies my son with two dolphins above his head Patrick Mc Nally.

The funeral happened, my brother Garrett flew over with his girlfriend and soon after that my brother was getting married in august.

I flew to Ireland to be around my family as all the time there was no one for me around me and all the Costa Rican side of things were Carmen's family for her. I continued to go to work and try and make her comfortable. My brother John was getting married and I did not tell him I was coming but I told my mother, I flew in the day before the wedding and woke him up; him and his wife to be were full of tears for Patrick and joy that I could make it. I got the suit and didn't want my being there ruin his plans and so I left it til last minute. It was not easy that day being in the church while the wedding ceremony was taking place as I had been making faces and mean thoughts and words to the statues of Jesus in the church, I thought it was all in my head but I guess Garrett could hear me calling Jesus a useless cunt... Many of the relatives gave their condolences to me that day and I tried to stay outside smoking at the drinks reception after wards, when we went to the hotel it was more drinks, as

John says laughing, Clontarf Castle the Vikings were driven out years ago and now John had invited them back with all the Swedish contingent in attendance. My buddy Donal hooked my brother up with photography with a quick email to call in a favour. That was two Mc Nally weddings now for my buddy Donal. I hung back outside on the terrace having a coke and a few smokes chatting with my brothers and few friends stopped by and shook my hand and then went back inside to the bar. Then we were called for the dining room where dinner will be served, we were last and when we got to the dining hall everyone was looking for their placing's at the tables, almost all were seated and I found my table, I was placed next to a high chair, a baby chair, the people at my table had a baby, I walked towards the top table in a hurry, my mother was there, under our breaths I said mam I have to go, they are after sitting me next to a baby I have to go.... I walked out, John and Ida were outside the door about to make their entrance, I hugged and told her she looked lovely and he said wait, I said enjoy I have to go. I left and walked the road home to catch a train to Skerries and then walked the road home from Skerries to Loughshinny, I had to break into my Na Na's house and sleep there for the night, I was in that horrible place again, alone, hurt and so much emotions the tears gave little reprieve. Life is cruel in an unusual way at the worst of times. I just buried my own beautiful baby three weeks prior and some dumb person could not know to keep away from a placing me where a baby would be. I mean come on I understand 100 people or whatever to be seated and I was not looking for any special treatment, I did not want to have anything to get in the way of John and Ida's special day, but Jesus Christ, think of one simple thing, and make sure John's brother is not sitting next to a baby. I thought to myself it would not have killed John to make a point of that to look out for me a little bit. I did not talk to the prick for a year over that one and even today I don't feel like talking to him much. Weird what we share, the phone calls about dad and then he had to break the news to me about Darra and he jumped in and flew me home when I was freaking out in Costa Rica, but now over this over sight I did not like him, I did not want to be his friend anymore. Don't know why exactly, it has something to do with the depth that occurs to the feelings when you lose your baby. Sensitivity takes on a whole new meaning and not in the normal run of things. I could sit and watch a bloody movie where they are hacking up bodies, not a problem I could watch look who's talking where it is all babies and no problem, now let me walk down the aisles of a supermarket and see a mommy grab her young child hard by the wrist and tug on them or pull on them really hard. I am ready to go and slap that lady because the child does not deserve it no matter what they did, they are a child, and it is the parent's responsibility to explain to the child right from wrong, not slap them across the head or drag them along a supermarket floor. For this I can get so worked up it just becomes tears. All my feelings now just become tears. I can be happy and cry, get all sensitive because the girl in the movie is re united with her father, Cry, look at the nature channel and see how the whales protect their calf, Cry, I am an adult I am a father with all the love to give my babies but my babies are not there, I feel the need to protect and take care of, but not there, my babies are in heaven or somewhere up there is the comfort I get, that they are comfortable and so I get on with it, get up every day go to work, try to shower and shave regularly and keep the house hold together.

Chapter 35.

My protections turn to Carmen and Luciano and my little family and making them comfortable in life. The devastating blow that has occurred is not easy to shake, I cannot use the bathroom properly for months and things are difficult, not able to sleep at night sometimes just afraid, because I did not want to wake up to a tragedy. 2014 surely was another messed up year and now all I do is go to work every day and try and deal with those stresses as a method to have something of focus and add normalness to a fucked up life I am living. In my relationship it is like the more I do the more she wants, I am trying to make her comfortable and keep her sheltered so as to allow her time to deal with the horrible loss, but I am neglecting myself. At the end of October that year we were in a discussion and I asked nicely that well I explained that these next few months are the hardest for me. Nov marks Darra's birthday, Dec marks his anniversary so Christmas I am not looking forward to, Jan marks my birthday and I cannot say I feel good about that for the past few years and Feb will mark the birthday for Patrick where we should be hugging and kissing him for his second birthday. Patrick by the way was a year and four months when he found his way out that morning to walk to his death by drowning in the pool. So in the conversation I had asked my partner to watch out for me as the tough months lie ahead and even though we both miss Patrick I find it tough too and need some space. I want to feel my way through this miserable time.

What someone does not realize in times of hurt and relationship difficulties that when being genuine and expressing to their partner that they want space or need time or the things they fear or the emotional pains, you are giving the partner the ammunition to hurt you even more or deeper. Darra's birthday came around on the 16 of November and I did have horrible feelings and did not do anything special or anything different just mope around go to work and go through the motions, on the 23rd of November I ended up with a full scale war with my partner as to she was packing her stuff and leaving me as I was too miserable to be around. Of course this was not happening in a normal way, she waited until I got home and went to bed for the night and then she started her screaming and shouting and the lights were turned on so I could not sleep and banging closet doors and filling plastic garbage bags with clothes. I said here let me help you and began to take the bags she had filled and moved them to the front room of the house, saying of course, that I will be glad to be rid of you. Now I was wrong to react but sometimes enough is enough. Well Carmen ran down the street to a neighbour's house and then played the victim I was throwing her out, the police were called and I was taken to jail for the night. She then started all she could try when the police came first, his passport is out of date he is illegal in the country he is this he is that. While in the jail cell I thought, I promised myself I would never be in jail again in my life when I was seventeen years of age and now here through some lies of my partner I am incarcerated again. The police explained to me that a judge will see me in the morning and tell me where we go from here. I was given a paper to sign telling me to stay away from Carmen and my home for one year and not to have any contact. I was escorted by police to my home to remove my personal belongings and was not to return. I left with my car loaded with junk and was late for work to the office, I went to the office and parked rear end to the wall hoping it was not obvious that everything was in turmoil by the back of my car being full of my belongings. I went to stay at a hotel that night and it was then the text messages came of how sorry she was and she did not want to lose me and that she would go to the doctors again and she was sorry. My replies were simple and to the same point that has always been the case. Get help to fight the demons inside you and I will carry you all the way, fight against me and I must stay away as now I have an official order to stay away from a judge. Carmen was so apologetic and said she did not know they would take me to jail she was sorry and wanted my help to attend the doctors. Carmen said she will go and remove the restriction with the judge first thing in the morning. Unfortunately the only way I could return would be to have officially that same restriction removed. I returned the next day to read the copy and the whole thing was squashed, Carmen had informed me that the judge was very clear on how she cannot play this game and she should get help of some kind also, Carmen had told the judge we are now going to seek help of a psychological nature. Restriction was lifted.

I pleaded with her to attend a doctor and a psychologist was sought out and the meeting we had was like dropping a rock on the poor doctor. I am sure that the doctor saw that we were a couple having problems and when my tears and our story of Patrick and Darra and all the crap we have been through, the doctor was also in a place of shock, but we agreed to begin some sessions and go from there. Therapy had started and it was time to look at some real issues for us both individually and as a couple. The therapy was us together then once each individually and then again together to discuss amongst ourselves the position we were in. that was the treatment plan.

In an effort to gain some form of security for Carmen I decided we should visit Ireland for Christmas as this could give her an opportunity to see where I come from and meet my close and dear friends and to see the beautiful country where I grew up, to see it is not like Costa Rica with prostitutes on every corner and family life is important, probably the single most important thing in Irish lives. My hope was she would gain an understanding and know that it is not in us the Irish to just be flimsy with our relationships and I come from a society where the concept of running to bars and meeting hookers is not the normal daily thing, yes the Irish run to the bars, but we like the atmosphere and the laugh and the craic and most of all the beer. My hidden agenda which I stated was that to get out of Costa Rica for Christmas would be great as we will not have Patrick and to put distraction between us and the sadness, a trip would do us good, I say hidden agenda because this was a runaway tactic to escape from the pain of Christmas and I could visit Darra's grave for Christmas and take time away from Costa Rica where lay Patrick.

I had told my mother over the phone what had happened to me in the jail and what Carmen had done and my mother was very upset and what would she do now as she was booked to visit Costa Rica starting December 9th for 5 days where we could spend the anniversary of Darra at Patrick's grave and be together just for a few days, but my mother didn't want to come, I explained to her look therapies have started and just go ahead with the trip it is paid for now. And so she came, the night I picked her up at the airport she was tired from travelling and to take a moment we sat by the pool at the house for my mother it was warm and so some air is what she wanted. I landed it on her, Mam I have booked a trip and we the three of us, please put our names in the pot for Christmas this year, we fly in on the 24th to Dublin and will leave January 7th, my birthday. Two weeks in Ireland is the plan. My mother was stunned but seemed happy and then we went ahead and entertained her for her stay, she went to the spa with Carmen and her sister and then a night out dancing salsa and it seemed my mother had a nice time even though only a few days really, but with taking care of my Na-Na all the time, it was all she could squeeze in for a mini break. It was a great way to assist in us that Santa Claus gifts were taken by my mam to Ireland December 15th and so when we travelled and woke up Christmas morning Santa Claus knew we were there and had brought Luciano gifts to Dublin Ireland, all worked out well.

We had a great Christmas in the cold and visiting the museums and touring the countryside and the joy of eating fresh fish and chips in Ireland and the tea and the butter and the sausages. Well I was home to gorge myself on Irish chocolates again and all the extras except this time Carmen and Luciano could enjoy the spoils of the Irish delights that I pined for year in and year out, nothing fancy just a good old cup of tea and some chocolate biscuits, life's little pleasures. With the cold and the friends and the Leopardstown races the leprechaun museum and a trip to cliffs of mother. A trip to Darra's grave Carmen and Luciano had a great trip.

They got to visit with my friend James and his family and he has a couple of younger children so they were delighted to play with Luciano, Donna and Keith entertained us a couple of nights and we visited with Donal and his wife Enda too. All in all they got to see my little slice of Ireland in a quick two weeks trip. The return flight was a one night stay over in Madrid and luckily it was not too cold, we walked the shopping streets and took a dinner for my birthday at the hotel. Real and Athletico were playing that night and Luciano had great fun with the idea I planted for him that he was all the way from Costa Rica just to see his big cousin Kaylor navas, the goalie for Madrid is Costa Rican ya see from a little town that Luciano knows only too well.

Carmen was so in love with Ireland and with me for this trip we seemed to be doing really well we had the day of celebrating Patrick's birthday in February and I had went for a drive one day with Carmen and we stumbled across an artist studio who made life like statues and I wanted to inquire as to what it would take to make a statue of our baby. The cost seemed high but myself and Carmen agreed it would be lovely to have a nice bronze statue, approx. cost about seven thousand dollars.

I then when researching some stuff on the internet found a beautiful little café for sale and decided we could buy it and make it a sandwich shop like an American deli style sandwich. To this we will call it Pat's Sandwiches, this will be Carmen's business to run and she and I can build maybe a chain of these and everybody will Know Pat's Sandwiches, they need not know why but our logo became a baby with a big sandwich in his hands as every picture we look at our baby Patrick, is him with some food in his hand, a cookie a tortilla something or other as Patrick loved to eat and snack away all day long.

I am sitting here writing at my desk and I look to my left and the dancing mickey mouse that Patrick loved is starring back at me, one of his Passport photographs sits beside me on my office phone and I think of him several times every day. Those photos of him in full flight doing anything with the food in his hands bring a warm smile across my body.

The sandwich shop was opened and my good friend from California who I befriended through Georges home service market when I lived in San Francisco, that's right Omar came to visit and help train Carmen and one staff member on how to make the deli sandwich just as they do in San Francisco. Omar had a week here to help me out and so it was on. The Deli will open, we served sandwiches of all kinds and gourmet products very tasty stuff and coffee and smoothies all fruit drinks healthy and delicious. It is an expensive venture to get something up and running like this but it was to go hand in hand with the therapies we were attending, I wanted to show Carmen how much I loved her and that we will be together for a long time so she could see how I was investing in our future. Funny thing was Carmen was now seeing how hard work it is just to gain pennies and me just funding her money all the time was coming to an end, she now had a business to run and needed to run it and make us money.

When the therapy came to a stop or an end as Carmen found some excuse that the lady was flirting with me and that going to these or referred to psychiatrists and all this psychology was nonsense, well then the abuse started again, Carmen saw fit to throw the coffee table in the air breaking everything and screaming and shouting around the house became a normal pattern. I had gone and stayed in a hotel again one night as the therapist had recommended I keep an overnight bag in my car at all times and when I see an episode building get out before it explodes. I pretended to everyone things were ok but they really were not.

I could not believe because I was to have a bad day, a bad day being I wanted to stay in bed and cry all day I was not allowed to that, my gripe became with Carmen that when I need time it seems as if I am not allowed, I am not allowed one single second for myself but you want to continue the abuse of me. I mean it was getting bad, she would roar and scream at me, things of horrible nature, "you are an imbecile, you are smelly get out of the room, I hate you" this kept going on and this idea of "you do not care about me and Luciano". We had been trying to make a baby through this time after Christmas and for some reason it did not seem to be working and I thought a lot of what I felt was we would never have another baby, for her I do not know but this idea of being cute and jealous had taken a whole new form. The episodes were becoming ridiculous. On an episode where she exploded and did not go to work at the coffee shop and decided she was leaving, she took off in the dark of night with her son, ran away to some friends house under the victim idea again she could not be with me anymore I am abusive. Oh was the story so reversed. I went to the court and asked them how I could protect myself from this kind of violence in the home and what could I do to make sure I am safe, I explained to the court I do not want to enforce it but I am in very difficult situation and need some sort of backup plan of protection. The system that exists takes your statement and then gives you a paper that says that the other person cannot be around you and in no form of physical or psychological way can they threaten you or do any damage to you. The court system then notifies the other person and a restriction order is then in place. I did not receive any notifications but as I later found out that in retaliation to my protection order Carmen went and filed for one also. I was told that could not be done, but it was done none the less. I went to work at the coffee shop and keep it going and paid the bills and the staff as it was a new business I needed to reach into my pocket a lot to keep it afloat

Through some persuasion and commitments from Carmen she again was sorry, this time I said strict therapies or nothing, if you saw no to therapy you say no to me, I cannot and will not help you anymore unless you start helping yourself. Carmen returned home and agreed to return to the doctor who again would refer her for further evaluations. In this time one evening when I went to fetch her and Luciano on a Saturday afternoon to close up early and we would go to the movies. I had stopped off at the local casino to take lunch with a business client and then headed to pick them up, I got there and the shop was closed already and they were waiting across the street, I said what the problem is and Carmen was furious. Why because I had been in the casino and I said three o clock and it was now three thirty. I said no you are mistaken I said three thirty and I am here on time, now drop the attitude and stop trying to ruin the day. Carmen continued screaming at me that the casino is full of hookers and whores and she cannot be with me and that lifestyle, that I was a filthy disgusting pig and she just wanted to go home, with that I pulled the car into a parking area in front of a pharmacy and told her she needed to get out and find her own way home. I was not going to put up with this anymore. I need it to stop but it has not and it cannot go on in front of Luciano and not me, Carmen started to punch me and slap me while in the car and she made a grab for the keys of the car, I caught her arm and removed the keys myself and I stepped out of the car to stand outside, I instructed to her get out of the car or I am calling the police, you are completely out of control and this has to stop. Luciano was in the back seat crying saying "mammy please stop please" but these were real tears he had, his poor day and the idea of a trip to the movies was now ruined. I looked at Luciano in the back seat with his seat belt on and saw his tears and it tore my heart out, I looked at him directly and said don't worry man we will go to the cinema just like I promised. Carmen said take me home and you guys can go to the cinema I don't feel like it anymore. She was calmer now and apologizing to her son and so I got into the car. I drove to the movie plex to buy the tickets and this is inside a big mall, we walked through the mall and while walking through there myself and Luciano were trying to make some fun and Carmen walked behind us with a sour face and attitude. The movies next show times were going to be seven and eight o clock as we had wanted something to eat the idea was we now had time to go home and shower and come back to the movies as there would be no traffic on a Saturday evening or take a meal somewhere around the shopping area and kill some time while waiting for the movie start time. I said I need a cigarette and the street is close to the movie theatre section so I walked outside, Carmen came to sit by a tree and Luciano too, I was smoking and I looked at her like nothing had happened. I said do you have any kind of apology, she replied "No for what we are fine now and going to the movies, why do you want to ruin that too" I asked again is there any form of apology or you do not see any wrong in what you have just done? The answer again was no, just drop it she said and stop trying to ruin everything. I turned on my heels and left them at the movie theatre, I went directly home and I went out and had some dinner myself by myself. I started to receive the text messages as to was I coming to the movie and eventually after trying to say, I will return to the movies and want nothing more than my family but the violence has no place anymore. The texts started to turn mean from Carmen and so I stopped responding, I then received a message that they were home and I was not there and typical I must be out "fucking whores" I replied I will be home shortly but you cannot be there you need to leave. When I returned home they had already turned in for the night and sitting there in the bed with her brave and bold face and attitude, I walked in and said "it is time to go, get your stuff and be gone, you need help beyond what I can provide for you and it is time to go, you cannot hit me and think it is ok, too many times now I am done with you" Carmen's reply was "fuck you I am going nowhere this is my house", I called the police and they came and took her out from my house.

I told the staff girl that I was not sure about Carmen may not be returning to the store. I changed the locks on my house by advice of the courts and I continued with my office Job.

I had no idea what was really going on but it was another fog of horrible feelings and I did not want to take on the hurt and the pain that was being caused I had enough on my plate. I saw the therapist by myself and she said well we can work on you only and how we can try and help heal some of the pain that I carry through my own grievance process.

I went to the coffee shop on Saturday just to check what was needed for Monday and that evening the locks had been changed. The shutters would not open and it appeared Carmen had changed the locks to lock me out of my business now too. This was a final straw for me and the idea to just forget about her and everything about her was now time. I felt horrible, I was probably at the lowest point I had ever been, I was reflecting on it all and trying to stay strong and pray for the strength to my two angels in heaven to come down and guide me please. This woman has made a big huge sucker out of me and cost me thousands upon thousands of dollars, I am losing clients at work as I am not focused, the fun was gone completely out of life, I bored the therapists with my long sessions of crying and pining for my love and how I now missed Luciano but I could not take the abuse anymore. I needed to take a moment to try and see was the business worth fighting for, was the whole issue of love that I wanted to be the super man and just rescue this girl and change her, or was it me and all my pain for the past few years had just become too much for me as a person. I had drank a few times over the past years and was this the time I would turn to alcohol again for comfort, could I start using drugs and give up, just give up on it all. Carmen at the time had some email exchanges with me where I said it was simply a matter of attending the doctors getting on some kind of treatment plan with doctors and that if a car does not work right we take it to a mechanic, if a person does not work right we take them to a psychiatrist or psychologist but something has to happen, she promised she would attend the new doctor referred by our therapist and she would show me she wanted me, but for these two weeks we were not together, she called to fight it seemed and so I stopped taking the calls but sent her some long heart felt emails as to the situation as I saw it and all we had been through and there is a problem, if she is ready to get honest and face it I will carry her through it, hand in hand we will walk side by side. I was losing the run of myself, I did not like the person I had become in the arguments with her and the pains I carried were already killing me slowly. I asked her why when she knows my heart is already been crushed in life she wishes to break it completely and shatter it to nothing, what have I ever done to you, what am I guilty of. In therapy I asked my doctor, tell me honestly what I have done, I have asked the family for help with this and no one wants to listen, no one seems to care. In the build up to the therapist to respond to me, was a smile and a smirk from her, she said well you asked,

I said yes I am finished my crying for today and really want to know what is my fault here what have I done, the doctor answered "you did not get out and run from this relationship sooner, that is your fault. You have stayed too long"

What a smack in the face, I was so confused in my life, I miss my babies, I love a girl that wants to hurt me, I only understand love as to how my father showed me love all my life, when I was a wayward teen he never stopped, he chased me and chased me through the end, he helped rescue me and I returned out of a life of potential death through drugs or guns, my father had shown me the deepest love I could ever know and how could I turn my back on someone that maybe needed me too. The harsh reality of life, who? Is more important, her or me. I can chase and try and attempt to get her to a point of treatment and dealing with a mental problem or walk away and leave her in her own misery and save myself. It was looking like the right route was save myself for the first time in life, save myself get some peace for the loss of my babies, look to take baby steps and rebuild myself, I was now a victim of domestic violence and immense abuse from my significant other. As a man there is a pride feeling that gets in the way to even acknowledge that, never mind speak the words, I am a victim of abuse at the hands of my woman. Not an easy pill to swallow. I made some more communications with Carmen that I was proud of her to attend the doctor and someday I hope we can be together as this is all I dream for the nice kind loving side of my partner to hold me and comfort me through my pains and ease off on the pressures and making demands of me. I told her I was proud of her to visit the doctors and that this would be good for us in the future. Then she and I had discussed that I would ship her belongings to where ever she is now and that perhaps a road of a different kind might help bring us together.

Carmen said she was sick and felt horrible and needed time and she now had Luciano in a school and she needed to figure out her life too and so we were officially apart now with unnecessary hurt in both our lives because when Carmen would have moments of clarity she would say she does not know why she hurts me and she does not want to hurt me, but it just never lasted and soon turned to rage and violence again. This particular day she said she thinks she might be pregnant and I cried when she told me this on the phone, I said we would need to make a blood test, she said she will try a pee test and see and she and I stayed on the phone while we waited to see one line or two. It is pregnant positive she said. I packed an overnight bag and ran to get a bus to the town where she was now staying with her father.

Chapter 36.

The local clinic was 24 hour service but the blood
tests for the pregnancy test were during business
hours, I went with her hand in hand that morning
and it was confirmed, pregnant. We are going to
have a baby, with this comes all those love feelings
all happiness and thoughts of the dreams but for us
major fears, and what and how it must be done right
this time. We knew we had to be together, there is
no other way, I said we will be together but it has to
be right, in my mind I always remember Carmen
always said, she feels so wonderful when she was
pregnant two times before and it brought me back to
the idea that maybe, there was something to the
doctor agreeing to recommend the blood tests and
lets look and see is there a hormone over load or
deficiency. Carmen did not want to return to the
house unless the court things were lifted and so for
a second time we would approach the judge and ask
her to lift the restriction that our circumstances have
changed and we want to do it right through therapy
and bring a baby into the world I went to the court
and spoke with the judge and said I am in no real
danger, but if the process exists to bring about some
therapy then maybe it would be a good thing. The
court setting was just in an office with a judge, it
was an option to speak in front of each other or
speak privately. I chose for privately as I did not

want to rock the boat by Carmen thinking I said something for any different reasons.

The judge said she would have an answer within a few days as in a hurry up situation so we could get on with our lives. Luciano was able to start another school but it was important that he finish the year or he might not graduate. His mother never seemed to care about this but I did and it was not right having him in three different schools within the same school year. Of course in the fights or arguments she would say, as soon as Luciano is finished school I am leaving and you will never see this baby and how she will take this baby from me and there will be nothing I can do.

I look back at how jealous she really was, when my friend Omar came from the states to help us with the setting up of the sandwich shop, Carmen was jealous of how I welcomed him and wanted to offer him a day trip to the volcanoes. My brother Patrick had visited from Australia and Carmen was extremely jealous when I took him on a fishing trip to go sword fishing for the day, yes it was an expensive trip but he was the only Patrick Mc Nally I had left, she screamed and shouted and made the house uncomfortable when both of these came to visit, just to be jealous of me and my time given to others, people I also cared about which turned in to be some idea I did not care about her. The tantrums were ridiculous. The fishing trip she said was a day on a boat full of hookers and strippers and that is just disgusting and I was a smelly Irish and who do I think I am and she would never sleep with me again, to me it was all madness and I was sick and tired of it, I pleaded with her many times, why do you do these things and say such horrible things, for this she never had an answer. I always said, I have had a ball of hurt in my life, I have the perfect excuse to sit on the side of the road begging for change and just swig out of a bottle for the rest of my life, who could fault me for that after what has gone on, but I get up every day to support you guys and you just keep spending money without a care, closed the business and cost me a fortune, had me thrown in jail what more do you want? WHY?

In October of that year 2015 we were seeing the doctor for the pregnancy updates and had taken a scan and listened to a heartbeat and Carmen had to get some new pregnancy clothes, I got Luciano a bike for his birthday and a nice bench for the front of the house, so Carmen would not have to go up and down the steps while pregnant.

The night she returned to live with me I had the entire bedroom filled with candles and asked her not to go into the bedroom until after dinner.

So that I could go ahead and light all the candles, she went in and lay in the bed and was so happy, I said just relax honey just relax, she did and things were looking up. But in October, for some reason the immigration came knocking on my door asking me to show my residency status and what was my current status in the country, they said somebody anonymously called their offices and said I was illegal in the country and that I need to prove to them my papers, I did indeed have a process going for two years now and was waiting I explained that to them and so they said well we are here to take you to our offices but we can just set an appointment for tomorrow. I was given an official appointment sheet of paper and told to show up at the immigration headquarters tomorrow and bring my lawyer and all paper work with me. By the time I got there my lawyer was already there dealing with it and they said all I needed to do was carry a proof of status with me and that cannot happen again, I blamed Carmen's father saying to her he is trying to do this to me because he does not want to pay back the money he borrowed from me, she said it was the lawyer she had gotten to fight against me for the Pat's sandwiches business as that lawyer had been sending her nasty messages saying to pay her, "he is not a real man, a real man would pay his woman's bills" I was beginning to think the whole country is nuts or full of them for real. I could not believe that the immigration was called on me. That is someone sick trying to hurt me.

November was here again and it was going to be Darra's nineteenth birthday, can you imagine my baby would turn nineteen this year, oh how time flew. As I could see Carmen's ways were not improving and when I asked for space and did not want to see or do anything together I think I will go and visit his grave, she said yes this would be a good break as we are not communicating properly right now and for sure I was not going back to jail was my feeling as last year around this time that is what happened and so I jetted off to Ireland with one goal in mind, set some flowers on Darra's grave. I thought if he were alive right now I would find a way to be with him and spend his birthday together so I should do the same and visit his grave, I visit Patrick's grave all the time and clean it and planted flowers and roses, so I should visit with Darra.

Through all the stress over the past twelve or more months my stomach had not been working right and now something really weird was happening it was like diabetes or something, I was peeing three and four times in the night and had a very dry thirsty feeling almost immediately after peeing, I did not know what it was but boarded the plane for Ireland anyway. I had spent many nights and evenings driving the roads and thinking to stay in a hotel and used the casino and playing slot machines as an escape many times to avoid being at home and listening to the screaming and the fight. Carmen had introduced a few times in therapy and I said well look at the why, there is nowhere else to go, I can be alone and nobody bothers me or wants to know who I am or why I am there, if you prefer maybe I should go to a strip bar and watch girls the next time as you accuse me of this anyway. You see the format of how things work is funny when distorted, I go to the casino is Carmen's big gripe, but I point out no, the casino has not been the problem, the casino I seek refuge in, so ask yourself why should I have to seek refuge at all that is the real problem so put things in their correct order please in some effort to see the real problem. If I am the gambling headache you think I am then let's look at it, not once has any bill not been paid the rent is paid on time always, all the bills are paid and there are more than an abundance of groceries in the presses, does not to me look like a household that is affected negatively by any form of gambling, add to that all the money wasted thus far, we had moved house after the embarrassment I received by being hauled off to jail and so we moved, I furnished the new house, ten thousand dollars, we took a European vacation for Christmas ten thousand dollars, I invested in a Sandwich business seventeen thousand dollars and still managed to buy gifts and nice things for our home and support us, did not to me look like gambling or escaping through playing slot machines was doing any financial damage. It is the fact I have somewhere to go when you decide to scream and shout at me that's the real problem, I cannot be controlled then I can walk out the door and get in my car and leave. That is the real problem. The anniversary of Darra's death came upon us December 12th again another year, four years dead my baby, Carmen asked if we should do something I said I have no plans but for now think I want to be alone. I will see how I feel this coming Saturday when the day comes, for now my plan will be work in the morning and see from there.

When I awoke on the 12th I did not feel good, it is not just to choose to feel miserable there is just some weird comfort in thinking of him and feeling the negative down awkwardness that goes with it, it does pass but it must be felt. Carmen and Luciano had left out of the house to I do not know where, and I headed for the casino to take a lunch, within moments of me reaching there the text messages came, we are going to light candles and we should be together as a family and you are wrong to exclude us from this, I was in humour to reply and did, I said all your screaming about we have to go to the beach this Christmas that is what all of Costa

Rica does and that I am just too cheap and I don't care. Well I asked for some space but you do not seem to understand this, LEAVE ME ALONE TODAY.

She replied how she did not need me and need to depend on me for shit and I would regret the day I turned her away. Go find somewhere else to sleep. I gambled that day and played some table games and blew off some steam but I was looking for an escape again and alcohol was not a form of escape that tasted good, I didn't want to go home and listen to abuse so I stayed in the casino. The next morning I woke up as I had been on the couch for my feeling was, I am not going to sleep with someone who wants to treat me bad and be the thorn who wants to ruin my personal days, I went to work in my office.

The office was the third bedroom of this new house as I had to move and work from home due to the crap I would listen to from my partner when she decided I was not in the office and I was seeing someone else and call me and say put someone from the office on the phone, I would say I have walked out the back to smoke as this is embarrassing I am supposed to be the boss and do not need my partner harassing me in the middle of the day. The easy fix for this was to move the office home and give in to her again and show her what I do and how I do it all day, every day in front of a computer. And so this day was like no other, I was upstairs working and I heard lunch being prepared it was a Sunday so I thought it was a good way for her to make a peace offering, why not I did most of the cooking in the household so I went to take a smoke break from the upstairs office, I would normally go to the pool area outside and then I noticed it was two plates set for lunch, Carmen and Luciano and none for me, oh well my fault I asked to be left alone. I finished out the day and there was no talk from to Carmen all day. They went out somewhere for the rest of the day and I finished my work duties. I fell asleep down stairs that night again in front of the television and the next day continued the same pattern, no speak between us and I continued my work in the office, the following day the same thing except Tuesday after I had seen only two placings for two days now at the dinner table, Luciano came to the office to ask me if I wanted to take lunch with them, due to reasons of being busy I said no thank you and they ate.

Carmen came into the office after they had eaten, she said in a direct tone "Are me and Luciano and this baby part of your life or not?" I said I do not want to answer this question right now, please continue to leave me alone. She started screaming at me that I was horrible and mean and deserve that my babies died and who do I think I am to treat her so bad, I am asking you for the last time she said "are me this baby and Luciano part of your life or not" I stood up out of my chair and looked out the window so she could not see my face, tears were coming down my cheeks, not for Darra, not for Patrick but for me, I was feeling so sad that my woman who I loved and tried in every way I know how to show love to is just abusive and has problems beyond my capabilities. I did not want her to see my face because she would know my answer was yes and I did not want to give an answer as it is not fair how she pushes me and wants her question answered and to get her way. I walked to leave the room and she stood in front of the door, and screamed at me, answer my question, I said, "you are now blocking my exit from the room please step aside" she said NO I am going to answer or stay here until I do " Carmen, you are blocking my exit from the room and not permitting me to leave the room, this is not fair and not right, please get out of my way and step aside please" Carmen flung the door open and headed for the main bedroom screaming insults at me in Spanish. I headed for the pool area and smoked a cigarette, I knew she was inside in a fit of rage and I didn't know what to do, I thought just go in and do your work and lock the door to the office and wait for her to calm down. I was not happy smoking my cigarette and I returned to the house, Carmen was now sitting down stairs in the front room, I walked to her with an effort to be firm and tell her she is not going to keep doing this, I stood in front of the coffee table behind which she was sitting on the couch, I said firmly " you listen to me," before I could finish speaking she was roaring back at me, she has listened to me for the last time and throwing candles that were on the coffee table at me, one hit the wall the other hit my leg and did not break I retreated to go up the stairs and she had jumped up and was smashing any ornaments she could grab, firing them at me up the stairs, I turned and said to her, you are completely out of control, I took my phone out to take pictures and stupidly I should have taken a video but picture it was, she continued to grab the candle that didn't break and throw it at me, when she saw the phone she charged at me up the stairs, and tried to grab it I turned towards the wall as to protect the camera/phone, she was grabbing for it and hitting me in the shoulder and back, I had been retreating to go upstairs and lock myself in the office but this rage was something else and I then with her pushing and hitting went quickly down the stairs and out the front door and I called the emergency services and said I was having a domestic dispute and I needed the police to come, which they did and rather quickly, while waiting for them I took a quick shower and took some more photographs of the mess of glass all over the floor. When the police came Carmen produced her papers of restriction that she had gotten earlier that year and told the police I just went crazy and broke the house up, that her papers were valid and they needed to take me to jail. I explained to the police that I too had the same papers and that she had broken everything and I did not need to go to jail that they needed to get a doctor and look at her mental state, she is six months pregnant and does not seem to care about that, there is a small child upstairs and he does not seem to be cared about by the mother either. The police said we both needed to go to the court as I do not have papers but she does, I said mine are in the house, I went to where the files were kept and they were gone, Carmen had taken and hid them or done something with them but my evidence was not there I had no court papers. So two patrol cars took me in one and Carmen and Luciano in the other to the court house, as it was close to the Christmas season there was no judge available as they had left early for the day from the domestic violence court, this left only one option the criminal court downstairs. Carmen went ahead and made a big song and dance of a statement against me and I was taken in handcuffs and placed in a jail cell, fully processed and awaiting a judge. My charges were mistreatment of a woman, assault of a woman and damage to the house with a threat to her life. I was placed in a cell and awaiting a judge which might be tomorrow or the next day they said. My lawyer had shown up and I was in front of a criminal judge that night at around one in the morning. The court required me to give them an alternate address for where I can be reached while awaiting trial and informed me at this night I do not have to enter any plea as to guilty or not guilty, I must remain contactable and an address was something I did not have, that I had to stay away from my home and that I would receive a letter which would inform the police to escort me to get my belongings for the time being. I explained it was my place of work and so I was allowed also to get my personal belongings along with my items of work from the office. My lawyer whispered to me and said she had an apartment at the back of her house behind the pool and I could use that address and so it was entered into the court, I was at that location should they need to find me for anything and I was released, the judge at the time was a lady judge and she finished the formal proceedings and turned off her micro phone and addressed me directly saying, to me do not respond to anyone if they call you, turn off your phone if someone you do not know calls and when you recognize the voice hang up. This is going to be tough she said but I will try and put in for a swift trial and make things happen fast for you ok. I said I appreciate it and I was brought back down stairs to the cells to await the official paper work for my release. Devastation all over again at the hands of this woman.

People analyse their life sometimes and they think they have it bad and they get down and depressed and miserable, funny word miserable this was a charge I was facing the threat to her life was that I said I will make her life miserable. Well there is absolutely nothing funny about the word really as it stands for completely the opposite and holds no bearing to fun at all, however in these circumstances yes I recall the week before the word had been used, I sat at home and said I am going to go out and hang out with my friend, she said where I said maybe the casino I do not know. She said no and got all upset, I said you just want to see me miserable, there is no room in this life right now for me to do or say anything that might make me happy, let's all just stay miserable. That was the conversation and now I was in a court proceeding for the use and taken out of context situation of using the word miserable. When people say as my father would have always said to me growing up when I was talking back and giving cheek, choose your words carefully. It is indeed a wise statement because words and when dealing with someone who has presented to maybe have some weakness of mind, taken out of context words can be a major mess to say the least.

My court dates came fast alright every other day were the dates, each day I did not know what was going on but on the second day of visiting the court the prosecution came to offer me a deal, maintain the restriction order and move from the house and the charges will all be dropped, this was what Carmen had said she would go for and drop the charges, my lawyer advised me to try and take any deal as the law in Costa Rica supports women fully. I said to my lawyer, I understand what you are saying and I appreciate your advice, can you keep your voice down because they think they are winning over there, when they hear you advising me to take a deal they think they have the upper hand and I should be grateful, it does not work like that. I want my house back she has to get out of my house, she is crazy and has problems I am innocent of this and she needs to make an apology and tell them all sorry for making such lies. The prosecutor returned to say she said no and she will vacate the house on the 15th of February not a day before it, my lawyer said ok I will inform my client. He informed as to the status Carmen was now taking with her father sitting beside her across the hall at the outside of the court rooms. I have to think this was December 21st maybe I cannot recall even though recently the exact dates as I was in such a state of emotional turmoil coupled with outright disgust, I mean seriously I was now faced with some horrible crimes and in a foreign country and the woman I had loved and cared for so much, I had given everything I knew possible to this relationship Money, my blood, my sweat and tears in every sense of the cliché I had given it my all to end up here with this predicament. My Lawyer was hopping up and down saying take the deal, the deal works like this in the legal system in Costa Rica, basically everyone charged with some form of crime or another will get a chance to make a deal should the prosecution deem it fit to be a case where a deal is probably better. They will offer some terms and conditions and you do not get any record, you must stay clear of any trouble or problems for five years from the time of the deal and then it drops off and goes away. In that five year period should you end up in front of a court room again for any reason you will go straight to jail no deals no outs nothing NADA this is Spanish for nothing and used quite often to explain a severe situation of nothing. I looked at my lawyer and said to him this, I am not guilty of anything this is all fabricated lies, if she is not willing to tell the truth then let the judge decide as I speak the truth. The prosecution approached and asked if we have a deal and the answer was no and so with attitude the prosecutor said ok let's go to court, the intimidations tactics were not working on me.

Court rooms were nothing new in my life I had been in court for horrible crimes, some I did commit and some I did not in my lifetime I was not about to bow down to a situation of blatant lies. The judge did not proceed as they outlined the case and set it down to recommence after the Christmas holiday and due to the holiday it would be a couple of days only, the judge instructed it should not have gone this far and without a translator to explain fully everything to me in English, I had mentioned my lawyers could translate but that is not allowed as your lawyer could actually be instructing you what to say and so an independent translator would be needed, so a delay in proceedings was the step taken that night. When I returned to my lawyer's home, just to clarify I had two lawyers sitting beside me on the bench, the one a friend of mine and a company lawyer for legal matters and a hired criminal defence lawyer. It was the criminal defence lawyer running my case. So upon returning home that night to the company lawyers house where I had been temporarily housed in the apartment out by the pool, I received a phone call as we had turned in the gate and were by the front entrance, I asked who is speaking as they were speaking in Spanish, it was Carmen's older brother Walter, rambling on in Spanish telling me to come out where are you??. Come outside I will kill you. I am here he said and rattled off the address of where I was listed as staying, come out, how dare you treat my sister who is pregnant.... I hung up. I turned to my lawyer friend and told her it is Carmen's brother he is here somewhere telling me to come outside, and then the phone rang again. Come out you little faggot and I will kill you, who you think you are, I said "it is all lies, now what do you want" I could hear the funniest thing right at that time, a dog barking in the background but I could hear it through the phone and in my back ground also and so I knew he was close, I hung up the phone and called the emergency number for the authorities. He must have heard me because he was gone by the time they showed up, I had to explain this to them and return to court the next day also. It became obvious immediately to me and my friend that once they did not get the deal they decided to take the law into their own hands, but unfortunately that is not how life is supposed to go. The only way Walter could have the exact address is that it was given to him from the court files by Carmen. This through another bout of sadness into the Christmas of misery I was already having, I could not believe she would carry and run with a lie so deep.

In court I gave a full declaration and because I am long winded and wanted to give the full and proper account of things, it took some one hour and a bit maybe, although the judge paid me full attention, I started at the beginning which was the day in question and tracked backwards to the fact this was not the first time this tactic had been used except this time I must explain all. The judge permitted me and I spoke the whole story. You see on the court steps the night before I explained to my lawyer that I did not take the deal as this was not justice and if I go to jail then he is no good at his job and that is the simple short of it for me, I think he was slightly insulted for me to put his abilities into question but my message to him was simple. I am Irish and if there is one thing we are used to is being the underdog, I believe in god I put my faith in a Costa Rica judicial system to find the truth as that is all I have to speak oh yeah and did I mention I am Irish, well this stubborn headed Irish man will fight to the death to defend his innocence and not bow down to anyone. My lawyer's response was tasteful "as your legal representative I have to advise you as to the legal system in Costa Rica is a tough one against men in the mal treatment of women, as a man I agree with you and I love the Irishness" and he shook my hand. We knew then there was one out, win the case. Seeing as I had now given my declaration it was up to us to introduce evidences and the prosecution likewise, then another delay and was scheduled for two days later. Again the courtroom before New Year's Eve and this time it was the witnesses to speak. I sat in total shock, the only feeling was disbelief and shock to hear Carmen speak the lies to the judge, though it was a little flimsy as she slightly contradicted her original statement as it was not a push merely a passing on the stairs and so it was not a push. The evidence of text messages and the likes showed nothing but an argument or two between a dysfunctional couple. The case was delayed again for another date after the New Year. We had gotten into the habit of taking a snack somewhere after the case each evening and this was no exception. Except this night I cried hard as to understand why she is doing this, I cried in the car with my lawyers as I could not understand the lies I had heard tonight, I was shocked to see Carmen swear to a judge to tell the truth and then lie, it was beyond my realm of comprehension. I had remembered the therapist saying to me their belief of what Carmen suffered from and I had been reading all kinds of articles on the internet about different disorders and the traits and how it plays out, well the disbelief did not end in the court that day or her brother being sent to kill me, although that was probably concocted by her father. I could not believe it as I read more and more on the internet and how to live with such a condition and the patterns that take form and how someone acts with such illness, I cried again and again, this was all text book procedures everything that was happening could be found on the internet of every stereo typical scenario of a certain type of mental illness. I prayed hard that Christmas for some resolve and immediate result and wanted this behind me but it would drag on another few court dates more.

7th of January 2016 my birthday my day to turn 40 what a great day, I am due in court at 5 pm to go and maybe be sentenced to 4 or 5 years in prison in Costa Rica, this is what the prosecution has presented as to sentencing requirements including to put the fact of Carmen being pregnant means there are two lives put at risk not just one. My fortieth whoop de doo, my lawyer friend came out around the pool that morning singing, "It's your birthday, it's your birthday" I could not even laugh. The court went through the procedural items and after I hurried to the outside steps, to be sure to be there as she exited the court, I thought she will surely give me a look or something to show she knows she is wrong and it has all gone too far but nothing she walked right past me like I did not exist, I throw my hands up to her father walking behind her and he bowed his head. That was it, the lawyers said we have to go and celebrate your birthday let's go for some food and off we went, while I was sitting in the restaurant I received a voice speaking message from a number I did not recognize, it was Luciano's voice on Carmen's sisters phone, he said in Spanish

"Aidan happy birthday, I miss you and love you" I had walked out to the parking lot to listen to the message and then the lawyers joined me for a cigarette, then came a text message from Carmen, "Happy birthday Aidan xxoxx" I showed it to the lawyers and they said we have to use this, she is not well, what is wrong with her testifying against you and then a happy birthday.

I felt like shit, her tactics were working I was being broken down in my battle, I did not want the battle but I had no choice but to defend myself. The case got more interesting as I had a copy of all my files through time and instructed my lawyer to use the part where Carmen admitted to hitting me in the head to the domestic violence judge, my lawyer had a copy of the file from the court for the case that his messenger had picked up some time over the Christmas from the court but he did not have that page, the page was missing. We re-entered the court this particular night and my lawyer to approach the judge and review her copy of the file and she too the judge that is was also missing the page, my lawyer called for a mistrial and miscarriage of justice as the file was incomplete and the judge was being misled. The judge stopped proceedings and ordered that the domestic violence judge on call for the night be summoned and the complete file be provided. The on call judge was available but did not have access to these files and so adjourned again.

Carmen sent me a message on what's app to tell me she is worried that her nephew has been staying over and he has chicken pox, she is not sure if she had them before as a child and if she contracts them the baby could be in grave jeopardy. I rushed to meet her that lunch time the next day as she had red dots on her belly, the bump where the baby was, she called her doctor and he gave advice to drink water and rest and if the bumps are there tomorrow she would go to see him. I should have really told you that a doctor's visit occurred during this trial and when Carmen gave her declaration of lies against me she did say, that I was the most wonderful step father to her son that she could have ever prayed for and she also stuck the dagger in my heart, she had been for an ultrasound and she mentioned it was a baby girl. The bitter sweet elements of those words were daunting. So I met with her and the court was to be tonight there were no more delays and I said to her, you still have one last chance to speak and you could make it count, she apologized and was sorry and admitted to me she didn't think it could go this far.

I told my lawyers on the steps of the court that evening that I had met with her and they were pissed, they understood about the emergency and the chicken pox but I said to them they needed to know so there could be no surprises inside the courtroom this evening. The Judge began and read through how the case had gone and what was produced and what the evidence and declarations were and after the whole readings of everything took a recess and said, we will return at 9.30 pm and sentencing will occur. We went for something to eat and all the lawyers jokes were about me going to prison, I said I do not think so I believed the Judged winked at me as exiting for recess, my lawyers said no way I said, well maybe not a wink, but as she was saying we will wrap this up tonight she gave a very clear look as she walked past, I was brimming with confidence.

On return the judge gave a complete run down of how Carmen possessed restrictions against me from a different address three cities away, Aidan has existing restrictions against Carmen for domestic violence. She said I had every right to my house, she also said on each of the counts I fully and completely absolve Aidan of any wrong doing, I do not believe her. The judge said there is no doubt an argument took place but for everything else there is grave doubt. There appears to be a manipulation of the justice system and I was acquitted completely. I walked out so happy I had told Carmen that day at lunch I will get out from this and you must promise therapy and treatment and we go forward, I will pray to forgive and the baby is the most important thing, she agreed.

I have a good friend here in Costa Rica who was supporting me by listening to my awful talk and long winded reasoning throughout the whole case process, he supported me in whatever decision I made, but strongly advised to get as far away from this woman as possible, I explained whole heartedly to him and my lawyers and anyone who wanted to listen, I know what she did is bad, I know what she did is wrong, but for the sake of love and the eyes of God I believe it is upon me to forgive her and accept her with her faults and if indeed she is really suffering and this is a cry for help it is my duty as a man and a husband and a father to take my love and provide for her the best help and care money can buy and go forward to rid my relationship and my family of the demons that seem to possess and have firm hold on my loved one. I have lost two babies before and the utmost importance is to protect and provide for my new baby. This will be baby number three and when someone has lost two as I have done there is no future but to slave and make a beautiful life for my new baby. It may seem harsh and strange or even intense but the feeling inside me to have the opportunity not to fail again, the opportunity to take it and grab on with two hands. I have the nice of Carmen and love her so much and so for this reason I must seek to help her and help myself to bring my family back together and so my friend my good friend Franklin said he thought I was more than a good man he admire the attitude for all the shit I had just taken and he supported me in this decision.

Chapter 37.

I went forward with the therapy and for the first session of therapy I loaded my car from my friend's apartment where I had been staying and headed to therapy, in the session Carmen admitted the truth and I made clear I was moving home and therapy would need to be every day or other day for all this to work. We took six session of therapy with a rocky patch in between and in the argument that day it was February 13th exactly as it marked two weeks before Patrick's birthday, I asked Carmen to please not start again, please bite your tongue for two weeks, my commitment I will not go to the casino as this was Carmen's biggest gripe. I wanted from her a promise that for two weeks, she will not scream she will not fight and she will not break anything in the house. This mostly came about that day as I was sitting in my office upstairs,

Carmen was doing homework with Luciano down stairs. I heard voices raised and I said the violence is no more, I am not having it in the house anymore, we argued and I said if you cannot control yourself you will have to leave, Carmen agreed to two weeks, she would do the two weeks and we would be a family and take a nice dinner to celebrate Patrick's 3rd birthday. Something didn't work right and buy February 25th it was all hell breaking loose as Carmen was calling me and questioning me as to where a certain pair of black pants were and how I am fucking someone else and that I needed to find somewhere to live. I needed to be a real man and leave, that she was disgusted to end up with someone like me and I must be using cocaine and fucking whores, all her words, I said you have to leave, be out of my house by 6pm this evening, this treatment is not going to happen, legally you are not supposed to be here, I began to load my car with TVs and anything she could possibly break, I went to the domestic violence court and asked them what I should do, they said leave voluntarily or call the police to remove her. She is eight months pregnant by this day and she is frantic like before just like Christmas, Luciano luckily was at school, she told me how if she were a man she would beat the shit out of me and I had not got the balls to call the police on her, I said if you keep daring me it is what is going to happen, she tried to make fun of me, and I explained to her, I do not know you anymore and do not know who you have become, I explained how the black pants that she was making a song and dance about were in the closet probably where they always are as I have not worn them in weeks. She submitted to this and said "I might be in error about the pants" I paused and waited and said then, that usually when someone realizes they made a mistake an apology is what follows but in your case never as you do no wrong. The screaming abuse at me continued and I decided to make a video as I could not believe I was here again. I went to go to my storage unit with all the items I had taken from the house, I had dismantled our bed and explained to her all the comforts are over, I do not need them in my house and am taking them to storage, that is she is not to rob anything from my house and to leave. I went to the storage, but through traffic and the time of day I did not make it on opening hours and so lugged all the stuff back again. When I returned home, my key did not work. I had seen the light get turned off when I drove up to the garage, I remembered her screaming today that if I did not leave the house she would call the police and I would go to jail just like at Christmas, laughing as she finished screaming the words. I went to the trunk of my car where I had kept the copies of the court files so I could have the paper copy to show them as I was not going to jail again no way. The files were gone they were not there; I thought I have seen this before. I called the emergency line and explained the situation. When the police came they observed my keys do not work and that there is someone inside, she did not open, they knocked again after ten minutes, Carmen appeared with her copy of the files and attempted to convince the police it is me that deserves to go to jail as she is pregnant and in fear of her life. The same story over again. I told the cops no way I am going to the courts and explained the whole Christmas saga, I insisted they go and demand her to produce my files as she has stolen them from my car, this alone shows the vindictiveness of what she is doing. The cop returned to say they are in the neighbour's car and the neighbour will return in twenty minutes, and so we wait. I asked can you guys not see what is going on here, who takes the files and hides them in the neighbours car? Who locks themselves in the house? Off we went to the court house 7pm at night and the prosecutors wanted me to press charges, I asked is there nothing you can do that where she does not have to go to a jail cell as now she was in the position I was in in December last. Their answer was if you press charges right now, we take her to jail but even though she is pregnant we do not want to, I agreed and so they said, just put the charges for the courts tomorrow and she does not have to go to jail. It was only at the point in their questioning when they asked who owns the house, I said it is a rental that they walked out to her, and explained her something. I heard her raising her voice and beginning to cry, saying "I have done nothing" the prosecutor walked back into his office where I sat and handed me the keys to my house and said she cannot return there and you are free to go to your home, if she goes to the house call the police. I went to the court the next morning and then started on the track of checking what exactly can I do to protect my unborn baby, I have seen her violence and I must protect.

I have lost two sons as is already explained and I was trying to hold this together but panicking at the same time as my baby was not born and how do I know she will not harm herself or my baby. Carmen went to the court a couple of days later to petition the rights to enter my house and get her belongings and in that was written, the baby's clothes and the toys and all her and her sons personal belongings. She stormed through the house with attitude and her sister was there to help if they could they would have taken everything, they took all my memories of Patrick as claiming this is what was meant by the babies clothes. I returned to the judge frantic the next day demanding to see the judge and asked why did you give such specifics, you were manipulated, these are the clothes of my dead son, my memories you cannot give an order to let her take these but she has to hurt me even more. The judge apologized and said that when she saw her pregnant it seemed obvious the baby's clothes. The judge gave me an order to go and get some of my belongings back and understood it was done to hurt me. I went to her sister's house with police to retrieve my pictures but was informed they were not there and they were stored at her father's maybe. Nothing I could do, I returned to the judge and explained and the judge gave me another order which was not specific to the address of her sisters to retrieve my property but what good is that.

I sat at home and questioned everything; her words were tough who knows if this baby is yours she said. Who knows if Patrick was mine, the only way I would ever be sure is go and dig up his grave and take DNA samples, then she laughed to herself and said of course he is mine, and this baby will never know you. I started to question everything the timing of when she had been away out of the house and returned to say she was pregnant. The deepest question of all and the shock of how she would try and put me in jail a third time, the immigration trying to remove me from the country trying to throw me in jail why try so hard to get me out of the picture so that the truth about our baby could never be found?

Chapter 38.

What is this whole pattern of events? What is the truth? What is really going on? Is this real? I am going to lose my baby, she is so sick she will keep me from my baby? These thoughts can screw your mind up. How could she take the computer and the files from my car, it had to be done while I was sleeping one morning, she went to the car with the keys from my pocket sneaking and took the items and hid them with the neighbour, my neighbour who had her own problems and I fed her kids because she was going through rough times. Is this all really happening?

What is really going on? I looked for the results of the investigation of my son Patrick's death and when I was finally able to find the office and jurisdiction of where it is, I read it for the first time and what I read brought heavy tears to my eyes, the interviews were lies, my heart hit the back of my throat, LIES, I am reading lies I cannot believe it, the interview of mine is a copy of Carmen's words. That day in July 2014, one to two minutes after laying Patrick to rest the detectives met us outside the door of the morgue and written in her statement is lies. How could this be so calculated, what exactly is going on? All the times she apologized and said she loved me are all lies? My baby's death is in his report lies. The money she had stolen from me over the times was all to give to her father, what are the lies? I have given this woman everything and beyond I have prayed hard to find forgiveness in my heart and help my one true love the mother of my babies and now there is all lies everywhere, Please god come down from the heavens and show me something please, I cannot believe what has happened and how her family after learning of the lies of Christmas just gone, they do not see the state of crisis that exists, it must just suit everybody to keep her messed up. I could not and do not figure what it all means or what it could mean but now I better fight for my new baby because this lady is a monster, there is no other way. There is not an illness that can be cured it is sad yet it is all true. Devastation and the fight to try and open doors and courts and child protection services, it all appears my efforts are discriminated against here in Costa Rica for the simple fact I am not from here, I am a foreigner and the legal system has many holes for a woman to hide behind, trouble is she lies and tries to take refuge in a system that actually is designed to save and protect women in real danger. The only danger she is in is the danger from herself.

I learned on March 29th 2016 my baby daughter was born, said to be a little premature but ok. I am searching for protection and the rights to protect my baby, the cycle of events that surround Carmen and her out bursts of rage followed by extreme lies now have thrown serious doubt of what happened my baby Patrick and for this reason I press every day to find a way my new baby born will not meet the same faith. I pray to god that some office here will take a real view of what I am faced with and the extent of the entire family I am against that wish for me to share the blame for Carmen's mental condition with me, as I told Carmen that day of our last fight, no I am not crazy I am just finally standing up to the mentalness I am faced with, this is me taking action. I need the worlds help to see my baby, to save my baby, I have not seen my baby since day of birth and have not been notified by one single person of her family as to the health or status of the birth, day, time weight. I learned from public records she was born March 11th 2016.   3/11/16, Patrick 2/27/13, Darra 11/16/96

I am the second son born on the 7th, two and seven, Darra is the first of mine born 11/16 equals twenty seven, two and seven, Patrick is the 2nd son born 2/27 2nd and two and seven, my little daughter my third child born 3 for the third and 11 and 16 again, twenty seven. There is something there for to find, I have across my heart tattooed Darra's birthday 11/16/96   well six from nine is three, it could easily say 3/11/16 the other way my new baby's birthday.

 Hope the world community can find a way to pray and help me save my baby, I cannot lose another one. I am not appealing for prayers here, but a few would always help. I need to be reunited and fulfil the life cycle of raising my child and protecting her from all the harms of the world. My full intentions are to find the truth as to Patrick's death and to make strong roads to fight every step of the way for my daughter. Hopefully God will not keep me from her too long but it is up to the legal process now. That is my story and though there are many areas I did not explain in detail now you know Aidan Mc Nally, in knowing me hopefully the power of prayer will unite me with my daughter and the evil of the world will not cause failure again, two sons too many.

Be sure to stop by and say Hi on facebook or come follow on twitter, you can find me @TWOsonsTOOmany.

Like all independent and self-published authors would like you to always leave a review.

You will find a blog of some provoking thoughts on Goodreads where the author writes his blog.

Enjoy your day and what life has to offer, no seriously go out there and ENJOY.....

Made in the USA
Columbia, SC
06 March 2018